ACL Workshop on Computing and Historical Phonology 2007, the 9th Meeting of the ACL Special Interest Group in Computational Morphology and Phonology

Held in conjunction with ACL 2007

Prague, Czech Republic
28 June 2007

ISBN: 978-1-61738-521-6

Printed from e-media with permission by:

Curran Associates, Inc.
57 Morehouse Lane
Red Hook, NY 12571
www.proceedings.com

Some format issues inherent in the e-media version may also appear in this print version.

Printed by Curran Associates, Inc. (2010)

Association for Computational Linguistics
209 N. Eighth Street
Stroudsburg, Pennsylvania 18360

Phone: 1-570-476-8006
Fax: 1-570-476-0860

acl@aclweb.org

Preface

Welcome to the ACL Workshop on Computing and Historical Phonology, the 9th Meeting of ACL Special Interest Group for Computational Morphology and Phonology, a meeting held in conjunction with the 45th Meeting of the ACL in Prague. An introductory article explains our motivation for holding the workshop, which attracted 16 submissions, all but one of which is included in this volume of proceedings. We are gratified not only by the level of interest, but also by the quality of submissions we received.

We hoped to attract interest not only in the computational linguistics community *sensu stricto* but also in the broader linguistics community, and in the group of geneticists who have begun to apply phylogenetic analysis to linguistic data. As the reader may verify in these proceedings, we were not disappointed in this hope. Perhaps it is worth adding that, while we are in principle interested in further meetings of this sort, there are at the time of this writing no concrete plans for follow-ups.

Our thanks are largely given in the acknowledgments section of the introductory article, but let's add thanks here to Simone Teufel, the workshop chair of the conference, who ushered us through the various steps from the proposal through the production of this publication, and also to the committee she chaired.

John Nerbonne, T. Mark Ellison and Grzegorz Kondrak (Chairs)

Organizers

Chairs:

John Nerbonne, University of Groningen
Grzegorz Kondrak, University of Alberta
T. Mark Ellison, University of Western Australia

Program Committee:

Chris Brew, Ohio State University
Pierre Darlu, Paris
Michael Dunn, Max Planck, Nijmegen
Sheila Embleton, York University, Toronto
Hans Goebl, Salzburg
Russell Gray, Auckland
Sheldon Harrison, Western Australia
Wilbert Heeringa, Groningen
Brian Joseph, Ohio State University
Brett Kessler, Washington University of St. Louis
Simon Kirby, Edinburgh
Bill Kretzschmar, Georgia
Franz Manni, Paris
Hermann Moisl, Newcastle
David Nash, Australian National University, Canberra
Michael Oakes, Sunderland
Jon Patrick, Sydney
Gerald Penn, Toronto
Janet Pierrehumbert, Northwestern
Thomas Pilz, Duisburg
Joe Salmons, Wisconsin
Tandy Warnow, University of Texas

Keynote Speaker:

Brett Kessler, Washington University of St. Louis

Other Reviewers:

Hans J. Holm, Hannover
Sebastian Kürschner, University of Groningen

Table of Contents

Workshop Program

Thursday, June 28, 2007

8:30–8:45 Opening
Computing and Historical Phonology
John Nerbonne, T. Mark Ellison and Grzegorz Kondrak

8:45–9:45 Keynote Speaker
Word Similarity Metrics and Multilateral Comparison
Brett Kessler

9:45–10:15 *Bayesian Identification of Cognates and Correspondences*
T. Mark Ellison

10:15–10:45 *Testing Cladistics on Dialect Networks and Phyla (Gallo-Romance Vowels, Southern Italo-Romance Diasystems and Mayan Languages)*
Antonella Gaillard-Corvaglia, Jean-Léo Léonard and Pierre Darlu

10:45–11:15 Break

11:15–11:45 *The Relative Divergence of Dutch Dialect Pronunciations from their Common Source: An Exploratory Study*
Wilbert Heeringa and Brian Joseph

11:45–12:15 *Can Corpus Based Measures be Used for Comparative Study of Languages?*
Anil Kumar Singh and Harshit Surana

12:15–12:45 *Inducing Sound Segment Differences Using Pair Hidden Markov Models*
Martijn Wieling, Therese Leinonen and John Nerbonne

12:45–14:15 Lunch

14:15–14:45 *Phonological Reconstruction of a Dead Language Using the Gradual Learning Algorithm*
Eric Smith

14:45–15:15 *Evolution, Optimization, and Language Change: The Case of Bengali Verb Inflections*
Monojit Choudhury, Vaibhav Jalan, Sudeshna Sarkar and Anupam Basu

Thursday, June 28, 2007 (continued)

15:15–15:45 Posters

On the Geolinguistic Change in Northern France between 1300 and 1900: A Dialectometrical Inquiry
Hans Goebl

Visualizing the Evaluation of Distance Measures
Thomas Pilz, Axel Philipsenburg and Wolfram Luther

Data Nonlinearity in Exploratory Multivariate Analysis of Language Corpora
Hermann Moisl

Emergence of Community Structures in Vowel Inventories: An Analysis Based on Complex Networks
Animesh Mukherjee, Monojit Choudhury, Anupam Basu and Niloy Ganguly

Cognate Identification and Alignment Using Practical Orthographies
Michael Cysouw and Hagen Jung

ParaMor: Minimally Supervised Induction of Paradigm Structure and Morphological Analysis
Christian Monson, Jaime Carbonell, Alon Lavie and Lori Levin

15:45–16:15 Break

16:15–16:45 *Dynamic Correspondences: An Object-Oriented Approach to Tracking Sound Reconstructions*
Tyler Peterson and Gessiane Picanco

16:45–17:15 *Creating a Comparative Dictionary of Totonac-Tepehua*
Grzegorz Kondrak, David Beck and Philip Dilts

17:15–17:45 Discussion

17:45–18:00 Closing

Computing and Historical Phonology

John Nerbonne
Alfa-Informatica
University of Groningen
j.nerbonne@rug.nl

T. Mark Ellison
Informatics
University of Western Australia
mark@markellison.net

Grzegorz Kondrak
Computing Science
University of Alberta
kondrak@cs.ualberta.ca

Abstract

We introduce the proceedings from the workshop 'Computing and Historical Phonology: 9th Meeting of the ACL Special Interest Group for Computational Morphology and Phonology'.

1 Background

Historical phonology is the study of how the sounds and sound systems of a language evolve, and includes research issues concerning the triggering of sound changes; their temporal and geographic propagation (including lexical diffusion); the regularity/irregularity of sound change, and its interaction with morphological change; the role of borrowing and analogy in sound change; the interaction of sound change with the phonemic system (potentially promoting certain changes, but also neutralizing phonemic distinctions); and the detection of these phenomena in historical documents.

There is a substantial and growing body of work applying computational techniques of various sorts to problems in historical phonology. We mention a few here to give the flavor of the sort of work we hoped to attract for presentation in a coherent SIGMORPHON workshop. Kessler (2001) estimates the likelihood of chance phonemic correspondences using permutation statistics; Kondrak (2002) develops algorithms to detect cognates and sound correspondences; McMahon and McMahon (2005) and also Nakhleh, Ringe and Warnow (2005) apply phylogenetic techniques to comparative reconstruction; and Ellison and Kirby (2006) suggest means of detecting relationships which do not depend on word by word comparisons. But we likewise wished to draw on the creativity of the computational linguistics (CL) community to see which other important problems in historical phonology might also be addressed computationally (see below).

There has recently been a good deal of computational work in historical linguistics involving phylogenetic inference, i.e., the inference to the genealogical tree which best explains the historical developments (Gray and Atkinson, 2003; Dunn et al., 2005). While the application of phylogenetic analysis has not universally been welcomed with open philological arms (Holm, 2007), it has attracted a good deal of attention, some of which we hoped to engage. We take no stand on these controversies here, but note that computing may be employed in historical linguistics, and in particular in historical phonology in a more versatile way, its uses extending well beyond phylogenetic inference.

2 Introduction

The workshop thus brings together researchers interested in applying computational techniques to problems in historical phonology. We deliberately defined the scope of the workshop broadly to include problems such as identifying spelling variants in older manuscripts, searching for cognates, hypothesizing and confirming sound changes and/or sound correspondences, modeling likely sound changes, the relation of synchronic social and geographic variation to historical change, the detection of phonetic signals of relatedness among potentially related languages, phylogenetic reconstruction based on sound correspondences among languages, dating

Proceedings of Ninth Meeting of the ACL Special Interest Group in Computational Morphology and Phonology, pages 1–5,
Prague, June 2007.

historical changes, or others.

We were emphatically open to proposals to apply techniques from other areas to problems in historical phonology such as applying work on confusable product names to the modeling of likely sound correspondences or the application of phylogenetic analysis from evolutionary biology to the problem of phonological reconstruction.

3 Papers

We provide a preview to some of the issues in the papers in this bundle.

Brett Kessler's invited contribution sketches the opportunities for multiple string alignment, which would be extremely useful in historical phonology, but which is also technically so challenging that Gusfield (1999, Ch. 14) refers to it as "the holy grail" (of algorithms on strings, trees, and sequences).

3.1 Identification of Cognates

T. Mark Ellison combines Bayes's theorem with gradient descent in a method for finding cognates and correspondences. A formal model of language is extended to include the notion of parent languages, and a mechanism whereby parent languages project onto their descendents. This model allows the quantification of the probability of word lists in two languages given a common ancestor which was the source for some of the words. Bayes's theorem reverses this expression into the evaluation of possible parent languages. Gradient descent finds the best, or at least a good one, of these. The method is shown to find cognates in data from Russian and Polish.

Grzegorz Kondrak, David Beck and Philip Dilts apply algorithms for the identification of cognates and recurrent sound correspondences proposed by Kondrak (2002) to the Totonac-Tepehua family of indigenous languages in Mexico. Their long-term objective is providing tools for rapid construction of comparative dictionaries for relatively unfamiliar language families. They show that by combining expert linguistic knowledge with computational analysis, it is possible to quickly identify a large number of cognate sets across related languages. The experiments led to the creation of the initial version of an etymological dictionary. The authors hope that the dictionary will facilitate the reconstruction of a more accurate Totonac-Tepehua family tree, and shed light on the problem of the family origins and migratory patterns.

Michael Cysouw and Hagen Jung use an iterative process of alignment between words in different languages in an attempt to identify cognates. Instead of using consistently coded phonemic (or phonetic) transciption, they use practical orthographies, which has the advantage of being applicable without expensive and error-prone manual processing. Proceeding from semantically equivalent words in the Intercontinental Dictionary Series (IDS) database, the program aligns letters using a variant of edit distance that includes correspondences of one letter with two or more, ("multi-n-gram"). Once initial alignments are obtained, segment replacement costs are inferred. This process of alignment and inferring segment replacement costs may then be iterated. They succeed in distinguishing noise on the one hand from borrowings and cognates on the other, and the authors speculate about being able to distinguish inherited cognates from borrowings.

3.2 A View from Dialectology

Several papers examined language change from the point of view of dialectology. While the latter studies variation in space, the former studies variation over time.

Hans Goebl, the author of hundreds of papers applying quantitative analysis to the analysis of linguistic varieties in dialects, applies his dialectometric techniques both to modern material (1900) from the *Atlas Linguistique de France* and to material dating from approximate 1300 provided by Dutch Romanists. Dialectometry aims primarily at establishing the aggregate distances (or conversely, similarities), and Goebl's analysis shows that these have remain relatively constant even while the French language has changed a good deal. The suggestion is that geography is extremely influential.

Wilbert Heeringa and Brian Joseph first reconstruct a protolanguage based on Dutch dialect data, which they compare to the proto-Germanic found in a recent dictionary, demonstrating that their reconstruction is quite similar to the proto-Germanic, even though it is only based on a single branch of a large family. They then apply a variant of edit distance to the pronunciation of the protolanguage, comparing it to the pronunciation in modern Dutch dialects, allowing on the one hand a quantitative evaluation of the degree to which "proto-Dutch" correlates with proto-Germanic ($r = 0.87$), and a sketch of conservative vs. innovative dialect areas in the Netherlands on the other.

Anil Singh and Harshit Surana ask whether corpus-based measures can be used to compare languages. Most research has proceeded from the assumption that lists of word pairs be available, as indeed they normally are in the case of dialect atlas data or as they often may be obtained by constructing lexicalizations of the concepts in the so-called "Swadesh" list. But such data is not always available, nor is it straightforward to construct. Singh and Surana construct n-gram models of order five (5), and compare Indo-Iranian and Dravidian languages based on symmetric cross-entropy.

Martijn Wieling, Therese Leinonen and John Nerbonne apply PAIR HIDDEN MARKOV MODELS (PHMM), introduced to CL by Mackay and Kondrak (2005), to a large collection of Dutch dialect pronunciations in an effort to learn the degree of segment differentiation. Essentially the PHMM regards frequently aligned segments as more similar, and Wieling et al. show that the induced similarity indeed corresponds to phonetic similarity in the case of vowels, whose acoustic properties facilitate the assessment of similarity.

3.3 Views from other Perspectives

Several papers examined diachronic change from well-developed perspectives outside of historical linguistics, including evolution and genetic algorithms, language learning, biological cladistics, and the structure of vowel systems.

Monojit Choudhury, Vaibhav Jalan, Sudeshna Sarkar and Anupam Basu distinguish two components in language developments, on the one hand functional forces or constraints including ease of articulation, perceptual contrast, and learnability, which are modeled by the fitness function of a genetic algorithm (GA). On the other hand, these functional forces operate against the background of linguistic structure, which the authors dub 'genotype–phenotype mapping', and which is realized by the set of forms in a given paradigm, and a small set of possible atomic changes which map from form set to form set. They apply these ideas to morphological changes in dialects of Bengali, an agglutinative Indic language, and they are able to show that some modern dialects are optimal solutions to the functional constraints in the sense that any further changes would be worse with respect to at least one of the constraints.

Eric Smith applies the gradual learning algorithm (GLA) developed in Optimality Theory by Paul Boersma to the problem of reconstructing a dead language. In particular the GLA is deployed to deduce the phonological representations of a dead language, Elamite, from the orthography, where the orthography is treated as the surface representation and the phonological representation as the underlying representation. Elamite was spoken in southwestern and central Iran, and survives in texts dating from 2400– 360 BCE, written in a cuneiform script borrowed from Sumerians and Akkadians. Special attention is paid to the difficult mapping between orthography and phonology, and to OT's Lexicon Optimization module.

Antonella Gaillard-Corvaglia, Jean-Léo Léonard and Pierre Darlu apply cladistic analysis to dialect networks and language phyla, using the detailed information in phonetic changes to increase the resolution beyond what is possible with simple word lists. They examine Gallo-Romance vowels, southern Italo-Romance dialects and Mayan languages, foregoing analyses of relatedness based on global resemblance between languages, and aiming instead to view recurrent phonological changes as first-class entities in the analysis of historical phonology with the ambition of including the probability of specific linguistic changes in analyses.

Animesh Mukherjee, Monojit Choudhury, Anupam Basu and Niloy Ganguly examine the structure of vowel systems by defining a weighted network where vowels are represented by the nodes and the likelihood of vowels' co-occurring in the languages of the world by weighted edges between nodes. Using data from the 451 languages in the UCLA Phonological Segment Inventory Database (UPSID), Mukherjee and colleagues seek high-frequency symmetric triplets (with similar co-occurrence weights). The vowel networks which emerged tend to organize themselves to maximize contrast between the vowels when inventories are small, but they tend to grow by systematically applying the same contrasts (short vs long, oral vs nasal) across the board when they grow larger.

3.4 Methodology

Finally, there were three papers focusing on more general methodological issues, one on non-linearity, one on a direct manipulation interface to cross-tabulation, and one on visualizing distance measures.

Hermann Moisl has worked a great deal with the Newcastle Electronic Corpus of Tyneside English (NECTE). NECTE is a corpus of dialect speech from Tyneside in North-East England which was collected in an effort to represent not only geographical, but also social variation in speech. In the contribution to this volume, Moisl addresses the problem of nonlinearity in data, using the distribution of variance in the frequency of phonemes in NECTE as an example. He suggests techniques for spotting nonlinearity as well as techniques for analyzing data which contains it.

Tyler Peterson and Gessiane Picanco experiment with cross tabulation as an aid to phonemic reconstruction. In particular they use PIVOT TABLES, which are cross tabulations supported by new database packages, and which allow direct manipulation, e.g., drag and drop methods of adding and removing new sets of data, including columns or rows. This makes it easier for the linguist to track e.g. phoneme correspondences and develop hypotheses about them. Tupí stock is a South American language family with about 60 members, mostly in Brazil, but also in Bolivia and Paraguay. Pivot tables were employed to examine this data, which resulted in a reconstruction a great deal like the only published reconstruction, but which nevertheless suggested new possibilities.

Thomas Pilz, Axel Philipsenburg and Wolfram Luther describe the development and use of an interface for visually evaluating distance measures. Using the problem of identifying intended modern spellings from manuscript spellings using various techniques, including edit distance, they note examples where the same distance measure performs well on one set of manuscripts but poorly on another. This motivates the need for easy evaluation of such measures. The authors use multidimensional scaling plots, histograms and tables to expose different levels of overview and detail.

3.5 Other

Although this meeting of SIGMORPHON focused on contributions to historical phonology, there was also one paper on synchronic morphology.

Christian Monson, Alon Lavie, Jaime Carbonell and Lori Levin describe ParaMor, a system aimed at minimally supervised morphological analysis that uses inflectional paradigms as its key concept. ParaMor gathers sets of suffixes and stems that co-occur, collecting each set of suffixes into a potential inflectional paradigm. These candidate paradigms then need to be compared and filtered to obtain a minimal set of paradigms. Since there are many hundreds of languages for which paradigm discovery would be a very useful tool, ParaMor may be interesting to researchers involved in language documentation. This paper sketches the authors' approach to the problem and presents evidence for good performance in Spanish and German.

4 Prospects

As pleasing as it to hear of the progress reported on in this volume, it is clear that there is a great deal of interesting work ahead for those interested in computing and historical phonology. This is immediately clear if one compares the list of potential topics noted in Sections 1-2 with the paper topics actually covered, e.g. by skimming Section 3 or the table of contents. For example we did not receive submissions on the treatment of older documents, on recognizing spelling variants, or on dating historical changes.

In addition interesting topics may just now be rising above the implementation horizon, e.g. computational techniques which strive to mimic internal reconstruction (Hock and Joseph, 1996), or those which aim at characterizing general sound changes, or perspectives which attempt to tease apart historical, areal and typological effects (Nerbonne, 2007). In short, we are optimistic about interest in follow-up workshops!

5 Acknowledgments

We are indebted to our program committee, to the incidental reviewers named in the organizational section of the book, and to some reviewers who remain anonymous. We also thank the SIGMORPHON chair Jason Eisner and secretary Richard Wicentowski for facilitating our organization of this workshop under the aegis of SIGMORPHON, the special interest group in morphology and phonology of the Association for Computational Linguistics.[1] We thank Peter Kleiweg for managing the production of the book. We are indebted to the Netherlands Organization for Scientific Research (NWO), grant 235-89-001, for cooperation between the Center for Language and Cognition, Groningen, and the *Department of Linguistics* The Ohio State University, for support of the work which is reported on here.

References

A. Michael Dunn, A. Terrill, Geert Reesink, and Stephen Levinson. 2005. Structural phylogenetics and the reconstruction of ancient language history. *Science*, 309(5743):2072–2075.

Mark Ellison and Simon Kirby. 2006. Measuring language divergence by intra-lexical divergence. In *Proc. of ACL/COLING 2006*, pages 273–280, Shroudsburg, PA. ACL.

Russell D. Gray and Quentin D. Atkinson. 2003. Language-tree divergence times support the Anatolian theory of Indo-European origin. *Nature*, 426(6965):435–439.

Dan Gusfield. 1999. *Algorithms on Strings, Trees, and Sequences: Computer Science and Computational Biology*. Cambridge Univesity Press, Cambridge.

Hans Henrich Hock and Brian D. Joseph. 1996. *Language History, Language Change, and Language Relationship : An Introduction to Historical and Comparative Linguistics*. Mouton de Gruyter, Berlin.

Hans J. Holm. 2007. The new arboretum of Indo-European "trees": Can new algorithms reveal the phylogeny and even prehistory of IE? *Journal of Quantitative Linguistics*, 14(2).

Brett Kessler. 2001. *The Significance of Word Lists*. CSLI Press, Stanford.

Grzegorz Kondrak. 2002. *Algorithms for Language Reconstruction*. Ph.D. thesis, University of Toronto.

Wesley Mackay and Grzegorz Kondrak. 2005. Comparing word similarity and identifying cognates with pair hidden markov models. In *Proceedings of the 9th Conference on Natural Language Learning (CoNLL)*, pages 40–47, Shroudsburg, PA. ACL.

April McMahon and Robert McMahon. 2005. *Language Classification by Numbers*. Oxford University Press, Oxford.

Luay Nakleh, Don Ringe, and Tandy Warnow. 2005. Perfect phylogentic networks: A new metholodology for reconstructing the evolutionary history of natural languages. *Language*, 81(2):382–420.

John Nerbonne. 2007. Review of April McMahon & Robert McMahon *Language Classification by Numbers*. Oxford: OUP, 2005. *Linguistic Typology*, 11.

[1] `http://nlp.cs.swarthmore.edu/sigphon/`

Word Similarity Metrics and Multilateral Comparison

Brett Kessler
Washington University in St. Louis
bkessler@wustl.edu

Abstract

Phylogenetic analyses of languages need to explicitly address whether the languages under consideration are related to each other at all. Recently developed permutation tests allow this question to be explored by testing whether words in one set of languages are significantly more similar to those in another set of languages when paired up by semantics than when paired up at random. Seven different phonetic similarity metrics are implemented and evaluated on their effectiveness within such multilateral comparison systems when deployed to detect genetic relations among the Indo-European and Uralic language families.

1 Introduction

Because the historical development of languages is analogous to the evolution of organisms, linguists and biologists have been able to share much of their cladistic theory and practice. But in at least one respect, linguists are at a disadvantage. While all cellular organisms on Earth are patently related to each other, no such assumption can be made for languages. It is possible that languages were invented multiple times, so that the proper cladistic analysis of all human languages comprises a forest rather than a single tree. Therefore historical linguists undertaking a cladistic analysis – more often referred to as *subgrouping* – have to ask a question that rarely arises at all in biology: Are the entities for which I am undertaking to draw a family tree related to each other in the first place?

The question of whether two or more languages are related is addressed by looking at characters that differ between languages and asking whether observed similarities in those characters are so great as to lead to the conclusion that the languages have a common ancestor. Researchers have investigated many types of characters for this purpose, including fairly abstract ones such as the structure of paradigms, but the most commonly used characters have been the individual morphemes of the language. Morphemes are associations between strings of phones and specific language functions such as lexical meanings or more general grammatical properties. Crucially, those associations are arbitrary to a very great extent. Knowing that a 'tree' is /strom/ in Czech will not help one figure out that it is /ets/ in Hebrew; nor should Hebrew speakers confronted with two Czech lexical morphemes, such as /strom/ vs /firad/, be able to guess which one means 'tree' and which one means 'castle'. An implication of this arbitrariness is that if one pairs morphemes by meaning between two languages, that set of pairs should not have any systematic phonetic property that would not be obtained if morphemes were paired up without regard to meaning. Thus, if one does observe some systematic phonetic property across the semantically paired morphemes, one can conclude that there is some historical contingency that gave those languages that property. Namely, one can conclude that at one time the languages shared the same morpheme for at least some of the meanings, either because of borrowing or because of descent from a common ancestor.

The most straightforward application of this prin-

Proceedings of Ninth Meeting of the ACL Special Interest Group in Computational Morphology and Phonology, pages 6–14,
Prague, June 2007.

ciple is to see whether the morphemes for the same concept in two different languages appear unusually similar to each other. Anyone seeing that the morpheme for 'all' was /æɑlː/ in Old English and /alː/ in Old High German, that 'animal' was /deːor/ and /tior/, respectively, and that 'back' was /hrydːʒ/ vs. /hrukː/, and so forth, might well conclude that the languages were related to each other, as indeed they were. Unfortunately, the universal properties of language mean that even unrelated morphemes have something in common; it is not always obvious whether the amount of similarity between semantically matched morphemes is significantly greater than that between semantically mismatched morphemes. For nearly two centuries now, the standard recourse in case of doubt has been the comparative method. One counts how many times the same pair of sounds match up in semantically matched morphemes; for example, Old English /d/ often corresponds to Old High German /t/. A large number of recurrent sound correspondences appearing in several positions in a large number of different words has been considered proof that languages are related. This method is more sophisticated than eyeballing similarities, not least because it recognizes the effect of phonetic apomorphies – sound changes – such as the change of /d/ to /t/ in Old High German. The standard methodology gives no concrete guidance as to how many recurrent sound correspondences constitute proof. However, there have been attempts to recast the comparative method in terms of modern statistical theory and experimental methodology, providing clearcut quantification of the magnitude and significance of the evidence that languages are related (see Kessler, 2001, for recent developments and a summary of earlier work).

One drawback to recent statistical adaptations of the comparative method is that they have been limited to comparing two languages at a time. It has been claimed, however, most prominently by Greenberg (e.g., 1993), that when one wishes to test whether a large set of languages are related, conducting a series of bilateral tests loses power: there may be information contained in a pattern of relations across three or more languages that is not manifest in the bilateral partitioning of the set of languages. Greenberg's approach to multilateral comparison was a step backward to the days before the development of the comparative method (Poser & Campbell, 1992). By his own account, he simply eyed the data and apparently never failed to conclude that languages were related.

Most linguists have rejected Greenberg's approach and many have written detailed refutations (e.g., Campbell, 1988; Matisoff, 1990; Ringe, 1996; Salmons, 1992). But Kessler and Lehtonen (2006) believed that multilateral comparison could be valid and advantageous if applied with some statistical rigour. Adapting Greenberg's basic approach, they developed a methodology that involved computing phonetic similarity between semantically matched morphemes across several languages at a time. This was different from the comparative method, because recurrent sound correspondences were not sought: large numbers of recurrences are not typically found across large numbers of languages. However, it is conceptually straightforward to aggregate similarity measures across morphemes in many languages. Crucially, the similarity across semantically matched morphemes was compared to that obtained across semantically mismatched morphemes. Thus, this application of multilateral comparison is based on the same principles about sound–meaning arbitrariness on which the comparative method was based. Because the similarity computations were completely algorithmic and applied to data collected in an unbiased fashion, the new methodology provided a way to reliably quantify and test the significance of phonetic similarity as evidence for historical connections between two sets of multiple languages. Kessler and Lehtonen demonstrated that the method was powerful enough to detect the relationship between 11 Indo-European languages and that between 4 Uralic languages, but it did not detect any connection between those two families.

The core of the multilateral comparison methodology is the phonetic similary metric. To my knowledge, Greenberg never specified any particular metric. However, many different phonetic comparison algoriths have been proposed for many purposes, including this task of looking for similarities between words (reviewed in Kessler, 2005); in particular, Baxter and Manaster Ramer (2000) and Oswalt (1998) developed algorithms expressly for investigating language relatedness, though only in bilateral tests. In this paper I explore several different phonetic comparison algorithms and evaluate how well they perform in Kessler and Lehtonen's (2006) multilateral comparison task for Indo-European and Uralic.

2 Multilateral Comparison

The basic multilateral algorithm is described in Kessler and Lehtonen (2006); here I give a summary of the relevant facts. For each of 15 languages, we collected all of the words expressing concepts in the Swadesh (1952) list of 200 concepts. However, words were discarded if they violated the key assumptions discussed in the introduction. For example, onomatopoeia and sound symbolism would violate the assumption of arbitrariness: languages could easily come up with similar words for the same concept if they both resorted to natural associations between sounds and their meanings. Grammatical words were rejected because they tend to have certain phonetic properties in common across languages, such as shortness; this also violates arbitrariness. Loanwords were discarded in order to focus on genetic relationships rather than other types of historical connection.

In addition to rejecting some words outright, we tagged others for their relative suitability for a historical analysis. The concepts themselves were scored for how much confidence other researchers have placed in their suitability for glottochronological studies. Some of the contribution to this score was quite subjective; other parts of it were derived from studies of retention rates: how long words expressing the concept tend to survive before being replaced by other words. The words were stripped down to their root morpheme, and then tagged for how concordant that root meaning is with the target concept; for example, if a word for 'dirty' literally means 'unclean', the root 'clean' does not express the concept 'dirty' very well. None of the conditions indicated by these suitability measures invalidates the use of a word, but low retention rates and complex semantic composition mean the word has a lower chance of being truly old and consequently of being a very good datum in a comparison of languages suspected of being only distantly related. These suitability scores were combined for each word in each language. Then, in any given comparison between languages, the suitability scores for each concept were aggregated across words, and the 100 concepts with the best rankings were selected for actual comparison. This technique both ensures the availability of a reasonably large amount of data and also attempts to ensure that the words themselves will be reasonably probative without biasing the test in either direction.

In any single multilateral test, it is assumed that we have a single specific hypothesis: whether one group of one or more languages is related to another group of one or more languages. The approach taken therefore is to determine for each concept how different the words in one group are to the words in the other group. If there are more than one word in each group, then all crosspairs are computed and their average is taken. This approach applies both to the situation where there are multiple languages in a group and multiple words for a given language. These averages are then summed across all 100 concepts, giving a single distance measure: a score of how different the two groups of languages are from each other.

It is important to note, however, that this distance measure is not meaningful in itself. Sets of languages could get relatively low distance measures just because their phonological inventories and phonotactics are very similar to each other's; such typological similarity is not, however, strong evidence for historical connectedness between languages. Rather, what is needed is a relative comparison: how dissimilar would the words be across the two sets of languages if they were not matched by semantics? This is computed by randomly matching concepts in one set of languages with concepts in another set of languages and recomputing the sum of the dissimilarity measures. Each such rearrangement may give a different total distance, which may not be representative, so this procedure is done 100,000 times and the distance is averaged across all those iterations, yielding a very close estimate of the phonetic difference between words that are not matched on semantics. From this one can compute the proportion by which the semantically matched distance is less than the semantically mismatched distance. This proportion is the magnitude m of the evidence in favour of the hypothesis that sets of languages are related to each other. At the same time that the magnitude is computed, one can also compute the significance level of the hypothesis, by counting what proportion of the 100,000 rearrangements has a total distance score that is at least as small as that between the semantically matched words. That number estimates how likely it is that the attested amount of evidence would have occurred by chance, given the phonology of the sets of languages. This paper follows the usual convention in the social sciences of considering significance levels, p, below .05 as being reasonably comfortable.

While each individual test can tell the probability that two sets of languages are related, specific studies may seek to find out which of three or more sets of languages are related. To investigate that, a nearest-neighbour hierarchical clustering is used. In each cycle of the procedure, comparisons are made between all pairs of sets of languages to see which pairs have significant evidence ($p < .05$) of being related. Of those, the pair with the highest magnitude m are combined to form a new, larger, set of languages. The cycles repeat until all languages are grouped into one large set, or no pair of sets have sufficiently significant evidence of being related.

3 Phonetic Distance Metrics

Phonetic distance metrics can be evaluated on several different principles. The ultimate goal is that they should result in p values that are very low when languages are related and high when they are not related. Unfortunately, that goal is only partly evaluable. There are no two languages known for sure not to be related; otherwise there would be no monogeneticists. The best one can test for is m values that correlate well with our incomplete knowledge of the degree of relatedness between languages.

Beyond basic engineering goals of simplicity and efficiency, therefore, a good algorithm should give a relatively low distance score for words or languages known to be related. To the extent possible, it should take minimal account of phonetic features that change quickly over time, and weight more heavily features that tend to be stable over time.

It is perhaps less obvious that a phonetic distance metric should be based on features that are widespread, both across the languages of the world and within individual languages. To take a clearly absurd example, a bad metric would give a distance of 0 if two words agree in whether or not they contained a click, and 1 otherwise. For the vast majority of languages, all word pairs would be assigned a distance 0, because neither word has a click. Such a metric would find no evidence that any pair of clickless languages are related, because the distance of the semantically matched pairs would be no less than the distance of the mismatched pairs. Similarly, even if a feature is found in both languages, it should be neither too common nor too rare. For example, many languages have a contrast between lateral and central sounds, but lateral sounds tend to be vastly less common than central sounds. A metric that compares sounds based on central/lateral distinctions may again end up finding little probative evidence. This observation may seem commonplace for statisticians, but is worth pointing out because the tradition in historical linguistics has always been to look for pieces of evidence that are individually spectacular for their rarity, such as a pair of words whose first five sounds are all identical. It is great to report such evidence when it is found, but bad to demand such evidence in advance, because typically any specific type of spectacular evidence will not show up even for related languages. In a statistical analysis it is much better to look for common pieces of evidence to ensure that their distribution in any particular study will be typical and therefore reasonably conducive to a reliable quantitative analysis.

A much more subtle danger is that a poorly chosen phonetic distance metric might be influenced by parts of the phonology that are not as completely arbitrary as one might like them to be. Because the arbitrariness hypothesis is almost always observed to be applicable in practice, and because it has attained the status of dogma, linguists do not know all there is to know about conditions in which the association between sound and meaning may not be entirely arbitrary and the ways in which that non-arbitrariness may repeat across languages, spuriously indicating that languages are related. However, one strong contender for non-arbitrariness is word length. It appears to be true that words that are longer in one language tend to be longer in another. If a phonetic distance metric is sensitive to word length, it could indicate that semantically matched words are more or less similar than mismatched words, just because their length is similar. This study attempts to minimize that effect by discarding grammatical words, which tend to be systematically shorter than lexical words. It also reduces words to their root morpheme, in part because crosslinguistic tendencies favouring longer words are probably due largely to a tendency to use more morphemes when building lower-frequency concepts. Nevertheless, even these steps are not proof against matching-length effects, and so it would be better for phonetic distance metrics not to be sensitive to word length.

3.1 Candidate Metrics

Seven different phonetic distance metrics were evaluated for this study.

C_1-place. The phonetic distance metric used by Kessler and Lehtonen (2006) was based on the observations that in language change, consonants tend to be more stable than vowels, the front of the word tends to be more stable than the end of the word, and place of articulation tends to be more stable than other features. Consequently it is based on the place feature of the first consonants (C_1) found in the comparanda; only if a comparandum has no consonant at all is its first vowel used instead. Places of articulation are assigned integer values from 0 (lips) to 10 (postvelar), and candidate phones are assigned a list of these values, which allows for secondary and double articulation. The phonetic distance between two sounds is the smallest absolute difference between the crosswise pairings of those place values. In addition, half a point is added if the two sounds are not identical. For example, when comparing the Old English word for 'child', /tʃild/, with the corresponding Old High German word, /kind/, the algorithm would extract the first consonants, /tʃ/ and /k/; assign the postalveolar /tʃ/ a place value of 4 and the velar /k/ a value of 9; and report the difference plus an extra 0.5 for being non-identical: 5.5.

P_1-Dolg. Baxter and Manaster Ramer (2000), in a demonstration of bilateral comparison, used a phonetic distance metric adapted fom Dolgopolsky (1986). Dolgopolsky grouped sounds into 10 classes, which were defined by a combination of place and manner of articulation. Two sounds were considered to have a distance of 0 between them if they fell in the same class; otherwise the distance was 1. Instead of using the first consonant in the word, the first phoneme (P_1) is used instead, but all vowels are put in the same class. Dolgopolsky's idea was to group together sounds that tend to change into each other over time; thus one class contains both velar stops and postalveolar affricates, because the sound change [k] $\rightarrow$ [tʃ] is common. Thus in the example of /tʃild/ vs. /kind/, the reported distance would be 0.

C_1-Dolg and P_1-place. These metrics were introduced in order to factor apart the two main differences between C_1-place and P_1-Dolg. C_1-Dolg uses Dolgopolsky classes but operates on the first consonant, if any, rather than on an initial vowel. P_1-place uses the place comparison metrics of C_1-place, but always operates on the first phoneme, even if it is a vowel. So many morphemes begin with a consonant that this is often a distinction without a difference, as in the 'child' example. But note how in comparing Old English /æːɣ/ with Latin /oːw/, both 'egg', the P_1 versions would compare /æː/ with /oː/, for a distance of 3.5 by the P_1-place metric (palatal vs. velar vowels) and 0 by the P_1-Dolg metric (all vowels are in the same class); whereas the C_1 metrics would compare /ɣ/ with /w/, for a distance of 0.5 by C_1-place (both sounds have velar components) and 1 by C_1-Dolg.

P_1-voice. This metric is designed to be as simple as possible. Two words have a distance of 0 if their first phones agree in voicing, 1 if they disagree. Breathy voice was counted as voiced. The idea here is that phonation contrast is reasonably universal, and it is a relatively simple matter to partition all known phones into two sets.

C*-DolgSeq. In the comparative method, the best evidence for genetic relatedness is considered to be the presence of several words that contain multiple sounds that all evince recurrent sound correspondences. In particular, multiple consonant matches between words are often sought as particularly probative evidence. This metric implements this desideratum by lining up all the consonants (C*) in the words sequentially (hence Seq). Each such pair of aligned consonants contributes a distance of 1 to the cumulative distance between the words if the consonants are not in the same Dolgopolsky class. If the one word has more consonants than the other word, alignment begins at the beginning of the word, and the extra consonants at the end are ignored. To avoid making this metric sensitive to word length, the total distance is divided by the number of consonant pairs. Continuing the 'child' example, /tʃ/ and /k/ contribute 0 because they are in the same Dolgopolsky class; /l/ and /n/ contribute 1 because they are in different classes; and /d/ and /d/ contribute 0; the sum 1 is averaged across 3 comparisons to give a score of 0.33.

C*-DolgCross. Although the C*-DolgSeq metric attempts to exploit information from multiple consonants in each pair of words, it fails to exploit all possible information. The extra consonants at the end of the longer word are ignored. Further, there is the possibility that the sequential alignment would fail under some fairly common situations. For example, if in one language a consonant is deleted or vocalized, the later consonants will not be aligned correctly. To address this issue, this metric examines all crosswise pairs of consonants and reports their average Dolgopolsky metric. In the example, /tʃ/ is compared to /k/ (0), /n/ (1), and /d/ (1); /l/ is compared to /k/ (1), /n/ (1), and /d/ (1); and /d/ is compared to /k/ (1), /n/ (1), and /d/ (0). Thus the metric is $7/9$, or 0.78.

3.2 Test

Data from 15 languages were used. These languages were selected to give a reasonably wide range of variation in their relatedness to each other. Eleven of the languages were Indo-European, and four were Uralic. Within both of those families there are subclades that are noticeably more closely related to each other than to other languages in the same family. The Indo-European set contains four Germanic languages (Old English, Old High German, Gothic and Old Norse) and two Balto-Slavic languages (Lithuanian and Old Church Slavonic); all the other languages are traditionally considered as belonging to separate branches of Indo-European: Latin, Albanian, Greek, Latin, Old Irish, and Sanskrit. The Uralic set contains three languages that subgroup in a clade called Finno-Ugric (Finnish, Hungarian, and Mari), which is rather distinct from the Samoyedic branch, which contains Nenets. Several linguists believe that the Indo-European and Uralic languages are related to each other (e.g., Bomhard, 1996; Greenberg, 2000; Kortlandt, 2002), though this hypothesis is far from being universally accepted. For each of the 15 languages, translation equivalents were found for each of the Swadesh 200 concepts, as described in Kessler and Lehtonen (2006).

The multilateral comparison algorithm described above was performed once with each of the above-described phonetic distance metrics. Each of the analyses comprised a complete hierarchical clustering of all 15 languages. For each metric, the main concern was whether a multilateral analysis performed with it would group together languages known to be related, however remotely. A second question was what similarity magnitudes would be reported for languages known to be related. In general one would expect a good phonetic distance metric to yield high magnitudes and low p values for languages known to be related, and that, all things being equal, magnitudes should increase the more closely related the languages are.

A large amount of information is available about each run of the program. The algorithm begins by performing bilateral comparisons for each pair of languages, and it might be somewhat interesting to compare those 105 data points across each of the seven metrics. Perhaps more interesting and decidedly more succinct is to focus on the numbers for each of the major clades described above (Table 1). Because almost all of the runs of the program created clusters that contained exactly the languages in each of the clades named in the column headers, it was possible to show the m value reported by the program when that cluster was formed: the degree of similarity between the two subsclusters that were joined to form the cluster in question. For example, when the algorithm using the C_1-place metric joined Old Norse up with a cluster containing Old English, Old High German, and Gothic, it reported an m value of .65 between those two groups. Because of the nature of the clustering algorithm, this represents the weakest link within the clade: in general, the similarity between languages in each of those two subclades will be higher than this number.

A striking feature of Table 1 is the stability of

Metric	Germanic	Balto-Slavic	Indo-European	Finno-Ugric	Uralic	Indo-Uralic
C_1-place	.65**	.43**	.12**	.23**	.09*	.00
C_1-Dolg	.65**	.42**	.12**	.26**	.09**	.02*
C*-DolgCross	.22**	.14**	.05**	.10**	.05**	.01
C*-DolgSeq	.57**	.37**	.09**	.22**	.07**	.02*
P_1-Dolg	.66**	.41**	.13**	.25**	.10**	.02
P_1-place	.66**	.45**	.13**	.31**	.09*	-.01
P_1-voice	.68**	.57**	(.19)	.37**	(.05)	(.05)

Table 1: Similarity Magnitudes Reported for Each Linguistic Clade. $*p < .05$. $**p < .001$. Numbers are the m values reported when the clade is constructed via clustering. If the algorithm does not posit the clade as a cluster, table reports in parentheses the average m reported for each pair of languages in the clade.

the algorithm across different phonetic distance metrics. All of them constructed the relatively easy subclades (Germanic, Balto-Slavic, and Finno-Ugric), reporting very strong significance values. All of them except P_1-voice constructed Indo-European and Uralic, which are both fairly difficult to identify; in fact P_1-voice nearly did so, except that it misclassed Nenets with the Indo-European languages. All of them assigned very low similarity magnitudes to a proposed Indo-Uralic grouping: that is, they found very little similarity between Indo-European and Uralic words for the same concept. Furthermore, the magnitudes for the various clades are all ranked in the same order. As one would hope, the subclades within each family are given much higher m values than the families themselves.

In direct comparisons between comparable version of the place metric and the Dolgopolsky metric (C_1-place vs. C_1-Dolg and P_1-place vs. P_1-Dolg), no very consistent patterns emerge. But the Dolgopolsky metrics tend to reveal the Uralic family with much higher significance levels than do the other measures, and they are also the only metrics that ever posit an Indo-Uralic clade at acceptable significance levels (C_1-Dolg at $p = .04$; C*-DolgSeq at $p = .02$). An optimistic explanation is that the Dolgopolsky classes are better at finding subtle evidence of language relatedness, and that this may be due to their being constructed eclectically. Sounds were claimed to have been grouped into classes based on the frequency with which they are known to develop into each other in the course of language change (Dolgopolsky, 1986:35), not based on any a priori principle; place of articulation clearly is a consideration, but there are many other factors involved. For example, one group comprises the coronal obstruents, except that sibilant fricatives are in a separate group of their own, and sibilant affricates are grouped with the velars. One might expect a system based on empirical data to perform better than one based on a monothetic property such as place of particulation. However, it must also be cautioned that Dolgopolsky did not explain how he gathered the statistics upon which his classes are based. Since the classes were introduced in a paper designed to show that Indo-European and Uralic, among other families, are related to each other, it is possible that the statistics were informed at least in part by patterns he perceived between those language families. There is therefore some small cause to be concerned that Dolgopolsky classes may be, if only inadvertently, somewhat tuned to the Indo-Uralic data and therefore not completely unbiased with respect to the research question.

A more consistent trend in the table is that the metrics that attempt to incorporate more information about the comparanda return lower similarity magnitudes. The C*-DolgSeq metric, which aligns the consonants and reports the average distance across all the pairs. gave substantially lower numbers than the metrics that analyze single phonemes. This observation applies even more strongly to the C*-DolgCross metric, which reported magnitudes a third the size of other measures. The result is not unexpected. It is common knowledge that initial consonants tend to be more stable than other consonants in the word; incorporating non-initial consonants into the metric means that a higher proportion of the data the metric looks at will be more dissimilar. This being the case, it may seem surprising that C*-DolgSeq and C*-DolgCross showed essentially the same connections between languages as did the other metrics, and at strong significance levels. Even though the similarity levels are close to background levels (those of semantically unmatched pairs), they are still measurably above background levels; the p values are only concerned with whether the matched data is more similar than the unmatched data, not by how much they are different.

P_1-voice was introduced to experiment with a metric that takes the other approach: instead of incorporating more material into the measure, it incorporates less. Being based on a single binary phonetic feature, P_1-voice is arguably the most minimal metric possible. Perhaps not unexpectedly, it has the opposite effect of that of C*-DolgSeq and C*-DolgCross: m measures are raised. At the same time, this metric too appears to reveal the known relations between languages. The several gaps in the table are due to a single odd choice that the algorithm made: it concluded that the Uralic language Nenets was quite similar to the Germanic languages, at least with respect to whether the first sound is voiced in semantically matched words. Presumably this connection was just a chance accident; indeed, saying that one is working with significance levels of .05 is another way of saying that one is willing to tolerate such errors about 5% of the time.

4 Conclusions

The evaluation of the methodology across 15 languages did not provide overwhelming evidence favouring one type of phonetic distance metric over another. Perhaps, by a small margin, the strongest results are obtained by comparing what Dolgopolsky classes the first consonants – or, equally well, the first phonemes – of the words fall into, but nothing seriously warns the researcher away from other approaches.

Conceivably further experiments with other data sets will reveal strengths and weaknesses of different metrics more convincingly. Until such time, however, it may be most useful to choose phonetic distance metrics primarily on theoretical, if not philosophical, criteria. Metrics that look at many parts of the word have the advantage of not missing information, even if it turns up in unusual places. It is not unknown for a branch of a language family to do something unusual like drop all initial consonants; in such an event, all the single-phoneme metrics explored here would fail entirely. One does not really wish to change one's metric for different sets of languages, because if one has the freedom to fish for different metrics until a test succeeds, one can almsot certainly – and spuriously – prove that almost all languages are related. So there is some advantage to having a metric that covers all the bases. But the similarity measures returned under such circumstances do tend to be small, and although such reduction in m did not seem to have any deleterious effect in the present experiment, it is not unreasonable to worry that weak similarity measures may cause problems in some data sets. Further, the more of a word one is looking at, the more likely it is that one will inadvertently encode length information into the metric.

The main conclusion to be drawn from this study is that the basic methodology is very hospitable to a variety of phonetic distance metrics and performs adequately and stably with any reasonable metric. Unlike parametric methods, this randomization-based methodology does not require the researcher to develop new formulas to compute strength and significance values for each new distance metric. The simple expedient of randomly rearranging the data a large number of times and recomputing the distance metric for each rearrangement provides the most literal and straightforward way of applying the key insight of the arbitrariness hypothesis: the phonetic similarity of semantically matched words will be no greater than that of semantically mismatched ones, unless some historical contingency such as descent from a common language is involved.

References

William Baxter and Alexis Manaster Ramer. 2000. Beyond lumping and splitting: probabilistic issues in historical linguistics. In *Time Depth in Historical Linguistics*, eds. C. Renfrew, A. McMahon., and L. Trask. McDonald Institute for Archaeological Research, Cambridge, England. 167–188.

Allan R. Bomhard. 1996. *Indo-European and the Nostratic Hypothesis.* SIGNUM Desktop Publishing, Charleston, SC.

Lyle Campbell. 1988. Review of Greenberg (1987). *Language* 64:591–615.

Aaron B. Dolgopolsky. 1986. A probabilistic hypothesis concerning the oldest relationships among the language families of northern Eurasia. In *Typology, Relationship, and Time: A Collection of Papers on Language Change and Relationship by Soviet Linguists*, eds. V. V. Shevoroshkin and T. L. Markey. Karoma, Ann Arbor, MI. 27–50.

Joseph H. Greenberg. 1993. Observations concerning Ringe's *Calculating the Factor of Chance in Language Comparison*. Proceedings of the American Philosophical Society, 137, 79–89.

Joseph H. Greenberg. 2000. *Indo-European and its Closest Relatives: the Eurasiatic Language Family: Grammar.* Stanford University Press, Stanford, CA.

Brett Kessler. 2001. *The Significance of Word Lists.* Center for the Study of Language and Information, Stanford, CA.

Brett Kessler. 2005. Phonetic comparison algorithms. *Transactions of the Philological Society* 103:243–260.

Brett Kessler and Annukka Lehtonen. 2006. Multilateral comparison and significance testing of the Indo-Uralic question. *Phylogenetic Methods and the Prehistory of Languages*, eds. P. Forster and C. Renfrew. McDonald Institute for Archaeological Research, Cambridge, England. 33–42.

Frederik Kortlandt. 2002. The Indo-Uralic verb. In *Finno-Ugrians and Indo-Europeans: Linguistic and Literary Contacts.* Shaker, Maastricht, 217–227.

James A. Matisoff. 1990. On megalocomparison. *Language* 66:106–120.

Robert L. Oswalt. 1998. A probabilistic evaluation of North Eurasiatic Nostratic. In *Nostratic: Sifting the Evidence.*, eds. J. C. Salmons and B.D. Joseph. Benjamins, Amsterdam. 199–216.

William J. Poser and Lyle Campbell. 1992. Indo-European practice and historical methodology. In *Proceedings of the Eighteenth Annual Meeting of the Berkeley Linguistics Society*, eds. L. A. Buszard-Welcher, L. Wee, and W. Weigel. Berkeley Linguistics Society, Berkeley, CA. 214–236.

Donald A. Ringe. 1996. The mathematics of 'Amerind'. *Diachronica* 13:135–154.

Joseph Salmons. 1992. A look at the data for a global etymology: *Tik 'finger'. In *Explanation in Historical Linguistics*, eds. G.W. Davis and G.K. Iverson. Benjamins, Amsterdam, 207–228.

Morris Swadesh. 1952. Lexico-statistic dating of prehistoric ethnic contacts. *Proceedings of the American Philosophical Society* 96:452–463.

Bayesian Identification of Cognates and Correspondences

T. Mark Ellison
Linguistics, University of Western Australia,
and Analith Ltd
mark@markellison.net

Abstract

This paper presents a Bayesian approach to comparing languages: identifying cognates and the regular correspondences that compose them. A simple model of language is extended to include these notions in an account of parent languages. An expression is developed for the posterior probability of child language forms given a parent language. Bayes' Theorem offers a schema for evaluating choices of cognates and correspondences to explain semantically matched data. An implementation optimising this value with gradient descent is shown to distinguish cognates from non-cognates in data from Polish and Russian.

Modern historical linguistics addresses questions like the following. How did language originate? What were historically-recorded languages like? How related are languages? What were the ancestors of modern languages like? Recently, computation has become a key tool in addressing such questions.

Kirby (2002) gives an overview of current current work on how language evolved, much of it based on computational models and simulations. Ellison (1992) presents a linguistically motivated method for classifying consonants as consonants or vowels. An unexpected result for the dead language Gothic provides added weight to one of two competing phonological interpretations of the orthography of this dead language.

Other recent work has applied computational methods for phylogenetics to measuring linguistic distances, and/or constructing taxonomic trees from distances between languages and dialects (Dyen et al., 1992; Ringe et al., 2002; Gray and Atkinson, 2003; McMahon and McMahon, 2003; Nakleh et al., 2005; Ellison and Kirby, 2006).

A central focus of historical linguistics is the reconstruction of parent languages from the evidence of their descendents. In historical linguistics proper, this is done by the comparative method (Jeffers and Lehiste, 1989; Hock, 1991) in which shared arbitrary structure is assumed to reflect common origin. At the phonological level, reconstruction identifies cognates and correspondences, and then constructs sound changes which explain them.

This paper presents a Bayesian approach to assessing cognates and correspondences. Best sets of cognates and correspondences can then be identified by gradient ascent on this evaluation measure. While the work is motivated by the eventual goal of offering software solutions to historical linguistics, it also hopes to show that Bayes' theorem applied to an explicit, simple model of language can lead to a principled and tractable method for identifying cognates.

The structure of the paper is as follows. The next section details the notions of historical linguistics needed for this paper. Section 2 formally defines a model of language and parent language. The subsequent section situates the work amongst similar work in the literature,

Proceedings of Ninth Meeting of the ACL Special Interest Group in Computational Morphology and Phonology, pages 15–22,
Prague, June 2007.

making use of concepts described in the earlier sections. Section 4 describes the calculation of the probability of wordlist data given a hypothesised parent language. This is combined with Bayes' theorem and gradient search in an algorithm to find the best parent language for the data. Section 5 describes the results of applying an implementation of the algorithm to data from Polish and Russian. The final section summarises the paper and suggests further work.

1 Cognates, Correspondences and Reconstruction

In the neo-Grammarian model of language change, a population speaking a uniform language divides, and then the two populations undergo separate language changes.

Word forms with continuous histories in respective daughter languages descending which from a common word-form ancestor are called **cognate**, no matter what has happened to their semantics. Cognate word forms may have undergone deformations to make them less similar to each other, these deformations resulting from regular, phonological changes. Note that in the fields of applied linguistics, second language acquisition, and machine translation, the term *cognate* is used to mean any words that are phonologically similar to each other. This is not the sense meant here.

Phonological change produces modifications to the segmental inventory, replacing one segment by another in all or only some contexts. This sometimes has the effect of collapsing segment types together. Other changes may divide one segment type into two, depending on a contextual condition. The relation of parent-language segments to daughter-language segments is, usually, a many-to-many relation.

Parent-child segmental relations are reflected in the correspondences between segment inventories in the daughter languages. **Correspondences** are pairings of segments from daughter languages which have derived from a common parent segment. For example, **p** in Latin frequently corresponds to **f** in English, as in words like **pater** and **father**. Both segments have developed from a (postulated) Proto-IndoEuropean ***p**. Because correspondences only occur between cognates, identifying the two is often a bootstrap process: corraling cognates helps find more correspondences, and forms sharing a number correspondences are probably cognate.

2 Formal Structures

The method presented in this paper is based on a formal model of language. This is described in section 2.1. The subsequent section extends the model to define a parent language, whose segmental inventory is correspondences and whose lexicon is cognates linking two descendent languages.

2.1 Language model

The language model is based on three assumptions.

Assumption 1 *There is a universal, discrete set M of meanings.*

Assumption 2 *A language L has its own set of segments $\Sigma(L)$.*

Assumption 3 *The lexicon λ of a language L is a partial map of meanings to strings of segments $\lambda : M \rightarrow \Sigma(L)^*$.*

On the basis of these assumptions, we can define a language L to be a triple $(M, \Sigma(L), \lambda(L))$ of meanings, segments and mappings from meanings onto strings of segments.

For example, consider written Polish. The set of meanings contains concepts as TO TAKE-perfect-infinitive, TREE-nominative-singular, and so on. The segmental inventory contains the 32 segments **a ą b c ć d e ę f g h i j k l ł m n ń o ó p r s ś t u w y z ż ź**, ignoring capitalisation. The lexicon matches meanings to strings of segments, TO TAKE-perfect-infinitive to **wziąć**, TREE-nominative-singular to **drzewo**.

2.2 Parent language model

Definition 1 *A degree-(u, v) **correspondence** between L_1 and L_2 is a pair of strings $(s, t) \in \Sigma(L_1) \times \Sigma(L_2)$ over the segments of L_1 and L_2*

respectively, with lengths at least u and no more than v.

As an example of a correspondence, consider the pair of small strings from Polish and Russian, **(ć,ть)**. This is a degree-$(1, 2)$ correspondence because its members have lengths as low as one and as high as two. It is also a degree-(u, v) correspondence for any $u \leq 1$ and $v \geq 2$.

Any correspondence can be mapped onto its components by projection functions.

Definition 2 *The* ***projections*** π_1 *and* π_2 *map a correspondence* (s, t) *onto its first* $\pi_1(s, t) = s$ *or second* $\pi_2(s, t) = t$ *component string respectively.*

The first projection function will map **(ć,ть)** onto **ć**, while the second maps **(ć,ть)** onto **ть**.

Correspondences can be formed into strings. These strings also have projections.

Definition 3 *The* ***projections*** π_1 *and* π_2 *map a string of correspondences* $c_1..c_k$ *onto the concatenation of the projections of each correspondence.*

$$\pi_1(c_1..c_k) = \pi_1(c_1)\pi_1(c_2)..\pi_1(c_k),$$

$$\pi_2(c_1..c_k) = \pi_2(c_1)\pi_2(c_2)..\pi_2(c_k)$$

Suppose we sequence four correspondences into the string **(w,в)(z,з)(ią,я)(ć,ть)**. This string has first and second projections, **wziąć** and **взять**, formed by concatenating the respective projections of each correspondence.

We can now define a parent language.

Definition 4 *A degree-(u, v)* ***parent*** L_0 *of two languages* L_1, L_2 *is a triple* $(M, \Sigma(L_0), \lambda(L_0))$ *where* $\Sigma(L_0)$ *is a set of degree-(u, v) correspondences between* L_1 *and* L_2*, excluding the pair of null strings, and* $\lambda(L_0)$ *is a partial mapping from* M *onto* $\Sigma(L_0)$ *which obeys*

$$\pi_1 \circ \lambda(L_0) \subseteq \lambda(L_1), \ \pi_2 \circ \lambda(L_0) \subseteq \lambda(L_2)$$

The circle stands for function composition.

Continuing our past example, we will focus on the two meanings TO TAKE-perfect-infinitive and TREE-nominative-singular. The segment inventory for the parent language contains degree-$(0, 2)$ correspondences: **(,e)**, **(ć,ть)**, **(d,д)**, **(e,e)**, **(ią,я)**, **(o,o)**, **(rz,p)**, **(w,в)**, **(z,з)**. The lexical function maps TO TAKE-perfect-infinitive onto the string of correspondences **(w,в) (z,з) (ią,я) (ć,ть)** while TREE-nominative-singular maps to **(d,д) (,e) (rz,p) (e,e) (w,в) (o,o)**.

The parent language condition is verified by checking the projections of the two correspondence strings. The first string has projections **wziąć** and **взять**, which are forms for the meaning TO TAKE-perfect-infinitive in Polish and Russian respectively. The second string has projections **drzewo** and **дерево**, which are forms for the meaning TREE-nominative-singular in Polish and Russian respectively. So the projection condition is satisfied. If the lexical function is only defined on these two meanings, then this is a valid parent language.

It is worth emphasising that the projection condition for qualifying as a parent language applies only for those meanings for which the parent lexical mapping is defined. The corresponding forms in the child languages are said to be **cognate** in this model. Where no parent form is reconstructed, the forms are not cognate, and are to be accounted for in some way other than the parent language.

3 Related Work

The current work is, of course, far from the first to seek to identify cognates and/or correspondences. Here is an abbreviated overview of previous work in the field[1]. More detailed surveys can be found in chapter 3 of Kondrak's (2002) PhD thesis or Lowe's online survey [2] of prior art in this field.

In perhaps the first computational work on historical linguistics, Kay (1964) described an algorithm for determining correspondences given a list of cognate pairs across two daughter languages. His method seeks to find the smallest set

[1]An anonymous reviewer suggests that the current work shares features with that of Kessler (2001). I have been unable to access this book in time to include discussion of it in this paper.

[2]linguistics.berkeley.edu/~jblowe/REWWW/PriorArt.html

of correspondences which allows a degree-$(1, \infty)$ alignment for each cognate pair. Unfortunately, the complexity of the problem has precluded its application to significant daa sets.

Frantz (1970) developed a PL/1 programming which returned numerical evaluations of correspondences and cognacy, given a list of possible cognate word-pairs. Each word pair must be supplied as a degree-$(0, 1)$ reconstruction, that is, aligning single segments with each other or with gaps.

Guy (1984; 1994) presented a program called COGNATE which finds regular correspondences and identifies cognates using statistical techniques.

For his Master's, Broza (1998) developed MDL-based software called *candid* which identifies correspondences from cognates and expresses these as contextual phonological transformation rules.

Kondrak's (2002) doctoral dissertation combines phonological and semantic similarity methods with correspondance-learning. The algorithms for learning correspondences are taken from Melamed's (2000) probabilistic methods for identifying word-word translation equivalence. These methods, like the current work, are Bayesian. Because Melamed's problem seeks partial rather than complete explanation of the inputs in terms of correspondences, the matching problem is somewhat more difficult theoretically. As a result, he does not arrive at the decomposition of the sum of the probability of two inputs given the set of possible correspondences, approximating this with a high probability alignment.

4 Conditional Probability of the Data

The core of any Bayesian model is the conditional probability of the data given the hypothesis. This section details how probabilities assigned to data, and the assumptions on which this assignment is based.

The data is the mapping of meanings onto forms in two daughter languages. If those two languages are L_1 and L_2, we want to determine $P(\lambda(L_1), \lambda(L_2)|h)$. The nature of h will be discussed in section 4.6.

For brevity, we will write λ_i for $\lambda(L_i)$.

4.1 Meaning independence

The first step in defining the conditional probability of the data is to decompose it into meaning-by-meaning probabilities. This can be achieved by adopting the following two assumptions.

Assumption 4 *In a given language, the forms for different meanings are selected independently.*

This assumption states that *within a single language* choosing, for example, a form **wziąć** for meaning TO TAKE-perfect-infinitive is no help in predicting the form which expresses TREE-nominative-singular.

Assumption 5 *Across different languages, the forms corresponding to different meanings are independent.*

According to this assumption, the Polish word **wziąć** and the Russian word **взять** can be structurally dependent because they express the same meaning. In contrast, we can only expect a chance relationship between the Russian word **взять** meaning TO TAKE-perfect-infinitive, and the Polish word **drzewo** expressing TREE-nominative-singular.

Together, these two assumptions imply that the only dependencies possible between any four forms expressing the two meanings m_1 and m_2 in two languages L_1 and L_2 are between $\lambda(m_1)$ and $\lambda(m_1)$ on the one hand and $\lambda(m_2)$ and $\lambda(m_2)$ on the other.

Consequently the probability of generating the word forms in two languages can be decomposed into the product of generating the two language-particular forms for each meaning.

$$P(\lambda_1, \lambda_2|h) = \prod_{m \in M} P(\lambda_1(m), \lambda_2(m)|h)$$

4.2 Cognacy and independence

The next assumption holds that structural correlation between corresponding forms should be explained as resulting from cognacy.

Assumption 6 *Across different languages, forms corresponding to the same meaning are dependent only if the forms are cognate.*

If the words for a particular meaning do not derive from a common ancestral form, then they are uncorrelated. To return to our Polish and Russian examples, we can expect dependencies in structure between the cognate words **drzewo** and **дерево**. But we should expect no such correlation in the non-cognate pair **pomarańcza** and **апельсин** meaning ORANGE-nominative-singular.

Let us write M_i for the domain of the lexical function in language L_i. This is the set of meanings for which this language has defined a word form. The set of cognates is the domain of the lexical function of the parent language, M_0. We can decompose the evidential words into three sets: M_0 of cognates, $M_1 \setminus M_0$ of meanings only expressed in language L_1, and $M_2 \setminus M_0$ of meanings only expressed in language L_2. Words in the second and third categories are non-cognate, and so probabilistically independent of each other.

The conditional probability of the data can thus be expressed as follows.

$$P(\lambda_1, \lambda_2|h) = \prod_{m \in M_0} P(\lambda_1(m), \lambda_2(m)|h)$$

$$\prod_{m \in M_1 \setminus M_0} P(\lambda_1(m)|h) \prod_{m \in M_2 \setminus M_0} P(\lambda_2(m)|h)$$

4.3 Probability of a word

We now turn to the probability of generating a string in a language. The first assumption defines the distribution over word-length.

Assumption 7 *The probability of a word having a particular length is negative exponential in that length.*

The second assumption allows segment probability to depend only on the segment identity, and not on its neighbourhood.

Assumption 8 *Segment choice is context-independent.*

These two assumptions together imply that the probability of strings is determined by a fixed distribution over $\Sigma(L_i) \cup \{\#\}$, where $\#$ is an end-of-word marker. For the descendent languages, this distribution can be taken as the relative frequencies of the segments and end-of-word marker. Denote this distribution for language L_i by f_i.

The probability of generating a word in a language, given relative frequencies f_i, is the product of the relative frequencies for each lettern in the word, multiplied by the relative frequency of the end-of-word marker.

$$P(\lambda_i(m)|h) = f_i(\#) \prod_{a \in \lambda_i(m)} f_i(a)$$

Note that this expression only holds for words that are independent of all others, such as components of non-cognate pairs.

4.4 Probability of generating a cognate pair

The probability of generating a cognate pair of words is similar to the above, because descendent forms are deterministically derivable from the parent forms. If $(\lambda_1(m), \lambda_2(m))$ are a pair of cognates derived from an ancestral form $\lambda_0(m)$, then there is unit probability that the descendent forms are what they are given the parent: $P(\lambda_1(m), \lambda_2(m)|\lambda_0(m)) = 1$.

Since a cognate pair is derivable from a parent form, the probability of a cognate pair is the sum of the probabilities of all parent forms which will generate the two descendents. Write $W(m) = W(\lambda_1(m), \lambda_2(m))$ for the set of possible correspondence strings in the parent which project onto wordforms $\lambda_1(m)$ and $\lambda_2(m)$. Then the probability of the word pair is given by:

$$P(\lambda_1(m), \lambda_2(m)|h) = \sum_{s \in W(m)} P(\lambda_0(m) = s|h)$$

The summation poses a slight problem, however. How do we sum over all possible strings with given projections? Fortunately, we can decompose the summation. Start by recognising that the parent language is also a language, and so the probability of forms in the language is determined by a distribution over segments — in this case correspondences — and the end-of-word marker. For consistency, we call this distribution f_0.

The only parent form which projects onto two empty strings is the empty string, consisting only of the end-of-word marker. For brevity, we will drop the lambdas, writing $P(x, y|h)$ for $P(\lambda_1(m) = x, \lambda_2(m) = y|h)$

$$P(0, 0|h) = f_0(\#)$$

We assume, without loss of generality, that the segmental inventory of the parent language consists of all degree-(u, v) correspondences between L_1 and L_2. Parent segments which are never used can be excluded by giving them zero relative frequency in f_0.

The function $Pre(s; u, v)$ returns the set of binary divisions (a, b) of the string s, such that the length of the first part a is at least u and at most v.

$$Pre(s; u, v) = \{(a, b)|ab = s, m \leq |a| \leq n\}$$

With this function, we can recursively define a function $W(s, t; u, v)$ on pairs of strings (s, t) which returns the set of all degree-(u, v) parent language strings which project onto s and t. For brevity, we will treat all u, v arguments as implicit.

$$W(0, 0) = \{0\}$$

By definition, the only parent language string which can map onto the empty string in both descendents is the empty string.

The recursive step breaks the strings s and t into all possible prefixes a and c respectively. The correspondence (a, c) is then preposed on all strings returned by W when it is applied to the remainders of s and t.

$$W(s, t) = \biguplus_{(a,b)\in Pre(s)} \biguplus_{(c,d)\in Pre(t)} (a, c)W(b, d)$$

Note that this is the set $W(m)$ we defined earlier.

$$W(m) = W(\lambda_1(m), \lambda_2(m); u, v)$$

The recursive definition of W in terms of disjoint unions and concatenation can be transformed into a recursive definition for the probability $P_0(s, t|h)$ of constructing a member of the set. Disjoint union is replaced by summation, concatenation by product. The probability of an individual correspondence (a, c) is its (unknown) relative frequency $f_0(a, c)$ in the parent language. Once again, we hide the implicit u, v parameters.

$$P_0(0, 0|h) = f_0(\#)$$

$$P_0(s, t|h) = \sum_{(a,b)\in Pre(s)} \sum_{(c,d)\in Pre(t)} f_0(a, c)P(b, d|h)$$

4.5 Probability of a form-pair

We now have the pieces to specify the probability of finding any particular form as the form-pair for the descendent languages. The probability of the pair in the case of cognacy is $P_0(\lambda_1(m), \lambda_2(m)|h)$. If the pair are not cognate, then they are independent, and their probability is $P_1(\lambda_1(m))P_2(\lambda_2(m)|h)$. If we write $c(m|h)$ for the likelihood that the pair is cognate, we can combine these two values to given a total probability of the two forms.

$$P_0(\lambda_1(m), \lambda_2(m)|h)c(m|h)$$

$$+P_1(\lambda_1(m))P_2(\lambda_2(m)|h)(1.0 - c(m|h))$$

Because the word-pairs are independent (assumption 4), the product of the above probability for each meaning m gives the probability of the data given the hypothesis.

4.6 Hypothesis

One burning question remains, however. What is the hypothesis? The simple answer is that it is exactly those free variables in the specification of the probability of the data

There were two groups of unknowns in the probability of the data. The first is the relative frequency f_0 assigned to correspondences in parent-language forms. The second is the likelihood of cognacy c, a vector of values between zero and one indexed by meanings.

A hypothesis is therefore any setting of values for the pair of vectors (f, c).

Note that while the degree variables u, v were not fixed in the above derivation, they will be held constant for any particular search, and thus do not define a dimension in the hypothesis space.

4.7 Search

In this section, we have derived $P(D|h)$, the likelihood of our data given a hypothesis.

For simplicity, we choose a flat prior over hypotheses, rendering the MAP Bayesian approach an instance of maximum likelihood determination. The value for the likelihood is differentiable in each of the parameters. Consequently, gradient descent can be used to find the hypothesis which maximises the probability of the data.

5 Results

In constructing the method, we made a number of assumptions about independence of forms. It is sensible that for testing, the method is applied to data that conforms reasonably well to these assumptions. The alternative is to apply it to data which contradicts its fundamental assumptions, consequently hampering its effectiveness.

5.1 The data

Polish and Russian were chosen to provide the data because they approximately obey assumption 6: words have dependent structures if and only if they are cognate. For our two languages, this means that borrowings from common sources are uncommon (numbering 45 in our data set), at least in comparison with the number of cognates (numbering 156).

The data was harvested from two online dictionaries (Wordgumbo, 2007a; Wordgumbo, 2007b), one English-Polish, the other English-Russian. Multiple translations were simplified, with the shortest translation retained. The English glosses were used as the meanings for the words. Where the gloss contained a capital letter, indicating a proper noun, this was eliminated from the data.

The data should also conform to assumption 4, that words for different meanings with a language are independent. So where two meanings in the data sets were realised with the same form, these meanings were deemed to be structurally dependent, and so only the first was retained in the wordlist.

The remaining data contains 407 aligned Polish-Russian word pairs.

Polish and Russian both use a great deal of derivational and inflectional morphology. The simple language model used here does not take this into account, so this will be a disturbing influence on the results.

5.2 Evaluation

The aligned wordlists were hand-tagged as cognate, common borrowing or non-cognate. A permissive rule of cognacy was used: if the roots of words in the two languages were cognate, they were cognate, even if represented with non-cognate derivational and/or inflectional morphology.

Figure 1 shows the evaluation of the program's performance on the data.

Borrowings as:	cognates	non-cognates
Found f	162	119
Missed m	41	37
Errant e	6	49
Accuracy $f/(f+e)$	96%	71%
Recall $f/(f+m)$	81%	76%

Figure 1: Evaluation of program performance on 407 meaning-matched pairs of Polish-Russian words. Common borrowings are scored as cognates in the first column, non-cognates in the second.

The scores show that the method works well in identifying cognates, particularly if common borrowings are accepted as cognates, or excluded manually. If common borrowings are scored as non-cognates, then the accuracy falls.

Of the correspondences found between Polish and Russian, 67 have a phonological basis. The remaining 27 result from mismatch morphology in cognates or differences in common borrowings.

6 Conclusion

This paper has presented a model of language which allows the calculation of the posterior probability of forms arising in the cases where they are cognate, and where they are not. Bayes' theorem relates these probabilities to the posterior likelihood of particular correspondences and cognacy relationships. Gradient descent can be used to search this space for the best distribution over correspondences, and best cognacy evaluations for meaning-paired words. The application to data from Polish and Russian shows remarkable success identifying both cognates and non-cognates.

Future work will proceed by relaxing constraints on the parent language. The parent inventory will be widened to include multisegment correspondences. Multiple parent languages will be permitted, to the end of separating borrowings from cognates. Finally, richer models of language, incorporating syllable structure, will allow more information to identify cognates.

References

Gil Broza. 1998. Inter-language regularity: the transformation learning problem. Master's thesis, Institute of Computer Science, Hebrew University of Jerusalem, October.

Isidore Dyen, Joseph B. Kruskal, and Paul Black. 1992. An Indo-European classification: a lexicostatistical experiment. *Transactions of the American Philosophical Society*, 82(5).

T. Mark Ellison and Simon Kirby. 2006. Measuring language divergence by intra-lexical comparison. In *ACL*, pages 273–280, Sydney.

T. Mark Ellison. 1992. *The Machine Learning of Phonological Structure.* Ph.D. thesis, University of Western Australia.

Donald G. Frantz. 1970. A PL/1 program to assist the comparative linguist. *Communications of the ACM*, 13(6):353–356.

Russell D. Gray and Quentin D. Atkinson. 2003. Language-tree divergence times support the anatolian theory of indo-european origin. *Nature*, 426:435–439.

Jacques B. M. Guy. 1984. An algorithm for identifying cognates between related languages. In *10th International Conference on Computational Linguistics and 22nd Annual Meeting of the Association for Computational Linguistics.* Available online as http://acl.ldc.upenn.edu/P/P84/P84-1091.pdf.

Jacques B. M. Guy. 1994. An algorithm for identifying cognates in bilingual wordlists and its applicability to machine translation. *Journal of Quantitative Linguistics*, 1(1):35–42.

Hans Heinrich Hock. 1991. *Principles of Historical Linguistics.* Mouton de Gruyter, Berlin.

Robert J. Jeffers and Ilse Lehiste. 1989. *Principles and Methods for Historical Linguistics.* MIT Press, Cambridge, MA.

Martin Kay. 1964. The logic of cognate recognition in historical linguistics. Technical Report RM-4224-PR, The RAND Corporation, Santa Monica, CA, September.

Brett Kessler. 2001. *The Significance of Word Lists.* CSLI Publications, Stanford, CA.

Simon Kirby. 2002. Natural language from artificial life. *Artificial Life*, 8(2):185–215.

Grzegorz Kondrak. 2002. *Algorithms for Language Reconstruction.* Ph.D. thesis, University of Toronto.

April McMahon and Robert McMahon. 2003. Finding families: quantitative methods in language classification. *Transactions of the Philological Society*, 101:7–55.

I. Dan Melamed. 2000. Models of translational equivalence among words. *Computational Linguistics*, 26(2):221–249.

Luay Nakleh, Tandy Warnow, Don Ringe, and Steven N. Evans. 2005. A comparison of phylogenetic reconstruction methods on an ie dataset. *Transactions of the Philological Society*, 103(2):171–192.

D. Ringe, Tandy Warnow, and A. Taylor. 2002. Indo-European and computational cladistics. *Transactions of the Philological Society*, 100(1):59–129.

Wordgumbo. 2007a. /ie/sla/pol/erengpol.htm. Website http://www.wordgumbo.com/.

Wordgumbo. 2007b. /ie/sla/rus/erengrus.htm. Website http://www.wordgumbo.com/.

Testing cladistics on dialect networks and phyla (gallo-romance and southern italo-romance).

Antonella GAILLARD-CORVAGLIA
EA270, Langues Romanes : acquisition, linguistique, didactique, Sorbonne Nouvelle – ParisIII
Antoc75@hotmail.com

Jean-Léo LEONARD
UMR 7018
Phonétique et Phonologie.
Sorbonne Nouvelle-ParisIII
75005 PARIS
leonard@idf.ext.jussieu.fr

Pierre DARLU
INSERM, U535
Epidémiologie génétique et structure des populations humaines
BP1000 Villejuif, F-94817
darlu@vjf.inserm.fr

Abstract

This present work deliberately abandons the purpose of capturing the global resemblance between languages and the ambition of giving a rational foundation to probability of changes in linguistics, to focus instead on cladistic approach, which was applied to different dialects and data (gallo-romance, southern italo-romance) through an original coding of philological derivations. Results show good congruence with linguistic classification and provide new insight on how tackle various dialectological problems as borrowings.

1 Introduction

In the last decades, theoretical developments in the field of the biological evolution of species and populations have been combined with increasing computer facilities, which are likely to change the practice of phylogeny reconstruction drastically. Attempts to shift such a practice in order to reconstruct the evolution of language have been proposed, since the middle of the 20th century, as evidenced by several publications that display the whole range of methodologies. One of these approaches, called Numerical Taxonomy, consists in estimating some linguistic distances between pairs of languages, from which evolutionary trees or networks are inferred to produce some linguistic classifications. This approach is classically used in dialectometry. (Evrard, 1964; Goebl, 1981, 1987, Scapoli et al., 2005, Ben Hamed, 2005). A more recent approach, based on Bayesian principles, suggests to attach some probabilities to each linguistic change (Gray et al, 2003), looking for the most likely tree, given the model and the observed data. Finally, the last kind of approach, inherited from XIXth century linguists, is the cladistic approach, as formalized by Hennig (1950) and clearly advocated by some linguists, although using various methodologies (Hoenigswald and Wiener, 1987; Wang, 1988; Holden, 2001; Ringe et al., 2002; Rexova et al., 2003; Nakhleh et al., 2005; Ben Hamed et al., 2005).

The present work is focusing on cladistics, abandoning the purpose of capturing the global resemblance between languages and the ambition of giving a rational foundation to probability of linguistic changes, adopting instead a strategy enabling us to integrate linguistic hypotheses before drawing inference on the evolution of linguistic traits and languages, and possibly to refute them. To check the heuristic value of this methodology, we endeavour to apply cladistics to dialectal data from different sources, hoping to bring forward and discuss some arguments on their diversification in space and time. As far as we know, cladistic is more often applied to language families than to dialect areas, so that our research is pioneering the field, raising the controversial question concerning the best representation of dialectal diversity: tree-like and/or networks.

2 The data

2.1 Oïl Dialect[1]. We began our experiment with the oïl dialects, our starting point being the

[1] Oïl Dialect indicates the branch of the gallo-Romance languages developed in the North of France, south of Belgium (Walloon Area) and inthe Anglo-Normans islands.

Proceedings of Ninth Meeting of the ACL Special Interest Group in Computational Morphology and Phonology, pages 23–30,
Prague, June 2007.

Linguistic Atlas of France (ALF, Gilliéron and Edmont,1902-1910, reprint: 1968) which has already been extensively exploited by others in a context of global resemblance (Goebl, 1981, 1992). In order to delimit a precise and homogeneous field, the characters observed are limited only to the vocalism of these dialects, mainly stressed and oral vowels, even if a few series of facts from nasal and unstressed vocalism are taken into account. As far as the Oïl data is concerned, the selected localities amount to 45, from East to West, in order to limit our scope in this first attempt (figure 2).

ALF	Beau <*bĕllum* (13); Bien<*bĕne* (8); Blé<*blātum* (11); Bœuf <*bŏvem* (5); Cher <*cārum* (9); Eau<*ăquam* (14); Fait <*făctum* (5); Faucille<*fălcīculam* (8); Faux<*fălcem* (15); Feuille<*fŏliam* (11); Fleurs <*flōres* (8); Lit<*lĕctum* (9); Mûr <*matūrum* (14); Mûre <*matūram* (7); Pain<*pănem* (15); Père<*pătrem* (7); Pied<*pĕdem* (13); Poing<*pŭgnum* (10); Pré<*prātum* (16); Puits<*pŭteus* (14);Seigle<*sĕcalem* (21); Tendre<*tĕndere* (7); Toile<*tēlam* (20);
ALI	Bocca < *bŭccam* (16); Braccio < *brăchium* (18); Capelli < *capēllos/pĭlos* (19); Dente < *dĕntem* (18); Dito < *dĭgĭtum* (16); Dolce < *dŭlcem* (17); Fegato < *fīcatum* (15); Forte < *fŏrte* (11); Ginocchio < *genŭculum* (16); Gengiva < *gĕngīvam* (19) Gomito < *cŭbĭtum* (18); Grasso < *grăssum* (10); Grida(lui) <*critāre/allocutāre* (12); Odore < *odōrem* (11); Piede < *pĕdem* (18); Ridere < *rīdĕre* (16); Sopracciglia <*supercĭlĭum* (19); Sudore < *sudōrem* (17); Vedere < *vĭdēre* (18); Voce < *vŏcem* (16)

Table 1. Selected words from ALF and ALI Atlases. In parentheses is the number of derivations (states) for each selected world

We selected 23 words from the ALF (Table 1), yielding a variable number of forms or phonetic changes, representing the stressed vocalism of the dialects of Oïl (short/long, high/mid/low vowels in open and close syllabic context).

2.2 Southern Italo-Romance (SIR). We then applied the same type of cladistic analysis to the dialects of the dialectal area of Southern Italo-Romance. We made use of the data relating to the consonant system of these dialects, with ALI (Atlante Linguistico dell' Italia, 1995) as a source. In this case, 21 localities were sampled for this analysis, picking up three varieties for each main dialect of these areas (northern, central, and southern: 3 for Campanian, Basilian, Apulian, Calabrian, Sicilian and Salentinian, including also three varieties of Sardinian). The lexical sample amounts to 20 words (Table 1).

3 Cladistic analysis

3.1 Linguistic prolegomena. From the quoted corpora, diachronic trees were created using the existing bibliography (Chauveau, 1989; Pignon, 1960). But we must reckon and point out that we had a very hard time in trying to make sense out of contradictory or underspecified accounts on chains of phonetic changes available in the literature. We found out – to our bewilderment – that most phonetic changes are quite often telescoped in handbooks of Romance dialectology, monographs, and Ph.D. dissertations, giving only the first and the last stage of phonetic changes: *A > D, instead of *A > *B > *C > D. We therefore had to rely on principles of areologic continuity, as the process of stepping is made hazardous by the vacuum on the successive stages of the sound changes in the literature, in particular in the peripheral varieties of oïl (except in Chauveau's monographs on western Oïl dialects). These principles are the following:

Pr.1. *Principle of areologic continuity*: implies a gradual theory of linguistic change whose stages can be reconstructed on the basis of areal configurations. It entails that stages *B and *C of a *A > D change are available on the maps in current dialects not far from a contiguous centre of gravity. For instance, in western oïl dialects, *e > oi goes through a *e > ei > ai > oi vowel shift whose *ai phase is still to be seen on the ALF maps in the neighbourhood, but it is not akin with the far distant *e > oi change in the East (in Romance lorrain), where the chain *e > ei >oi does not entail an *ai phase.

Pr.2. *Principle of parsimony*: it claims that the vocalic system develops with parsimony the strategies of change; not more than two or three major structural options from which the later evolutions unfold.

Pr.3. *Principle of unitarianism and naturalness*: dialectal idiosyncrasies should be rare upstream and abundant downstream. In other words, change is strongly constrained typologically closer to the root of the stepping tree, and gets more and more free at the end of the branches. One should be cautious with the intricate complexity of explanations found in monographs and handbooks on idiosyncrasy of changes in local dialects. More simply, one could state that changes are constrained according to UG (Universal Grammar) principles on the first hand, and specified by local, language or dialect-specific parameters on the second hand.

3.2. Cladistic procedure. In order to apply cladistic procedure to linguistic data, one has first to find a way to code the trees of philological derivations through a coding procedure which takes into account all the hypotheses assumed by the linguists. In a second step, the field observations have to be coded, and, finally, tree building algorithms are implemented to meet optimal criteria, i.e. parsimony in this context. However, within the framework of this necessarily short paper, we will only discuss tree structure, tackling briefly the feasible reconstruction of ancestral state at nodes, but keeping detailed development for further presentation.

3.2.1 *Character coding*

Figure 1a shows how the relationships between vocalic variations of a given word ("Père", as an example) are coded. Each variant takes the value 0 or 1 depending on its place within the tree derivation. First, a matrix is built (figure 1b), where rows stand for the coding of the variants, whereas columns hold for the transformations from a plesiomorphic variant (the initial diachronic state, or etymon) to an apomorphic one (the terminal state, or synchronic reflexes). For example, the inferred variant, *aé (lettered A), derived from the late latin variant of the A[[2] variable, is coded by the vector [0000000], being the ancestral variant, while its derived reflexes are all coded 1, in the first column. Likewise, the apomorphic variant é:é (lettered F) is coded by the vector [1001100], the first 1 indicates that this variant is derived from the é variant (B), and the fourth and fifth 1 indicate that it is also derived successively from –é– to –à:é– (B–>E) and from –à:é– to – é:é– (E–>F).

[2] A[reads as classical latin low vowel in open syllable as in PA-TREM, MA-REM (noted < [>, whereas <] > stands for a closed syllabe as in –AR- : AR-CUM, AR-TEM).

(a)

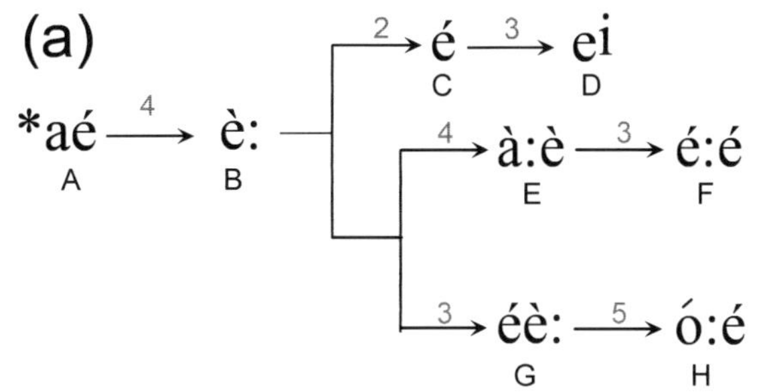

(b)

	A->B	B->C	C->D	B->E	E->F	B->G	G->H
W	4	2	3	4	3	3	5
A	0	0	0	0	0	0	0
B	1	0	0	0	0	0	0
C	1	1	0	0	0	0	0
D	1	1	1	0	0	0	0
E	1	0	0	1	0	0	0
F	1	0	0	1	1	0	0
G	1	0	0	0	0	1	0
H	1	0	0	0	0	1	1

(c)

From \ to ->	A	B	C	D	E	F	G	H
A	.	4	6	9	8	11	7	12
B	i	.	2	5	4	7	3	8
C	i	i	.	3	i	i	i	i
D	i	i	i	.	i	i	i	i
E	i	i	i	i	.	3	i	i
F	i	i	i	i	i	.	i	i
G	i	i	i	i	i	i	.	5
H	i	i	i	i	i	i	i	.

Figure 1: tree of derivation of the word "Père" (a), its factorized (c) and matrix (d) representations. Each column in (b) corresponds to a change in the tree derivation. The vector W allows a weighting of each shift (example of a 423433 weight-chain, values being expressed above each arrow, and in red colour). The arrows indicate the orientation of changes. Backward changes have an infinity weight. The (c) matrix provides equivalent information, with i holding for infinity weight. (b) and (c) representations are fitted for PHYLIP and PAUP respectively.

Since the transformations can be estimated to be more or less current in term of phonological naturalness, they can be weighed by giving heavy weights for natural or rare transformations and light weights for easy transformations. In this work, character weight was ranged on a scale between 1 and 5 (e.g. w [423433], figure 1).

Lastly, since the transformations are polarized, meaning that we hypothesize the absence of backward changes, we allocate an infinite weight for reversal transformation (i.e. no reversion allowed). This kind of coding is routinely used by phylogeneticists (see PHYLIP or PAUP software). All the derivation trees are available on request.

3.2.2. *Data coding and tree reconstruction*

Once the character coding step is performed for all the words investigated (23 different words for the Oïl data (ALF), 20 for SIR (ALI)), each area or dialect is coded according to the previous coding. In the example of the Oïl investigation, data were collected for 45 geographical different areas (figure 2), each of them having its own way to pronounce each of the 23 words of the sample. For example (Table 2), the row « 16Bourg [3]» has the variant C for the first word ("Père") described on the first column. This means that this area as well as the area numbered 45, 59, 65, and 143 share the same derived variant: –é– (labelled C, figure 1), while the rows labelled 108 and 153 share the –è:– reflex variant (B), variants that they inherited either from some common ancestor or because of geographical proximity.

16Bourg	CGLCREJB?NIFFDDEDDDJBBF
45FrCom	CBB?FGEEENCIGIDEDEFJBCF
59LorrRom	CILEMJFBEOFFDCHEDEFEDEF
65FrcomE	CAB?HGE?GNNGKIHEDEFB?BF
108BerNE	BILCGCGEENTFGBECDDDJ?MF
146Champ	CJNHQHLHE?JGGGGEADDF?GC
153Lorr	BILCEHCCEHGJJHHEGEED?BD

Table 2: Part of the data matrix from the ALF sample. First column is "Père" coding.

Finally, each letter of this data matrix is replaced by its coding (figure 1b), as it has been done in the previous step (character coding). For instance the letter C, column 1 (figure 2) is replaced by the vector [1100000], the letter B by [1000000]. The tree building reconstruction is carried out from this final matrix which sums up all the linguistic hypotheses (tree of philological derivation, polarity of changes, weighting, and geographic variants).

Factorisation are performed with FACTOR software (Felsenstein, 2004), parsimonious trees being obtained with PAUP* (v4.0) (Swofford, 2002), using TBR (tree-bisection-reconnection), random agglomeration option (100), holding 6 best trees at each steps. Tree length, consistency index and retention index are also estimated. The most parsimonious trees are then plotted figures 3 and 4. An example of inferred parallelism is also shown on figure 3. Once clades are well characterized, it becomes possible to count the number of parallelisms that are shared within each clade and those that are shared between clades, giving an estimation of the intensity of borrowing.

Figure 2: localization of the Oïl and SIR dialect samplings. Contour lines (upper map) correspond to clades from the figure 3.

4 Results

4.1. In the *Oïl dialects tree* (figures 2 and 3), the central varieties appear as a clade (C1, from 251Champagne NO to 478Noirmoutier, fuchsia and yellow clades), which gathers the dialects of the Paris basin and those of the mid-west plains, and includes peripheral spots, like Noirmoutier (478) or Saintongeais (518Saintonge). This major node (Center-Western macro-area) makes up a unit of the great mid-west, having the subset Normano-Picardo-Gallo (C2 and C3) as a peripheral compact core. Opposite to this, a very consistent and geographically gradual unit clustering the Franc-Comtois and the Walloon (C4, from 153Lorraine S to 197Wallon O, green clade) varieties, in the Eastern part of the macro-dialect network of Northern Gallo-Romance (i.e., oïl), together with

[3] Number refers to the ALF or ALI areas

the Romance Lorraine[4] dialects. In addition to these great divisions between Central-Western oïl and Peripheric Eastern oïl, which is fairly consistent with current classifications of oïl dialects (Goebl, 1984, 2002), the advantage of this tree lies in the consistency of the inner structures of the major or intermediate clades.

Table 3 gives the estimation of the number of parallelisms and/or borrowings within and between clades. Clearly the number of parallelism observed within each clades turns out to be more intense within than between clades.

	C1	C2	C3	C4
C1: Fuchsia+Yellow	3.66	1.47	.084	1.19
C2: Red	1.47	4.59	1.53	1.22
C3: Blue	0.84	1.53	9.38	1.68
C4: Green	1.19	1.22	1.68	6.19

Table 3: Estimation of the number of parallelisms and/or borrowings within (diagonal) and between clades, standardized by the number of possible exchanges. Clades are defined as figure 3.

4.2. Concerning the *Southern Italo-Romance* (SIR), from Naples to Sicily and Sardinia, the congruence between the cladistic tree (figure 4) and the philological classifications is satisfactory (Goebl, 1984; Grassi et al., 1997), and most of novelties lay in the inner structures of the tree. The phylogram of the SIR shows three major divisions (figure 4): two peripheries, the first one gathering Sardinian Central-Southerner varieties (786 and 748) and the southernmost apulien (818) (red cluster), and the second one (fuchsia) grouping the central-northern apulian (846,828)) as an external branch with the southernmost basilian and central salentino (868 and 917) This last branch is connected to an inner group which separates the branch from Sicilian-Sardinian-Salentino (in blue) from the campano-calabro-basilian (green and yellow). A most interesting detail is the place of 818Apul, a Gallo-Romance francoprovençal dialect settled in two villages (Faeto and Celle) San Vito by the Angevine dynasty in Northern Apulia during the 13th century. This dialect, previously spoken in the Ain and Isère departments in France, got into close, symbiotic contact with Apulian, a dialect of the SIR type. The cladistic procedure grasped accurately its allogenic structure, clustering it in the upper branch, along with Sardinian – also a distinct language as compared to SIR- which should therefore considered as a "foreign languages branch" rather than a peripheric node of the SIR continuum.

[4] As opposed to German Lorrain dialects (Lower-German type) spoken around Metz, whereas Romance Lorrain oïl dialects are or were spoken around Nancy and in the Vosges hills.

5 Discussion

The cladistic approach developed here provides a convenient way to integrate and test various hypotheses concerning the linguistic changes. Particularly, the rare or relative absence of backmutation in phonological characters is correctly taken into account by forbidden reverse changes, and complex relationships between states of traits are easily handled, unlike most of the other methods (as network approaches). The parsimony criterion consists to optimise the tree in minimising parallelism. The residual inferred parallelisms could clearly be visualized simply by looking at the places they occur along the tree (as exemplified figure 3). A way to circumvent the parallelism problem, when several parsimonious trees are found, would be using a successive weighting process which looks for parsimonious trees by assigning to each trait a weight inversely proportional to its degree of homoplasy (only parallelism in our case since reversion are not allowed) (Farris 1969). No such a process was necessary with our dataset since only one parsimonious tree was found. However, the robustness of the parsimonious tree remains difficult to evaluate, as long as only few words are integrated in our dataset (only 23 and 20 for Oil and SIR data respectively), particularly to appropriately implement resampling procedures (bootstrap or jackknife).

At this stage of interpretation, one cannot differentiate between parallel development and borrowing, unless some *a priori* are introduced to do so. In our data set, parallelisms are frequent (leading to a weak CI) although our two parsimonious trees are unique and well resolved (actually, there is no simple relation between CI and tree resolution) preventing us using various

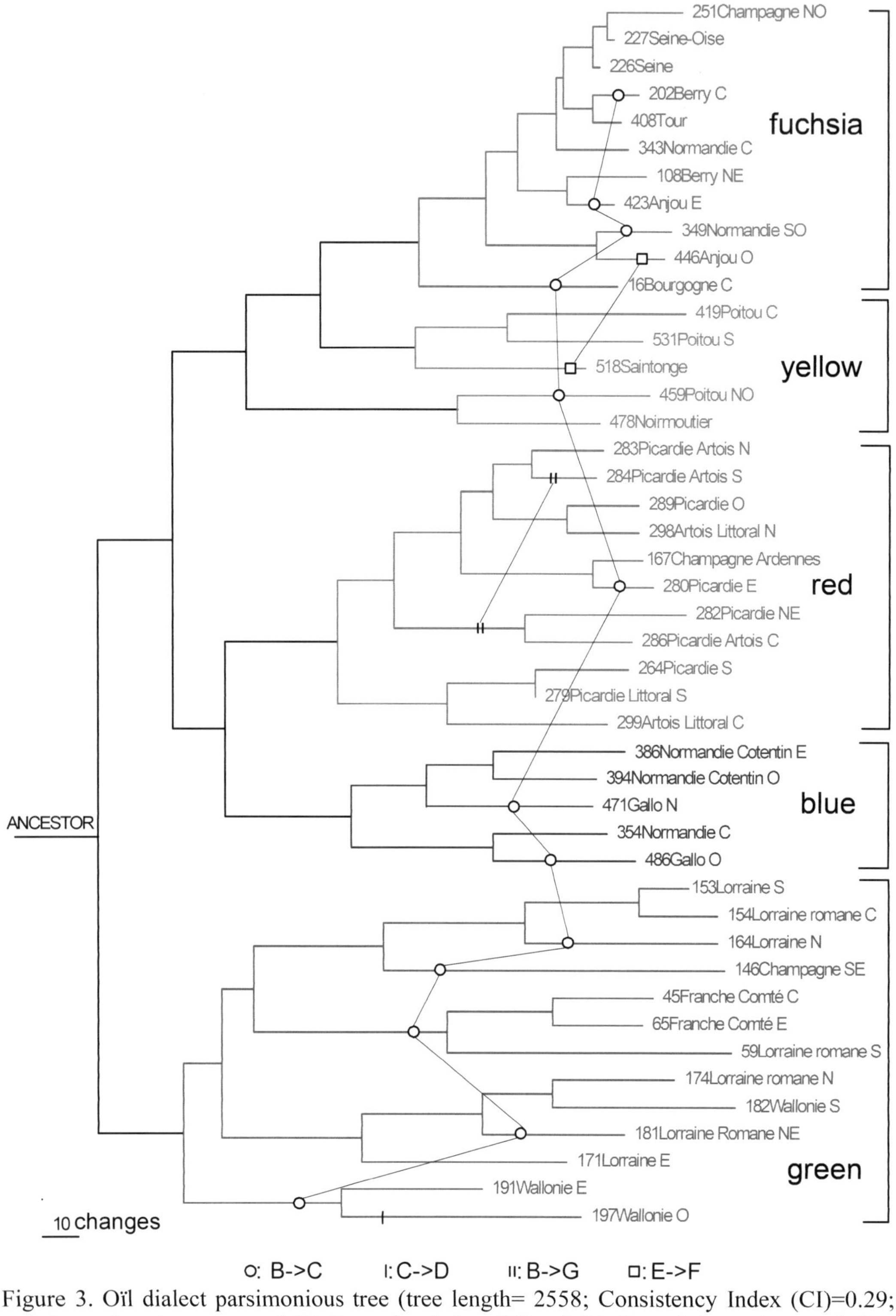

Figure 3. Oïl dialect parsimonious tree (tree length= 2558; Consistency Index (CI)=0.29; CI excluding uninformative characters = 0.22. Retention index (RI) = 0.74; Rescaled consistency index (RC) = 0.21). Branch lengths are proportional to the number of changes. Dialect numbers are labelled as in ALF. Parallel changes for "Père" are localized on the branches (see also figure 1)

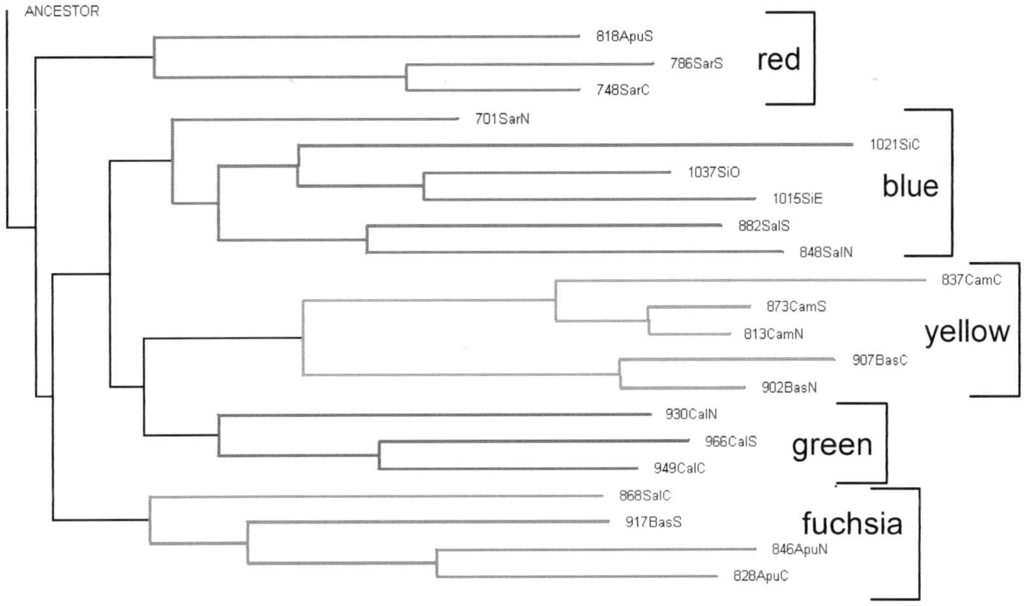

Figure 4 : SIR's parsimonious tree (Parsimonious tree: length = 1529, Consistency index (CI) = 0.59 ; CI excluding uninformative characters =0.40 ; Retention index (RI) = 0.53 ; Rescaled consistency index (RC) = 0.32) (Apu: Apulian;Si:Sicilian; Sar:Sardinian; Cal:Calabrian; Cam:Campanian; Bas: Basilian. N: North; C: Centre; S:South. (see also figure 2)

network approaches[5] (median network or median joining based on characters, definitively excluding neighbornet method which is based on global resemblance and is in any way cladistic). These approaches are not able, as far as we know, to handle large amount of polarized changes and complex weighted multistate relationships. On the other hand, our strategy turns out to be quite different from the one proposed by Nakhelh et al (2006) which first apply compatibility method to select the best traits allowing to retain few trees considered as "almost perfect phylogenies" (missing the phylogenetic information brought by the other traits), and then to parsimoniously handle the remaining traits as possible edges representing borrowing, (but not giving the possibility of modifying the tree structure accordingly). An additional advantage (only lightly evoked in this paper) of the cladistic approach is to allow inferring changes of the traits along the tree, suggesting some linguistic scenarios, as correlated changes, borrowings …

[5] See SPLITTREE and NETWORK packages in ref.

6 Conclusions

We shall conclude this pioneering cladistic survey of phyla and dialect networks pointing out at three main assets of our data processing : i) unlike most of current and past research in taxonomy applied to linguistic data, we tried to do much more than merely computing distance and similarity between lists of lexical cognates with a binary procedure: we processed data according to geolinguistic analysis, using area linguistic procedures and phonological markedness theory in endowing weight to reflexes, ii) our results are mainly congruent and consistent with current classification, but intricate patterns in the inner structures of cladistic nodes also challenging these classifications, iii) In spite of the small number of words presently studied here, but thanks to accurate data and proper sampling from the ALF and ALI database, it turns out that, by applying cladistics, for long advocated by linguists, one can obtain consistent, reliable (and possibly refutable) results. This is not always the case in the processing of fuzzy data and mere lists of words.

Linguists and cladisticians should therefore be cautious about word-lists, and should as well rely on linguistic atlases, which provide the widest array of sampling, and high quality data gathered through fieldwork by highly trained professionals. In other words, to put it straightforwardly, well managed empiricism is *a sine qua non* condition for reliable results in quantitative linguistics, especially as far as cladistics is concerned, due to the powerfulness of the procedure.

7 References

ALI, *Atlante Linguistico Italiano*. 1995-1996. Istituto Poligrafico dello Stato, vol. I-II.

ALF, Gilliéron J, Edmont E. 1902-1910. *Atlas linguistique de France*, Paris, 10 vol. (re-edition: Boulogne 1968)

Ben Hamed M., Darlu P., Vallée N. 2005. On Cladistic reconstruction of linguistic trees through vocalic data. *J. of Quantitative Linguistics*,12(1) :79-109

Ben Hamed M., 2005. Neighbour-nets portray the Chinese dialect continuum and the linguistic legacy of China's demic history. *Proceedings of the Royal Society of London B* , 272:1015–1022.

Chauveau J.-P. 1989. *Evolutions phonétiques en gallo,* Paris : CNRS (coll. Sciences du Langage) ,293 p.

Evrard E. 1964. Etude statistique sur les affinités de cinquante-huit dialectes Bantous." in: *Statistique et Analyse linguistique*, Colloque de Strasbourg 20-22 avril 1964. Presses Universitaires de France, 1966

Farris J.S. 1969. A successive approximations approach to character weighting. *Sys Zool* 18:374-85

Felsenstein J. 2004. PHYLIP (Phylogeny Inference Package) version 3.6b. Department of Genome Sciences, University of Washington, Seattle.

Goebl H. 1981. Eléments d'analyse dialéctometrique (avec application à l'AIS). *Revue de Linguistique Romane*, 45, 349-420

Goebl H 1984. Dialektometrische Studien. Anhand italoromanischer, rätoromanischer und gallo-romanischer Sprachmaterialien aus AIS und ALF, Tübingen (Niemeyer), 3 vol. 254S., 379S., 289S.

Goebl H. 1987. Points chauds de 'analyse dialectométrique: pondération et visualization. *Revue de Linguistique Romane*, 51 :63-118.

Goebl H 1992. Problèmes et méthodes de la dialectométrie actuelle. *IKER 7*. Euskaltzaindia. Real Academia de la lengua Vasca, Bilbao, pp429-475.

Goebl H 2002. Analyse dialectométrique des structures de profondeur de l'ALF. *Revue de linguistique romane*. 261-262 : 5-64

Grassi C, Sobrero A, Telmon T, 1997. Fondamenti di dialettologia italiana, Editori Laterza, Bari.

Gray R.D, Atkinson Q.D. 2003. Language-tree divergence times support the Anatolian theory of Indo-European origin. *Nature* |(426): 435-437

Hennig W 1950. *Grundzüge einer Theorie der Phylogenetischen Systematik*. Deutscher Zentralverlag (Berlin)

Hoenigswald M. H. and Wiener F L 1987. *Biological Metaphor and Cladistic Classification: An Interdisciplinary Perspective.* University of Pennsylvania Press, Philadelphia.

Holden C.J. 2001. Bantu language trees reflect the spread of farming across sub-saharian Africa: a maximum parsimony analysis. *Proceeding of the Royal Society (London)* 269:793-799.

Nakhleh L.; Ring D., Warnow T. 2005. Perfect phylogenetic networks: a new methodology for reconstructing the evolutionary history of natural languages. *Language* 11(2):382-420.

NETWORK v4.2.0.1, 2007. www.fluxusengineering.com/network_terms.html

Pignon E. 1960. L'évolution phonétique des parlers du Poitou (Vienne et Deux-Sèvres). Editions d'Artrey, Paris.

Rexova K., Frynta D., Zrzavy J. 2003. Cladistic analysis of languages: Indo-European classification based on lexicostatistical data. *Cladistics* (19):120-127.

Ringe D, Warnow T., Taylor A., 2002. Indo-European and computational cladistics. *Transaction of the philological society.* 100(1):59-129.

Scapoli C., Goebl H., Sobota S., Mamolini E., Rodriguez-Larralde A., Barraï I. 2005. Surnames and dialects in France: piopulation structure and cultural evolution. *J Theor Biol.* 237(1):75-86.

SPLITTREEv4beta. 2005. www.splittree.org

Swofford, D.L. 2002. PAUP*. Phylogenetic Analysis Using Parsimony (*and other methods). Version 4.0. Sinauer Associates, Sunderland, Massachusetts.

Wang W.S.Y. 1987. Representing languages relationships. In: Hoenigswald, M. H. and Wiener, F. L. (1987) " *Biological Metaphor and Cladistic Classification : An Interdisciplinary Perspective*" University of Pennsylvania Press, Philadelphia

The relative divergence of Dutch dialect pronunciations from their common source: an exploratory study

Wilbert Heeringa
Department of Humanities Computing
University of Groningen
Groningen, The Netherlands
w.j.heeringa@rug.nl

Brian Joseph
Department of Linguistics
The Ohio State University
Columbus, Ohio, USA
bjoseph@ling.ohio-state.edu

Abstract

In this paper we use the *Reeks Nederlandse Dialectatlassen* as a source for the reconstruction of a 'proto-language' of Dutch dialects. We used 360 dialects from locations in the Netherlands, the northern part of Belgium and French-Flanders. The density of dialect locations is about the same everywhere. For each dialect we reconstructed 85 words. For the reconstruction of vowels we used knowledge of Dutch history, and for the reconstruction of consonants we used well-known tendencies found in most textbooks about historical linguistics. We validated results by comparing the reconstructed forms with pronunciations according to a proto-Germanic dictionary (Köbler, 2003). For 46% of the words we reconstructed the same vowel or the closest possible vowel when the vowel to be reconstructed was not found in the dialect material. For 52% of the words all consonants we reconstructed were the same. For 42% of the words, only one consonant was differently reconstructed. We measured the divergence of Dutch dialects from their 'proto-language'. We measured pronunciation distances to the proto-language we reconstructed ourselves and correlated them with pronunciation distances we measured to proto-Germanic based on the dictionary. Pronunciation distances were measured using Levenshtein distance, a string edit distance measure. We found a relatively strong correlation (r=0.87).

1 Introduction

In Dutch dialectology the *Reeks Nederlandse Dialectatlassen* (RND), compiled by Blancquaert & Pée (1925-1982) is an invaluable data source. The atlases cover the Dutch language area. The Dutch area comprises The Netherlands, the northern part of Belgium (Flanders), a smaller northwestern part of France, and the German county of Bentheim. The RND contains 1956 varieties, which can be found in 16 volumes. For each dialect 139 sentences are translated and transcribed in phonetic script. Blancquaert mentions that the questionnaire used for this atlas was conceived of as a range of sentences with words that illustrate particular sounds. The design was such that, e.g., various changes of older Germanic vowels, diphthongs and consonants are represented in the questionnaire (Blancquaert 1948, p. 13). We exploit here the historical information in this atlas.

The goals of this paper are twofold. First we aim to reconstruct a 'proto-language' on the basis of the RND dialect material and see how close we come to the protoforms found in Gerhard Köbler's *neuhochdeutsch-germanisches Wörterbuch* (Köbler, 2003). We recognize that we actually reconstruct a stage that would never have existed in prehistory. In practice, however, we are usually forced to use incomplete data, since data collections -- such as the RND – are restricted by political boundaries, and often some varieties are lost. In this paper we show the usefulness of a data source like the RND.

Second we want to measure the divergence of Dutch dialects compared to their proto-language. We measure the divergence of the dialect pronunciations. We do not measure the number of changes that happened in the course of time. For

Proceedings of Ninth Meeting of the ACL Special Interest Group in Computational Morphology and Phonology, pages 31–39,
Prague, June 2007.

example if a [u] changed into a [y] and then the [y] changed into a [u], we simply compare the [u] to the proto-language pronunciation. However, we do compare Dutch dialects to both the proto-language we reconstruct ourselves, which we call ***P**roto-**L**anguage **R**econstructed* (PLR), and to the Proto-language according to the proto-Germanic Dictionary, which we call ***P**roto-**G**ermanic according to the **D**ictionary* (PGD).

2 Reconstructing the proto-language

From the nearly 2000 varieties in the RND we selected 360 representative dialects from locations in the Dutch language area. The density of locations is about the same everywhere.

In the RND, the same 141 sentences are translated and transcribed in phonetic script for each dialect. Since digitizing the phonetic texts is time-consuming on the one hand, and since our procedure for measuring pronunciation distances is a word-based method on the other hand, we initially selected from the text only 125 words. Each set represents a set of potential cognates, inasmuch as they were taken from translations of the same sentence in each case. In Köbler's dictionary we found translations of 85 words only; therefore our analyses are based on those 85 words.

We use the *comparative method* (CM) as the main tool for reconstructing a proto-form on the basis of the RND material. In the following subsections we discuss the reconstruction of vowels and consonants respectively.

2.1 Vowels

For the reconstruction of vowels we used knowledge about sound developments in the history of Dutch. In Old Dutch the diphthongs /ai/ and /au/ turned into monophthongs /eː/ and /oː/ respectively (Quak & van der Horst 2002, p. 32). Van Bree (1996) mentions the tendencies that lead /eː/ and /oː/ to change into /iː/ and /uː/ respectively. From these data we find the following chains:

ɑi	→	ɛi	→	e	→	i
ɑu	→	ɔu	→	o	→	u

An example is *twee* 'two' which has the vowel [ɑ] in 11% of the dialects, the [ɛ] in 14% of the dialects, the [e] in 43% of the dialects and the [i] in 20% of the dialects. [1] According to the *neuhochdeutsch-germanisches Wörterbuch* the [ɑ] or [ɑi] is the original sound. Our data show that simply reconstructing the most frequent sound, which is the [e], would not give the original sound, but using the chain the original sound is easily found.

To get evidence that the /ɑi/ has raised to /e/ (and probably later to /i/) in a particular word, we need evidence that the /e/ was part of the chain. Below we discuss another chain where the /i/ has lowered to /ai/, and where the /e/ is missing in the chain. To be sure that the /e/ *was* part of the chain, we consider the frequency of the /e/, i.e. the number of dialects with /e/ in that particular word. The frequency of /e/ should be higher than the frequency of /ɛ/ and/or higher than the frequency of /i/. Similarly for the change from /ɑu/ to /o/ we consider the frequency of /o/.

Another development mentioned by Van Bree is that high monophthongs diphthongize. In the transition from middle Dutch to modern Dutch, the monophthong /iː/ changed into /ɛi/, and the monophthong /yː/ changed into either /œy/ or /ɔi/ (Van der Wal, 1994). According to Van Bree (1996, p. 99), diphthongs have the tendency to lower. This can be observed in Polder Dutch where /ɛi/ and /œy/ are lowered to /ai/ and /au/ (Stroop 1998). We recognize the following chains:

i	→	ɛi	→	ɑi
y	→	œy/ɔi	→	ɑu
u	→	ɔu	→	ɑu

Different from the chains mentioned above, we do not find the /e/ and /o/ respectively in these chains. To get evidence for these chains, the frequency of /e/ should be lower than both the frequency of /ɛ/ and /i/, and the frequency of /o/ should be lower than both /ɔ/ and /u/.

Sweet (1888, p. 20) observes that vowels have the tendency to move from back to front. Back

[1] The sounds mentioned may be either monophthongs or diphthongs.

vowels favour rounding, and front vowels unrounding. From this, we derive five chains:

i	←	y	←	u
ɪ	←	ʏ	←	ʊ
e	←	ø	←	o
ɛ	←	œ	←	ɔ
a	←	←	←	ɑ

However, unrounded front vowels might become rounded under influence from a labial or labiodental consonant. For example *vijf* 'five' is sometimes pronounced as [vif] and sometimes as [vyf]. The [i] has been changed into [y] under influence of the labiodental [v] and [f].

Sweet (1888, p. 22) writes that the dropping of unstressed vowels is generally preceded by various weakenings in the direction of a vowel close to schwa. In our data we found that the word *mijn* 'my' is sometimes [i] and sometimes [ə]. A noncentral unstressed vowel might change into a central vowel which in turn might be dropped. In general we assume that deletion of vowels is more likely than insertion of vowels.

Most words in our data have one syllable. For each word we made an inventory of the vowels used across the 360 varieties. We might recognize a chain in the data on the basis of vowels which appear at least two times in the data. For 37 words we could apply the tendencies mentioned above. In the other cases, we reconstruct the vowel by using the vowel found most frequently among the 360 varieties, working with Occam's Razor as a guiding principle. When both monophthongs and diphthongs are found among the data, we choose the most frequent monophthong. Sweet (1888, p. 21) writes that isolative diphthongizaton "mainly affects long vowels, evidently because of the difficulty of prolonging the same position without change."

2.2 Consonants

For the reconstruction of consonants we used ten tendencies which we discuss one by one below.

Initial and medial voiceless obstruents become voiced when (preceded and) followed by a voiced sound. Hock & Joseph (1996) write that weakening (or lenition) "occurs most commonly in a medial voiced environment (just like Verner's law), but may be found in other contexts as well." In our data set *zes* 'six' is pronounced with a initial [z] in most cases and with an initial [s] in the dialects of Stiens and Dokkum. We reconstructed [s].[2]

Final voiced obstruents of an utterance become voiceless. Sweet (1888, p. 18) writes that the natural isolative tendency is to change voice into unvoiced. He also writes that the "tendency to unvoicing is shown most strongly in the stops." Hock & Joseph (1996, p. 129) write that final devoicing "is not confined to utterance-final position but applies word-finally as well."[3] In our data set we found that for example the word-final consonant in *op* 'on' is sometimes a [p] and sometimes a [b]. Based on this tendency, we reconstruct the [b].

Plosives become fricatives between vowels, before vowels or sonorants (when initial), or after vowels (when final). Sweet writes that the "opening of stops generally seems to begin between vowels…" (p. 23). Somewhat further he writes that in Dutch the *g* has everywhere become a fricative while in German the initial *g* remained a stop. For example *goed* 'good' is pronounced as [guˑᵊt] in Frisian dialects, while other dialects have initial [ɣ] or [x]. Following the tendency, we consider the [g] to be the older sound. Related to this is the pronunciation of words like *schip* 'ship' and *school* 'school'. As initial consonants we found [sk], [sx] and [ʃ]. In cases like this we consider the [sk] as the original form, although the [k] is not found *between* vowels, but only *before* a vowel.

Oral vowels become nasalized before nasals. Sweet (1888) writes that "nothing is more common than the nasalizing influence of a nasal on a preceding vowels" and that there "is a tendency to drop the following nasal consonant as superfluous" when "the nasality of a vowel is clearly developed" and "the nasal consonant is final, or stands before another consonant." (p. 38) For example *gaan* 'to go' is pronounced as [gɑ̝ n] in the dialect of Dok-

[2] In essence, in this and other such cases, a version of the manuscript-editing principle of choosing the "lectio difficilior" was our guiding principle.

[3] We do feel, however, that word-final devoicing, even though common cross-linguistically, is, as Hock 1976 emphasizes, not phonetically determined but rather reflects the generalization of utterance-final developments into word-final position, owing to the overlap between utterance-finality and word-finality.

kum, and as [gẽ ᵊ̃] in the dialect of Stiens. The nasalized [ẽ ᵊ] in the pronunciation of Stiens already indicates the deletion of a following nasal.

Consonants become palatalized before front vowels. According to Campbell (2004) "palatalization often takes place before or after *i* and *j* or before other front vowels, depending on the language, although unconditioned palatalization can also take place." An example might be *vuur* which is pronounced like [fjuˑᵊr] in Frisian varieties, while most other varieties have initial [f] or [v] followed by [i] or [y].

Superfluous sounds are dropped. Sweet (1888) introduced this principle as one of the principles of economy (p. 49). He especially mentioned that in [ŋg] the superfluous [g] is often dropped (p. 42). In our data we found that *krom* 'curved' is pronounced [krʊˑm] in most cases, but as [krʊ̃ mp] in the dialect of Houthalen. In the reconstructed form we posit the final [p].

Medial [h] deletes between vowels, and initial [h] before vowels. The word *hart* 'heart' is sometimes pronounced with and sometimes without initial [h]. According to this principle we reconstruct the [h].

[r] changes to [ʀ]. According to Hock and Joseph (1996) the substitution of uvular [ʀ] for trilled (post-)dental [r] is an example of an occasional change apparently resulting from misperception. In the word *rijp* 'ripe' we find initial [r] in most cases and [ʀ] in the dialects of Echt and Baelen. We reconstructed [r].

Syllable initial [w] changes in [ʋ]. Under 'Lip to Lip-teeth' Sweet (1888) writes that in "the change of *p* into *f*, *w* into *v*, we may always assume an intermediate [ɸ], [β], the latter being the Middle German *w*" (p. 26), and that the "loss of back modification is shown in the frequent change of (w) into (v) through [β], as in Gm." Since *v* – meant as "voiced lip-to-teeth fricative" – is close to [ʋ] – lip-to-teeth sonorant – we reconstruct [w] if both [w] and [ʋ] are found in the dialect pronunciations. This happens for example in the word *wijn* 'wine'.

The cluster ol+d/t diphthongizes to ou + d/t. For example English *old* and German *alt* have a /l/ before the /d/ and /t/ respectively. In Old Dutch *ol* changed into *ou* (Van Loey 1967, p. 43, Van Bree 1987, p. 135/136). Therefore we reconstruct the /l/ with preceding /o/ or /ɑ/.

3 The proto-language according to the dictionary

The dictionary of Köbler (2003) provides Germanic proto-forms. In our Dutch dialect data set we have transcriptions of 125 words per dialect. We found 85 words in the dictionary. Other words were missing, especially plural nouns, and verb forms other than infinitives are not included in this dictionary.

For most words, many proto-Germanic forms are given. We used the forms in italics only since these are the main forms according to the author. If different lexical forms are given for the same word, we selected only variants of those lexical forms which appear in standard Dutch or in one of the Dutch dialects.

The proto-forms are given in a semi-phonetic script. We converted them to phonetic script in order to make them as comparable as possible to the existing Dutch dialect transcriptions. This necessitated some interpretation. We made the following interpretation for monophthongs:

spelling	**phonetic**	**spelling**	**phonetic**	**spelling**	**phonetic**
i	ɪ	***æ***	æ	***u***	u
ī	i:	***ǣ***	æ:	***ū***	u:
e	ɛ	***a***	ɑ	***o***	ɔ
ē	e:	***ā***	a:	***ō***	o:

Diphthongs are interpreted as follows:

spelling	**phonetic**	**spelling**	**phonetic**
ai	ɑˑⁱ	***ei***	ɛˑⁱ
au	ɑˑᵘ	***eu***	ɛˑᵘ

We interpreted the consonants according to the following scheme:

spel-ling	pho-netic	spel-ling	pho-netic	spel-ling	pho-netic
p	p	***f***	f	***m***	m
b	b, v	***þ***	t	***n***	n, ŋ
t	t	***s***	s	***ng***	ŋ
d	d	***z***	z	***w***	w
k	k	***h***	x, h	***r***	r
g	g, ɣ			***l***	l
				j	j

Lehmann (2005-2007) writes that in the early stage of Proto-Germanic "each of the obstruents had the same pronunciation in its various locations…". "Later, /b d g/ had fricative allophones when medial between vowels. Lehmann (1994) writes that in Gothic "/b, d, g/ has stop articulation initially, finally and when doubled, fricative articulation between vowels." We adopted this scheme, but were restricted by the RND consonant set. The fricative articulation of /b/ would be [β] or [v]. We selected the [v] since this sound is included in the RND set. The fricative articulation of /d/ would be [ð], but this consonant is not in the RND set. We therefore used the [d] which we judge perceptually to be closer to the [ð] than to the [z]. The fricative articulation of /g/ is /ɣ/ which was available in the RND set.

We interpreted the *h* as [h] in initial position, and as [x] in medial and final positions. An *n* before *k*, *g* or *h* is interpreted as [ŋ], and as [n] in all other cases. The *þ* should actually be interpreted as [θ], but this sound in not found in the RND set. Just as we use [d] for [ð], analogously we use [t] for [θ]. We interpret double consonants are geminates, and transcribe them as single long consonants. For example *nn* becomes [nː].

Several words end in a '-' in Köbler's dictionary, meaning that the final sounds are unknown or irrelevant to root and stem reconstructions. In our transcriptions, we simply note nothing.

4 Measuring divergence of Dutch dialect pronunciations with respect to their proto-language

Once a protolanguage is reconstructed, we are able to measure the divergence of the pronunciations of descendant varieties with respect to that protolanguage. For this purpose we use Levenshtein distance, which is explained in Section 4.1. In Sections 4.2 the Dutch dialects are compared to PLR and PGD respectively. In Section 4.3 we compare PLR with PGD.

4.1 Levenshtein distance

In 1995 Kessler introduced the Levenshtein distance as a tool for measuring linguistic distances between language varieties. The Levenshtein distance is a string edit distance measure, and Kessler applied this algorithm to the comparison of Irish dialects. Later the same technique was successfully applied to Dutch (Nerbonne et al. 1996; Heeringa 2004: 213–278). Below, we give a brief explanation of the methodology. For a more extensive explanation see Heeringa (2004: 121–135).

4.1.1 Algorithm

Using the Levenshtein distance, two varieties are compared by measuring the pronunciation of words in the first variety against the pronunciation of the same words in the second. We determine how one pronunciation might be transformed into the other by inserting, deleting or substituting sounds. Weights are assigned to these three operations. In the simplest form of the algorithm, all operations have the same cost, e.g., 1.

Assume the Dutch word *hart* 'heart' is pronounced as [hɑrt] in the dialect of Vianen (The Netherlands) and as [ærtə] in the dialect of Nazareth (Belgium). Changing one pronunciation into the other can be done as follows:

hɑrt	delete h	1
ɑrt	subst. ɑ/æ	1
ært	insert ə	1
ærtə		
		3

In fact many string operations map [hɑrt] to [ærtə]. The power of the Levenshtein algorithm is that it always finds the least costly mapping.

To deal with syllabification in words, the Levenshtein algorithm is adapted so that only a vowel may match with a vowel, a consonant with a consonant, the [j] or [w] with a vowel (or opposite), the [i] or [u] with a consonant (or opposite), and a central vowel (in our research only the schwa) with a sonorant (or opposite). In this way unlikely matches (e.g. a [p] with an [a]) are prevented.[4] The longest alignment has the greatest number of matches. In our example we thus have the following alignment:

h	ɑ	r	t	
	æ	r	t	ə
1	1			1

4.1.2 Operations weights

The simplest versions of this method are based on a notion of phonetic distance in which phonetic overlap is binary: non-identical phones contribute to phonetic distance, identical ones do not. Thus the pair [i,ɒ] counts as different to the same degree as [i,ɪ]. The version of the Levenshtein algorithm which we use in this paper is based on the comparison of spectrograms of the sounds. Since a spectrogram is the visual representation of the acoustical signal, the visual differences between the spectrograms are reflections of the acoustical differences. The spectrograms were made on the basis of recordings of the sounds of the International Phonetic Alphabet as pronounced by John Wells and Jill House on the cassette The Sounds of the International Phonetic Alphabet from 1995.[5] The different sounds were isolated from the recordings and monotonized at the mean pitch of each of the two speakers with the program PRAAT[6] (Boersma & Weenink, 2005). Next, for each sound a spectrogram was made with PRAAT using the so-called Barkfilter, a perceptually oriented model. On the basis of the Barkfilter representation, segment distances were calculated. Inserted or deleted segments are compared to silence, and silence is represented as a spectrogram in which all intensities of all frequencies are equal to 0. We found that the [ʔ] is closest to silence and the [a] is most distant. This approach is described extensively in Heeringa (2004, pp. 79-119).

In perception, small differences in pronunciation may play a relatively strong role in comparison to larger differences. Therefore we used logarithmic segment distances. The effect of using logarithmic distances is that small distances are weighted relatively more heavily than large distances.

4.1.3 Processing RND data

The RND transcribers use slightly different notations. In order to minimize the effect of these differences, we normalized the data for them. The consistency problems and the way we solved them are extensively discussed in Heeringa (2001) and Heeringa (2004). Here we mention one problem which is highly relevant in the context of this paper. In the RND the *ee* before *r* is transcribed as [eː] by some transcribers and as [ɪˑ] by other transcribers, although they mean the same pronunciation as appears from the introductions of the different atlas volumes. A similar problem is found for *oo* before *r* which is transcribed either as [oː] or [ʊˑ], and the *eu* before *r* which is transcribed as [øː] or [ʏˑ]. Since similar problems may occur in other contexts as well, the best solution to overcome all of these problems appeared to replace all [ɪ]'s by [e]'s, all [ʊ]'s by [o]'s, and all [ʏ]'s by [ø]'s, even though meaningful distinctions get lost.

Especially suprasegmentals and diacritics might be used diffferently by the transcribers. We process the diacritics *voiceless*, *voiced* and *nasal* only. For details see Heeringa (2004, p. 110-111).

The distance between a monophthong and a diphthong is calculated as the mean of the distance between the monophthong and the first element of

---

[4] Rather than matching a vowel with a consonant, the algorithm will consider one of them as an insertion and another as a deletion.

[5] See http://www.phon.ucl.ac.uk/home/wells/cassette.htm.

[6] The program PRAAT is a free public-domain program developed by Paul Boersma and David Weenink at the Institute of Pronunciation Sciences of the University of Amsterdam and is available at http://www.fon.hum.uva.nl/praat.

the diphthong and the distance between the monophthong and the second element of the diphthong. The distance between two diphthongs is calculated as the mean of the distance between the first elements and the distance between the second elements. Details are given in Heeringa (2004, p. 108).

4.2 Measuring divergence from the proto-languages

The Levenshtein distance enables us to compare each of the 360 Dutch dialects to PLR and PGD. Since we reconstructed 85 words, the distance between a dialect and a proto-language is equal to the average of the distances of 85 word pairs.

Figures 1 and 2 show the distances to PLR and PGD respectively. Dialects with a small distance are represented by a lighter color and those with a large distance by a darker color. In the map, dialects are represented by polygons, geographic dialect islands are represented by colored dots, and linguistic dialect islands are represented by diamonds. The darker a polygon, dot or diamond, the greater the distance to the proto-language.

The two maps show similar patterns. The dialects in the Northwest (Friesland), the West (Noord-Holland, Zuid-Holland, Utrecht) and in the middle (Noord-Brabant) are relatively close to the proto-languages. More distant are dialects in the Northeast (Groningen, Drenthe, Overijssel), in the Southeast (Limburg), close to the middle part of the Flemish/Walloon border (Brabant) and in the southwest close to the Belgian/French state border (West-Vlaanderen).

According to Weijnen (1966), the Frisian, Limburg and West-Flemish dialects are conservative. Our maps shows that Frisian is relatively close to proto-Germanic, but Limburg and West-Flemish are relatively distant. We therefore created two maps, one which shows distances to PGD based on vowel substitutions in stressed syllables only, and another showing distances to PGD on the basis of consonant substitutions only.[7]

Looking at the map based on vowel substitutions we find the vowels of the Dutch province of Limburg and the eastern part of the province Noord-Brabant relatively close to PGD. Looking at the map based on consonant substitutions we find the consonants of the Limburg varieties distant to PGD. The Limburg dialects have shared in the High German Consonant Shift. Both the Belgium and Dutch Limburg dialects are found east of the Uerdinger Line between Dutch *ik/ook/-lijk* and High German *ich/auch/-lich*. The Dutch Limburg dialects are found east of the Panninger Line between Dutch *sl/sm/sn/sp/st/zw* and High German *schl/schm/schn/schp/scht/schw* (Weijnen 1966). The Limburg dialects are also characterized by the uvular [ʀ] while most Dutch dialects have the alveolar [r]. All of this shows that Limburg consonants are innovative.

The map based on vowel substitutions shows that Frisian vowels are not particularly close to PGD. Frisian is influenced by the Ingvaeonic sound shift. Among other changes, the [ʏ] changed into [ɪ], which in turn changed into [ɛ] in some cases (Dutch *dun* 'thin' is Frisian *tin*) (Van Bree 1987, p. 69).[8] Besides, Frisian is characterized by its falling diphthongs, which are an innovation as well. When we consulted the map based on consonant substitutions, we found the Frisian consonants close to PGD. For example the initial /g/ is still pronounced as a plosive as in most other Germanic varieties, but in Dutch dialects – and in standard Dutch – as a fricative.

When we consider West-Flemish, we find the vowels closer to PGD than the consonants, but they are still relatively distant to PGD.

4.3 PLR versus PGD

When correlating the 360 dialect distances to PLR with the 360 dialect distances to PGD, we obtained a correlation of r=0.87 (p<0.0001)[9]. This is a significant, but not perfect correlation. Therefore we compared the word transcriptions of PLR with those of PGD.

[7] The maps are not included in this paper.

[8] The Ingvaeonic sound shift affected mainly Frisian and English, and to a lesser degree Dutch. We mention here the phenomenon found in our data most frequently.

[9] For finding the *p*-values we used with thanks: *VassarStats: Website for Statistical Computation* at: http://faculty.vassar.edu/lowry/VassarStats.html.

Figure 1. Distances of 360 Dutch dialects compared to PLR. Dialects are represented by polygons, geographic dialect islands are represented by colored dots, and linguistic dialect islands are represented by diamonds. Lighter polygons, dots or diamonds represent more conservative dialects and darker ones more innovative dialects.

Figure 2. Distances of 360 Dutch dialects compared to PGD. Dialects are represented by polygons, geographic dialect islands are represented by colored dots, and linguistic dialect islands are represented by diamonds. Lighter polygons, dots or diamonds represent more conservative dialects and darker ones more innovative dialects.

First we focus on the reconstruction of vowels. We find 28 words for which the reconstructed vowel of the stressed syllable was the same as in PGD[10]. In 15 cases, this was the result of applying the tendencies discussed in Section 2.1. In 13 cases this was the result of simply choosing the vowel found most frequently among the 360 word pronunciations. When we do not use tendencies, but simply always choose the most frequent vowel, we obtain a correlation which is significantly lower (r=0.74, p=0).
We found 29 words for which vowel was reconstructed different from the one in PGD, although the PGD vowel was found among at least two dialects. For 28 words the vowel in the PGD form was not found among the 360 dialects, or only one time. For 11 of these words, the closest vowel found in the inventory of that word, was reconstructed. For example the vowel in *ook* 'too' is [ɑu] in PGD, while we reconstructed [ɔu].

Looking at the consonants, we found 44 words which have the same consonants as in PGD.[11] For 36 words only one consonant was different, where most words have at least two consonants. This shows that the reconstruction of consonants works much better than the reconstruction of vowels.

5 Conclusions

In this paper we tried to reconstruct a 'proto-language' on the basis of the RND dialect material and see how close we come to the protoforms found in Köbler's proto-Germanic dictionary. We reconstructed the same vowel as in PGD or the closest possible vowel for 46% of the words. Therefore, the reconstruction of vowels still needs to be improved further.

The reconstructions of consonants worked well. For 52% of the words all consonants reconstructed are the same as in PGD. For 42% of the words, only one consonant was differently reconstructed.

And, as a second goal, we measured the divergence of Dutch dialects compared to their proto-

[10] For some words PGD gives multiple pronunciations. We count the number of words which has the same vowel in at least one of the PGD pronunciations.

[11] When PGD has multiple pronunciations, we count the number of words for which the consonants are the same as in at least one of the PGD pronunciations.

language. We calculated dialect distances to PLR and PGD, and found a correlation of r=0.87 between the PLR distances and PGD distances. The high correlation shows the relative influence of wrongly reconstructed sounds.

When we compared dialects to PLR and PGD, we found especially Frisian close to proto-Germanic. When we distinguished between vowels and consonants, it appeared that southeastern dialects (Dutch Limburg and the eastern part of Noord-Brabant) have vowels close to proto-Germanic. Frisian is relatively close to proto-Germanic because of its consonants.

Acknowledgements

We thank Peter Kleiweg for letting us use the programs which he developed for the representation of the maps. We would like to thank Prof. Gerhard Köbler for the use of his *neuhochdeutsch-germanisches Wörterbuch* and his explanation about this dictionary and Gary Taylor for his explanation about proto-Germanic pronunciation. We also thank the members of the Groningen Dialectometry group for useful comments on a earlier version of this paper. We are grateful to the anonymous reviewers for their valuable suggestions. This research was carried out within the framework of a *talentgrant* project, which is supported by a fellowship (number S 30-624) from the Netherlands Organisation of Scientific Research (NWO).

References

Edgar Blancquaert & Willem Pée, eds. 1925-1982. *Reeks Nederlandse Dialectatlassen*. De Sikkel, Antwerpen.

Paul Boersma & David Weenink 2005. *Praat: doing phonetics bycomputer*. Computer program retrieved from http://www.praat.org.

Cor van Bree. 1987. *Historische Grammatica van het Nederlands*. Foris Publications, Dordrecht.

Cor van Bree. 1996. *Historische Taalkunde*. Acco, Leuven.

Wilbert Heeringa. 2001. De selectie en digitalisatie van dialecten en woorden uit de Reeks Nederlandse Dialectatlassen. *TABU: Bulletin voor taalwetenschap*, 31(1/2):61-103.

Wilbert Heeringa. 2004. *Measuring Dialect Pronunciation Differences using Levenshtein Distance*. PhD thesis, Rijksuniversiteit Groningen, Groningen. Available at: http://www.let.rug.nl/~heeringa/dialectology/thesis.

Hans Henrich Hock & Brian D. Joseph. 1996. *Language History, Language Change, and Language Relationship: an Introduction to Historical and Comparative Linguistics*. Mouton de Gruyter, Berlin etc.

Brett Kessler. 1995. Computational dialectology in Irish Gaelic. *Proceedings of the 7th Conference of the European Chapter of the Association for Computational Linguistics*, 60-67. EACL, Dublin.

Gerhard Köbler. 2003. *Neuhochdeutsch-germanisches Wörterbuch*. Available at: http://www.koeblergerhard.de/germwbhinw.html.

Winfred P. Lehmann. 1994. Ghotic and the Reconstruction of Proto-Germanic. In: Ekkehard König & Johan van der Auwera, eds. *The Germanic Languages*, 19-37. Routledge, London & New York.

Winfred P. Lehmann. 2005-2007. *A Grammar of Proto-Germanic*. Online books edited by Jonathan Slocum. Available at: http://www.utexas.edu/cola/centers/lrc/books/pgmc00.html.

Adolphe C. H. van Loey. 1967. *Inleiding tot de historische klankleer van het Nederlands*. N.V. W.J. Thieme & Cie, Zutphen.

John Nerbonne & Wilbert Heeringa & Erik van den Hout & Peter van der Kooi & Simone Otten & Willem van de Vis. 1996. Phonetic Distance between Dutch Dialects. In: Gert Durieux & Walter Daelemans & Steven Gillis, eds. *CLIN VI, Papers from the sixth CLIN meeting*, 185-202. University of Antwerp, Center for Dutch Language and Speech, Antwerpen.

Arend Quak & Johannes Martinus van der Horst. 2002. *Inleiding Oudnederlands*. Leuven University Press, Leuven.

Jan Stroop. 1998. *Poldernederlands; Waardoor het ABN verdwijnt*, Bakker, Amsterdam.

Henry Sweet. 1888. *A History of English Sounds from the Earliest Period*. Clarendon Press, Oxford.

Marijke van der Wal together with Cor van Bree. 1994. *Geschiedenis van het Nederlands*. Aula-boeken. Het Spectrum, Utrecht, 2nd edition.

Antonius A. Weijnen. 1966. *Nederlandse dialectkunde*. Studia Theodisca. Van Gorcum, Assen, 2nd edition.

Can Corpus Based Measures be Used for Comparative Study of Languages?

Anil Kumar Singh
Language Tech. Research Centre
Int'l Inst. of Information Tech.
Hyderabad, India
anil@research.iiit.net

Harshit Surana
Language Tech. Research Centre
Int'l Inst. of Information Tech.
Hyderabad, India
surana.h@gmail.com

Abstract

Quantitative measurement of inter-language distance is a useful technique for studying diachronic and synchronic relations between languages. Such measures have been used successfully for purposes like deriving language taxonomies and language reconstruction, but they have mostly been applied to handcrafted word lists. Can we instead use corpus based measures for comparative study of languages? In this paper we try to answer this question. We use three corpus based measures and present the results obtained from them and show how these results relate to linguistic and historical knowledge. We argue that the answer is yes and that such studies can provide or validate linguistic and computational insights.

1 Introduction

Crosslingual and multilingual processing is acquiring importance in the computational linguistics community. As a result, semi-automatic crosslingual comparison of languages is also becoming a fruitful area of study. Among the fundamental tools for crosslingual comparison are measures of inter-language distances. In linguistics, the study of inter-language distances, especially for language classification, has a long history (Swadesh, 1952; Ellison and Kirby, 2006). Basically, the work on this problem has been along linguistic, archaeological and computational streams. Like in other disciplines, computational methods are increasingly being combined with other more conventional approaches (Dyen et al., 1992; Nerbonne and Heeringa, 1997; Kondrak, 2002; Ellison and Kirby, 2006). The work being presented in this paper belongs to the computational stream.

Even in the computational stream, most of the previous work on inter-language distances had a strong linguistic dimension. For example, most of the quantitative measures of inter-language distance have been applied on handcrafted word lists (Swadesh, 1952; Dyen et al., 1992). However, with increasing use of computational techniques and the availability of electronic data, a natural question arises: Can languages be linguistically compared based on word lists extracted from corpora. A natural counter-question is whether such comparison will be valid from linguistic and psycholinguistic points of view. The aim of this paper is to examine such questions.

To calculate inter-language distances on the basis of words in corpora, we propose two corpus based distance measures. They internally use a more linguistically grounded distance measure for comparing strings. We also present the results obtained with one purely statistical measure, just to show that even naive corpus based measures can be useful. The main contribution is to show that even noisy corpora can be used for comparative study of languages. Different measures can give different kinds of insights.

2 Related Work

Typology or history of languages can be studied using spoken data or text. There has been work on the former (Remmel, 1980; Kondrak, 2002), but we

Proceedings of Ninth Meeting of the ACL Special Interest Group in Computational Morphology and Phonology, pages 40–47,
Prague, June 2007.

will focus only on text. An example of a major work on text based similarity is the paper by Kondrak and Sherif (Kondrak and Sherif, 2006). They have evaluated various phonetic similarity algorithms for aligning cognates. They found that learning based algorithms outperform manually constructed schemes, but only when large training data is used.

A recent work on applications of such techniques for linguistic study is by Heeringa et al. (Heeringa et al., 2006). They performed a study on different variations of string distance algorithms for dialectology and concluded that order sensitivity is important while scaling with length is not. It may be noted that Ellison and Kirby (Ellison and Kirby, 2006) have shown that scaling by distance does give significantly better results. Nakleh et al. (Nakleh et al., 2005) have written about using phylogenetic techniques in historical linguistics as mentioned by Nerbonne (Nerbonne, 2005) in the review of the book titled 'Language Classification by Numbers' by McMahon and McMahon (McMahon and McMahon, 2005). All these works are about using quantitative techniques for language typology and classification etc.

3 Inter-Language Comparison

Inter-language comparison is more general than measuring inter-language distance. In addition to the overall linguistic distance, the comparison can be of more specific characteristics like the proportion of cognates derived vertically and horizontally. Or it can be of specific phonetic features (Nerbonne, 2005; McMahon and McMahon, 2005). Quantitative measures for comparing languages can first be classified according to the form of data being compared, i.e., speech, written text or electronic text. Assuming that the text is in electronic form, the most common measures are based on word lists. These lists are usually prepared by linguists and they are often in some special notation, e.g. more or less a phonetic transcription.

The measures can be based on inter-lingual or on intra-lingual comparison of phonetic forms (Ellison and Kirby, 2006). They may or may not use statistical techniques like measures of distributional similarity (cross entropy, KL-divergence, etc.). These characteristics of measures may imply some linguistic or psycholinguistic assumptions. One of these is about a common phonetic space.

4 Common Phonetic Space

Language distance can be calculated through crosslingual as well as intra-lingual comparison. Many earlier attempts (Nerbonne and Heeringa, 1997; Kondrak, 2002) were based on crosslingual comparison of phonetic forms, but some researchers have argued against the possibility of obtaining meaningful results from crosslingual comparison of phonetic forms. This is related to the idea of a common phonetic space. Port and Leary (Port and Leary, 2005) have argued against it. Ellison and Kirby (Ellison and Kirby, 2006) argue that even if there is a common space, language specific categorization of sound often restructures this space. They conclude that if there is no language-independent common phonetic space with an equally common similarity measure, there can be no principled approach to comparing forms in one language with another. They suggest that language-internal comparison of forms is better and psychologically more well-grounded.

This may be true, but should we really abandon the approach based on crosslingual comparison? As even Ellison and Kirby say, it is possible to argue that there is a common phonetic space. After all, the sounds produced by humans are determined by human physiology. The only matter of debate is whether common phonetic space makes sense from the cognitive point of view. We argue that it does. In psychology, there has been a long debate about a similar problem which can be stated in terms of a common chromatic space. Do humans in different cultures see the same colors? There is still no conclusive answer, but many computational techniques have been tried to solve real world problems like classifying human faces, seemingly with the implicit assumption that there is a common chromatic space. Such techniques have shown some success (sheng Chen and kai Liu, 2003).

Could it be that we are defining the notion of a common chromatic (or phonetic) space too strictly? Or that the way we define it is not relevant for computational techniques? In our view the answer is yes. We will give a simple, not very novel, example. The phoneme t as in the English word *battery* is not present in many languages of the world. When a Thai speaker can not say *battery*, with the correct t, he will say *battery* with t as in the French word *entre*. Such substitution will be very regular. The point is that even if phonetic space is restructured for a particular language, we can still find which segments or sections of two differently structured phonetic spaces are close. $Cyan$ may span different ranges (on the spectrum) in different cultures, but the ranges are likely to be near to one another. Even if some culture has no color which can be called $cyan$, one or two of the colors that it does have will be closer to $cyan$ than the others. The same is true for all the other colors and also for sounds. If we use fuzzy similarity measures to take care of such differently structured cognitive spaces, cross-lingual comparison may still be meaningful for certain purposes. This argument is in defence of cross-lingual comparison, not against intra-lingual comparison.

5 Common Orthographic Space

Writing systems used by languages differ very widely. This can be taken to mean that there is no common orthographic space for meaningful crosslingual comparison of orthographic forms. This may be true in general, but for sets of languages using related scripts, we can assume a similar orthographic space. For example, most of the major South Asian languages use scripts derived from Brahmi. The similarity among these scripts is so much that crosslingual comparison of text is possible for various purposes such as identifying cognates without any phonetic transcription. This is in spite of the fact that the letter shapes differ so much that they are not mutually identifiable. Such similarity is relevant for corpus based measures.

6 Corpus Based Measures

Since we use (non-parallel) corpora of the two languages for finding out the cognates and hence comparing two languages, the validity of the results depends on how representative the corpora are. However, if they are of enough size, we might still be able to make meaningful, even if limited, comparison among languages. We restrict ourselves to word list based comparison. In such a case, corpus based measures can be effective if the corpora contain a representative portion of the vocabulary, or even of word segments. The second case (of segments) is relevant for the n-gram measure described in section-7.

This category of measures have to incorporate more linguistic information if they are to provide good results. Designing such measures can be a challenging problem as we will be mainly relying on the corpus for our information. Knowledge about similarities and differences of writing systems can play an important role here. The two cognate based measures described in sections 9 and 10 are an attempt at this. But first we describe a simple n-gram based measure.

7 Symmetric Cross Entropy (SCE)

The first measure is purely a letter n-gram based measure similar to the one used by Singh (Singh, 2006b) for language and encoding identification. To calculate the distance, we first prepare letter 5-gram models from the corpora of the languages to be compared. Then we combine n-grams of all orders and rank them according to their probability in descending order. Only the top N n-grams are retained and the rest are pruned. [1] Now we have two probability distributions which can be compared by a measure of distributional similarity. We have used symmetric cross entropy as such a measure:

$$d_{sce} = \sum_{g_l = g_m} \left(p(g_l) \, log \, q(g_m) + q(g_m) \, log \, p(g_l) \right) \tag{1}$$

where p and q are the probability distributions for the two languages and g_l and g_m are n-grams in languages l and m, respectively.

The disadvantage of this measure is that it does not use any linguistic (e.g., phonetic) information, but the advantage is that it can measure the similarity of distributions of n-grams. Such measures have proved to be very effective in automatically identifying languages of text, with accuracies nearing 100% for fairly small amounts of training and test data (Adams and Resnik, 1997; Singh, 2006b).

[1] This is based on the results obtained by Cavnar (Cavnar and Trenkle, 1994) and our own studies, which show that the top N (300 according to Cavnar) n-grams have a high correlation with the identity of the language.

8 Method for Cognate Identification

The other two measures are based on cognates, inherited as well as borrowed. Both of them use an algorithm for identification of cognates. Many such algorithms have been proposed. Estimates of *surface similarity* can be used for finding cognate words across languages for related languages. By surface similarity we mean the orthographic, phonetic and (possibly) morphological similarity of two words or strings. In spite of the name, surface similarity is deeper than string similarity as calculated by edit distances. Ribeiro et al. (Ribeiro et al., 2001) have surveyed some of the algorithms for cognate alignment. However, since they studied methods based on parallel text, we cannot use them directly.

For identifying cognates, we are using the computational model of scripts or CPMS (Singh, 2006a). This model takes into account the characteristics of Brahmi origin scripts and calculates surface similarity in a fuzzy way. This is achieved by using a stepped distance function (SDF) and a dynamic programming (DP) algorithm. We have adapted the CPMS for identifying cognates.

Different researchers have argued about the importance of order sensitivity and scaling in using string comparison algorithms (Heeringa et al., 2006; Ellison and Kirby, 2006). The CPMS takes both of these into account, as well as using knowledge about the script. In general, the distance between two strings can be defined as:

$$c_{lm} = f_p(w_l, w_m) \tag{2}$$

where f_p is the function which calculates surface similarity based cost between the word w_l of language l and the word w_m of language m.

Those word pairs are identified as cognates which have the least cost.

9 Cognate Coverage Distance (CCD)

The second measure used by us is a corpus based estimate of the coverage of cognates across two languages. Cognate coverage is defined as the number of words (out of the vocabularies of the two languages) which are of the same origin. The decision about whether two words are cognates or not is made on the basis of surface similarity of the two words as described in the previous section. We use (non-parallel) corpora of the two languages for identifying the cognates.

The normalized distance between two languages is defined as:

$$t'_{lm} = 1 - \frac{t_{lm}}{max(t)} \tag{3}$$

where t_{lm} and t_{ml} are the number of cognates found when comparing from language l to m and from language m to l, respectively.

Since the CPMS based measure of surface lexical similarity is asymmetric, we calculate the average number of unidirectional cognates:

$$d^{ccd} = \frac{t'_{lm} + t'_{ml}}{2} \tag{4}$$

10 Phonetic Distance of Cognates (PDC)

Simply finding the coverage of cognates may indicate the distance between two languages, but a measure based solely on this information does not take into account the variation between the cognates themselves. To include this variation into the estimate of distance, we use another measure based on the sum of the CPMS based cost of n cognates found between two languages:

$$C^{pdc}_{lm} = \sum_{i=0}^{n} c_{lm} \tag{5}$$

where n is the minimum of t_{lm} for all the language pairs compared.

The normalized distance can be defined as:

$$C'_{lm} = \frac{C^{pdc}_{lm}}{max(C^{pdc})} \tag{6}$$

A symmetric version of this cost is then calculated:

$$d_{pdc} = \frac{C'_{lm} + C'_{ml}}{2} \tag{7}$$

11 Experimental Setup

For synchronic comparison, we selected ten languages for our experiment (table-1), mainly because sufficient corpora were available for these languages. These languages, though belonging to two different families (Indo-Iranian and Dravidian), have

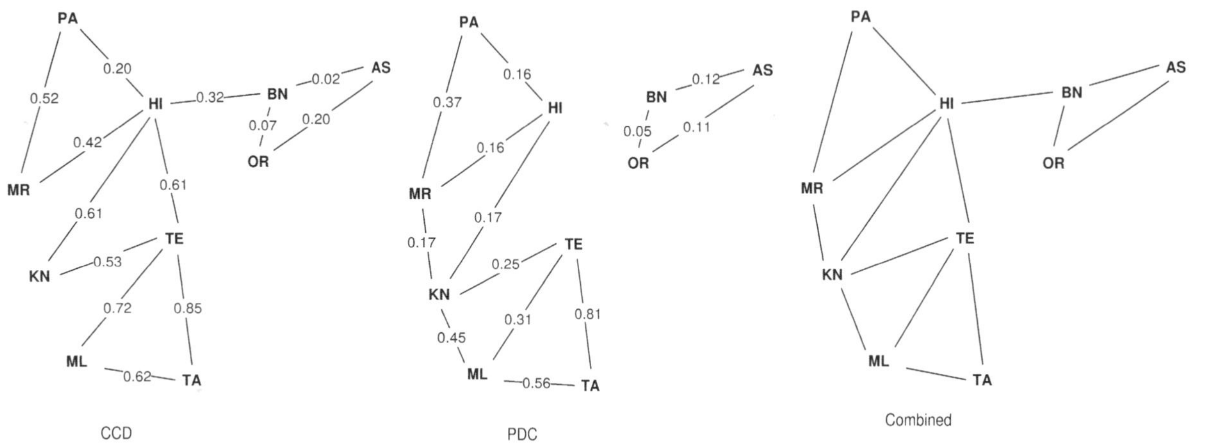

Figure 1: Graphical view of synchronic comparison among ten major South Asian languages using CCD and PDC measures. The layout of the graph is modeled on the geographical locations of these languages. The connections among the nodes of the graph are obtained by joining each node to its two closest neighbors in terms of the values obtained by using the two measures.

a lot of similarities (Emeneau, 1956). The cognate words among them are loanwords as well as inherited words. In fact, the similarity among these languages is due to common origin (intra-family) as well as contact and borrowing over thousands of years (intra- and inter-family). Moreover, they also use scripts derived from the same origin (Brahmi), which allows us to use the CPMS for identifying cognates. The corpora used for these ten languages are all part of the CIIL (Central Institute of Indian Languages) multilingual corpus. This corpus is a collection of documents from different domains and is one of best known corpora for Indian languages. Still, the representativeness of this corpus may be a matter of debate as it is not as large and diverse as the BNC (British National Corpus) corpus for English.

For the cognate measures (CCD and PDC), the only information we are extracting from the corpora are the word types and their frequencies. Thus, in a way, we are also working with word lists, but our word lists are extracted from corpora. Word lists handcrafted by linguists may be very useful, but they are not always available for all kinds of inter-language or inter-dialectal comparison, whereas electronic corpora are more likely to be available. Currently we are not doing any preprocessing or stemming on the word lists before running the cognate extraction algorithm. For SCE, n-gram models are being prepared as described in section-7. For all three measures, we calculate the distances among all possible pairs of the languages.

For diachronic comparison, we selected modern standard Hindi, medieval Hindi (actually, Avadhi) and Sanskrit. The corpus for modern Hindi was the same as that used for synchronic comparison. The medieval Hindi we have experimented with is of two different periods. These are the varieties used by two great poets of that period, namely Jaayasi (1477-1542 A.D.) and Tulsidas (1532-1623 A.D.). We took some of their major works available in electronic form as the corpora. For Sanskrit, we used the electronic version of Mahabharata (compiled during the period 1000 B.C. to 500 A.D. approximately) as the corpus. We calculate the distances among all possible pairs of the four varieties using the three measures. We also compare the ten modern languages with Sanskrit using the same Mahabharata corpus.

For synchronic comparison, we first extract the list of word types with frequencies from the corpus. Then we rank them according to frequency. Top N of these are retained. This is done because otherwise a lot of less relevant word types like proper nouns get included. We are interested in comparing the core vocabulary of languages. The assumption is that words in the core vocabulary are likely to be more frequent. Another reason for restricting the experiments to the top N word types is that there

	BN	HI	KN	ML	MR	OR	PA	TA	TE
AS	0.02 0.12 0.05	0.39 0.25 0.30	0.71 0.39 0.51	0.86 0.61 0.50	0.61 0.45 0.43	0.20 0.11 0.18	0.61 0.58 0.42	0.93 0.95 0.70	0.73 0.46 0.64
BN		0.32 0.29 0.29	0.68 0.42 0.47	0.86 0.64 0.45	0.57 0.42 0.43	0.07 0.05 0.14	0.56 0.56 0.42	0.96 0.90 0.74	0.70 0.50 0.43
HI			0.61 0.17 0.43	0.81 0.56 0.46	0.42 0.16 0.16	0.40 0.27 0.33	0.20 0.16 0.20	0.93 0.87 0.74	0.61 0.38 0.34
KN				0.77 0.45 0.18	0.68 0.17 0.38	0.75 0.31 0.52	0.73 0.50 0.58	0.88 0.82 0.42	0.53 0.25 0.09
ML					0.89 0.65 0.42	0.88 0.59 0.53	0.88 0.77 0.55	0.62 0.56 0.07	0.72 0.31 0.19
MR						0.64 0.40 0.34	0.52 0.37 0.39	0.95 0.94 0.60	0.68 0.46 0.30
OR							0.63 0.45 0.65	0.98 0.89 0.83	0.74 0.44 0.64
PA								0.90 0.90 0.92	0.71 0.59 0.48
TA									0.85 0.81 0.39

Table 1: Inter-language comparison among ten major South Asian languages using three corpus based measures. The values have been normalized and scaled to be somewhat comparable. Each cell contains three values: by CCD, PDC and SCE.

are huge differences in sizes of corpora of different languages. In the next step we identify the cognates among these word lists. No language specific features or thresholds are used. Only common thresholds are used. We now branch out to using either CCD or PDC.

The method used for diachronic comparison is similar except that N is much smaller because the amount of classical corpus being used (Jaayasi, Tulsidas) is also much smaller. Two letter codes are used for ten languages and four varieties[2].

12 Analysis of Results

The results of our experiments are shown tables 1 to 3 and figures 1 and 2. Table-1 shows the distances among pairs of languages using the three measures. Figure-1 shows a graph showing the distances according to CCD and PDC. Figure-2 shows the effect of the size of word lists (N) on comparison for three linguistically close language pairs. Table-2 shows the comparison of ten languages with Sanskrit. Table-3 gives the diachronic comparison among four historical varieties.

12.1 Synchronic Comparison

As table-1 shows, all three measures give results which correspond well to the linguistic knowledge about differences among these languages. Cognate based measures give better results, but even the n-gram based measure gives good results. However, there are some differences among the values obtained with different measures. These differences are also in accordance with linguistic insights. For example, the distance between Hindi and Telugu was given as 0.61 by CCD and 0.38 by PDC. Similarly, the distance between Hindi and Kannada was given as 0.61 by CCD and 0.17 by PDC. These values, in relative terms, indicate that the number of cognates between these languages is in the medium range as compared to other pairs. But less PDC cost shows that top N cognates are very similar. This is because most cognates are *tatsam* words directly borrowed from Sanskrit without any change.

The results presented in the table have been normalized on all language pairs using the maximum and minimum cost. The results would be different and more comparable if we normalize over language families (Indo-Iranian and Dravidian). With such normalization, Punjabi-Oriya and Marathi-Assamese are identified as the farthest language pairs with costs of 0.92 and 0.90, respectively. This corresponds well with the actual geographical and linguistic distances.

While comparing with Sanskrit, it is clear that different languages have different levels of cognate coverage. However, except for Punjabi and Tamil, all languages have very similar PDC cost with the Mahabharata corpus. This again shows that the closest cognates among these languages are *tatsam* words. These results agree well with linguistic knowledge, even though the Sanskrit corpus (Mahabharata) is highly biased.

Figure-1 makes the results clearer. It shows that just by connecting each node to its nearest two

[2]**AS:** Assamese, **BN:** Bengali, **HI:** Hindi, **KN:** Kannada, **ML:** Malayalam, **MR:** Marathi, **OR:** Oriya, **PA:** Punjabi, **TA:** Tamil, **TE:** Telugu, **TL:** Avadhi (Tulsidas), **JY:** Avadhi (Jaayasi), **MB:** Sanskrit (Mahabharata)

Distance	AS	BN	HI	KN	ML	MR	OR	PA	TA	TE
CCD	0.71	0.70	0.65	0.78	0.87	0.73	0.71	0.78	0.94	0.77
PDC	0.37	0.38	0.40	0.43	0.37	0.41	0.37	0.50	0.63	0.30

Table 2: Comparison with Sanskrit (Mahabharata)

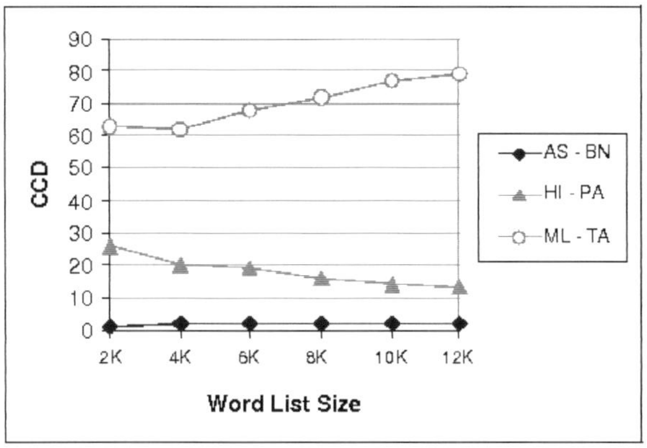

Figure 2: Effect of the size of word lists on inter-language comparison.

	TL	JY	MB
HI	0.45	0.54	0.82
	0.45	0.42	0.70
	0.64	0.56	0.49
TL		0.01	0.84
		0.02	0.72
		0.16	0.91
JY			0.98
			0.95
			0.81

Table 3: Diachronic comparison among four historical varieties.

neighbors we can get a very good graphical representation of the differences among languages. It also shows that different measures capture different aspects. For example, CCD fails to connect Marathi with Kannada and Kannada with Malayalam. Similarly, PDC fails to connect Bengali with Hindi. We get this missing information by combining the graphs obtained with the two measures. More sophisticated methods for creating such graphs may give better results. Note that the Hindi-Telugu and Marathi-Kannada connections are valid as these language pairs are close, even though they are not genetically related. The results indicate closeness between two languages, but they do not distinguish between inheritance and borrowing.

We also experimented with several word list sizes. In figure-2 the CCD values are plotted against word list sizes for three close language pairs. There is variation for Hindi-Punjabi and Malayalam-Telugu, but not for Assamese-Bengali. The following observations can be derived from the three lines on the plot. Malayalam-Telugu share a lot of common core words but not less common words. Hindi-Punjabi share a lot of less common words, but core words are not exactly similar. Finally, Assamese-Bengali share both core as well as less common words.

12.2 Diachronic Comparison

Table-4 shows the results. We can see that Hindi is closer to Tulsidas than to Jaayasi by the CCD measure. PDC gives almost similar results for both. Tulsidas and Jaayasi are the nearest. Tulsidas is much nearer to Mahabharata than Jaayasi, chiefly because Tulsidas' language has more Sanskrit origin words. Our results put Tulsidas nearest to Hindi, followed by Jaayasi and then Sanskrit. This is historically as well as linguistically correct.

13 Conclusions and Further Work

In this paper we first discussed the possibility and validity of using corpus based measures for comparative study of languages. We presented some arguments in favor of this possibility. We then described three corpus based measures for comparative study of languages. The first measure was symmetric cross entropy of letter n-grams. This measure uses the least amount of linguistic information. The second and third measures were cognate coverage distance and phonetic distance of cognates, respectively. These two are more linguistically grounded. Using these measures, we presented a synchronic comparison of ten major South Asian languages and a diachronic comparison of four historical varieties. The results of our experiments show that even these simple measures based on crosslingual comparison and on the data extracted from not very representative and noisy corpora can be used for obtaining or validating useful linguistic insights about language divergence, classification etc.

These measures can be tried for more languages to see whether they have any validity for less related languages than the languages we experimented with. We can also try to design measures and find methods for distinguishing between borrowed and inherited words. Proper combination of synchronic and diachronic comparison might help us in doing this. Other possible applications could be for language reconstruction, classification, dialectology etc.

Better versions of the two cognate based measures can be defined by using the idea of confusion probabilities (Ellison and Kirby, 2006) and the idea of distributional similarity. If intra-lingual comparison is more meaningful than inter-lingual comparison, then these modified versions should be even more useful for comparative study of languages.

References

Gary Adams and Philip Resnik. 1997. A language identification application built on the Java client-server platform. In Jill Burstein and Claudia Leacock, editors, *From Research to Commercial Applications: Making NLP Work in Practice*, pages 43–47. Association for Computational Linguistics.

William B. Cavnar and John M. Trenkle. 1994. N-gram-based text categorization. In *Proceedings of SDAIR-94, 3rd Annual Symposium on Document Analysis and Information Retrieval*, pages 161–175, Las Vegas, US.

I. Dyen, J.B. Kruskal, and P. Black. 1992. An indo-european classification: A lexicostatistical experiment. In *Transactions of the American Philosophical Society, 82:1-132.*

T. Mark Ellison and Simon Kirby. 2006. Measuring language divergence by intra-lexical comparison. In *Proceedings of the 21st International Conference on Computational Linguistics and 44th Annual Meeting of the Association for Computational Linguistics*, Sydney, Australia. Association for Computational Linguistics.

M. B. Emeneau. 1956. India as a linguistic area. In *Linguistics 32:3-16.*

W. Heeringa, P. Kleiweg, C. Gooskens, and J. Nerbonne. 2006. Evaluation of String Distance Algorithms for Dialectology. In *Proc. of ACL Workshop on Linguistic Distances.*

G. Kondrak and T. Sherif. 2006. Evaluation of Several Phonetic Similarity Algorithms on the Task of Cognate Identification. In *Proc. of ACL Workshop on Linguistic Distances.*

Grzegorz Kondrak. 2002. *Algorithms for language reconstruction.* Ph.D. thesis. Adviser-Graeme Hirst.

April McMahon and Robert McMahon. 2005. *Language Classification by the Numbers.* Oxford University Press, Oxford.

Luay Nakleh, Don Ringe, and Tandy Warnow. 2005. Perfect phylogentic networks: A new methodology for reconstructing the evolutionary history of natural languages. pages 81–2:382–420.

J. Nerbonne and W. Heeringa. 1997. Measuring dialect distance phonetically. In *Proceedings of SIGPHON-97: 3rd Meeting of the ACL Special Interest Group in Computational Phonology.*

J. Nerbonne. 2005. Review of 'language classification by the numbers' by april mcmahon and robert mcmahon.

B. Port and A. Leary. 2005. Against formal phonology. pages 81(4):927–964.

M. Remmel. 1980. Computers in the historical phonetics and phonology of Balto-Finnic languages: problems and perspectives. In *Communication présentée au 5th International Finno-Ugric Congress, Turku.*

A. Ribeiro, G. Dias, G. Lopes, and J. Mexia. 2001. Cognates alignment. *Machine Translation Summit VIII, Machine Translation in The Information Age*, pages 287–292.

Duan sheng Chen and Zheng kai Liu. 2003. A novel approach to detect and correct highlighted face region in color image. In *AVSS '03: Proceedings of the IEEE Conference on Advanced Video and Signal Based Surveillance*, page 7, Washington, DC, USA. IEEE Computer Society.

Anil Kumar Singh. 2006a. A computational phonetic model for indian language scripts. In *Constraints on Spelling Changes: Fifth International Workshop on Writing Systems*, Nijmegen, The Netherlands.

Anil Kumar Singh. 2006b. Study of some distance measures for language and encoding identification. In *Proceedings of ACL 2006 Workshop on Linguistic Distance*, Sydney, Australia.

M. Swadesh. 1952. Lexico-dating of prehistoric ethnic contacts. In *Proceedings of the American philosophical society, 96(4).*

Inducing Sound Segment Differences using Pair Hidden Markov Models

Martijn Wieling
Alfa-Informatica
University of Groningen
wieling@gmail.com

Therese Leinonen
Alfa-Informatica
University of Groningen
t.leinonen@rug.nl

John Nerbonne
Alfa-Informatica
University of Groningen
j.nerbonne@rug.nl

Abstract

Pair Hidden Markov Models (PairHMMs) are trained to align the pronunciation transcriptions of a large contemporary collection of Dutch dialect material, the Goeman-Taeldeman-Van Reenen-Project (GTRP, collected 1980–1995). We focus on the question of how to incorporate information about sound segment distances to improve sequence distance measures for use in dialect comparison. PairHMMs induce segment distances via expectation maximisation (EM). Our analysis uses a phonologically comparable subset of 562 items for all 424 localities in the Netherlands. We evaluate the work first via comparison to analyses obtained using the Levenshtein distance on the same dataset and second, by comparing the quality of the induced vowel distances to acoustic differences.

1 Introduction

Dialectology catalogues the geographic distribution of the linguistic variation that is a necessary condition for language change (Wolfram and Schilling-Estes, 2003), and is sometimes successful in identifying geographic correlates of historical developments (Labov, 2001). Computational methods for studying dialect pronunciation variation have been successful using various edit distance and related string distance measures, but unsuccessful in using segment differences to improve these (Heeringa, 2004). The most successful techniques distinguish consonants and vowels, but treat e.g. all the vowel differences as the same. Ignoring the special treatment of vowels vs. consonants, the techniques regard segments in a binary fashion—as alike or different—in spite of the overwhelming consensus that some sounds are much more alike than others. There have been many attempts to incorporate more sensitive segment differences, which do not necessarily perform worse in validation, but they fail to show significant improvement (Heeringa, 2004).

Instead of using segment distances as these are (incompletely) suggested by phonetic or phonological theory, we can also attempt to acquire these automatically. Mackay and Kondrak (2005) introduce Pair Hidden Markov Models (PairHMMs) to language studies, applying them to the problem of recognising "cognates" in the sense of machine translation, i.e. pairs of words in different languages that are similar enough in sound and meaning to serve as translation equivalents. Such words may be cognate in the sense of historical linguistics, but they may also be borrowings from a third language. We apply PairHMMs to dialect data for the first time in this paper. Like Mackay and Kondrak (2005) we evaluate the results both on a specific task, in our case, dialect classification, and also via examination of the segment substitution probabilities induced by the PairHMM training procedures. We suggest using the acoustic distances between vowels as a probe to explore the segment substitution probabilities induced by the PairHMMs.

Naturally, this validation procedure only makes sense if dialects are using acoustically more similar sounds in their variation, rather than, for example,

Proceedings of Ninth Meeting of the ACL Special Interest Group in Computational Morphology and Phonology, pages 48–56,
Prague, June 2007.

randomly varied sounds. But why should linguistic and geographic proximity be mirrored by frequency of correspondence? Historical linguistics suggests that sound changes propagate geographically, which means that nearby localities should on average share the most changes. In addition some changes are convergent to local varieties, increasing the tendency toward local similarity. The overall effect in both cases strengthens the similarity of nearby varieties. Correspondences among more distant varieties are more easily disturbed by intervening changes and decreasing strength of propagation.

2 Material

In this study the most recent Dutch dialect data source is used: data from the Goeman-Taeldeman-Van Reenen-project (GTRP; Goeman and Taeldeman, 1996). The GTRP consists of digital transcriptions for 613 dialect varieties in the Netherlands (424 varieties) and Belgium (189 varieties), gathered during the period 1980–1995. For every variety, a maximum of 1876 items was narrowly transcribed according to the International Phonetic Alphabet. The items consisted of separate words and word groups, including pronominals, adjectives and nouns. A more detailed overview of the data collection is given in Taeldeman and Verleyen (1999).

Since the GTRP was compiled with a view to documenting both phonological and morphological variation (De Schutter et al., 2005) and our purpose here is the analysis of variation in pronunciation, many items of the GTRP are ignored. We use the same 562 item subset as introduced and discussed in depth by Wieling et al. (2007). In short, the 1876 item word list was filtered by selecting only single word items, plural nouns (the singular form was preceded by an article and therefore not included), base forms of adjectives instead of comparative forms and the first-person plural verb instead of other forms. We omit words whose variation is primarily morphological as we wish to focus on pronunciation.

Because the GTRP transcriptions of Belgian varieties are fundamentally different from transcriptions of Netherlandic varieties (Wieling et al., 2007), we will focus our analysis on the 424 varieties in the Netherlands. The geographic distribution of these varieties is shown in Figure 1. Furthermore, note that we will not look at diacritics, but only at the phonetic symbols (82 in total).

Figure 1. Distribution of GTRP localities.

3 The Pair Hidden Markov Model

In this study we will use a Pair Hidden Markov Model (PairHMM), which is essentially a Hidden Markov Model (HMM) adapted to assign similarity scores to word pairs and to use these similarity scores to compute string distances. In general an HMM generates an observation sequence (output) by starting in one of the available states based on the initial probabilities, going from state to state based on the transition probabilities while emitting an output symbol in each state based on the emission probability of that output symbol in that state. The probability of an observation sequence given the HMM can be calculated by using well known HMM algorithms such as the Forward algorithm and the Viterbi algorithms (e.g., see Rabiner, 1989).

The only difference between the PairHMM and the HMM is that it outputs a pair of symbols instead of only one symbol. Hence it generates two (aligned) observation streams instead of one. The PairHMM was originally proposed by Durbin et al. (1998) and has successfully been used for aligning

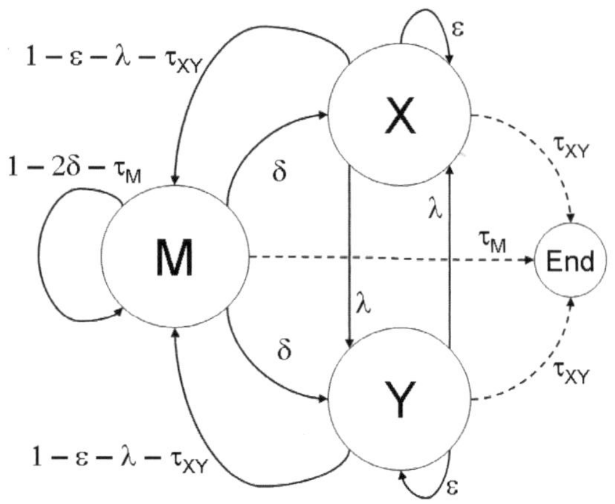

Figure 2. Pair Hidden Markov Model. Image courtesy of Mackay and Kondrak (2005).

biological sequences. Mackay and Kondrak (2005) adapted the algorithm to calculate similarity scores for word pairs in orthographic form, focusing on identifying translation equivalents in bilingual corpora.

Their modified PairHMM has three states representing the basic edit operations: a substitution state (M), a deletion state (X) and an insertion state (Y). In the substitution state two symbols are emitted, while in the other two states a gap and a symbol are emitted, corresponding with a deletion and an insertion, respectively. The model is shown in Figure 2. The four transition parameters are specified by λ, δ, ε and τ. There is no explicit start state; the probability of starting in one of the three states is equal to the probability of going from the substitution state to that state. In our case we use the PairHMM to align phonetically transcribed words. A possible alignment (including the state sequence) for the two observation streams [mɔəlkə] and [mɛlək] (Dutch dialectal variants of the word 'milk') is given by:

m	ɔ	ə	l		k	ə
m	ɛ		l	ə	k	
M	M	X	M	Y	M	X

We have several ways to calculate the similarity score for a given word pair when the transition and emission probabilities are known. First, we can use the Viterbi algorithm to calculate the probability of the best alignment and use this probability as a similarity score (after correcting for length; see Mackay and Kondrak, 2005). Second, we can use the Forward algorithm, which takes all possible alignments into account, to calculate the probability of the observation sequence given the PairHMM and use this probability as a similarity score (again corrected for length; see Mackay, 2004 for the adapted PairHMM Viterbi and Forward algorithms).

A third method to calculate the similarity score is using the log-odds algorithm (Durbin et al., 1998). The log-odds algorithm uses a random model to represent how likely it is that a pair of words occur together while they have no underlying relationship. Because we are looking at word alignments, this means an alignment consisting of no substitutions but only insertions and deletions. Mackay and Kondrak (2005) propose a random model which has only insertion and deletion states and generates one word completely before the other, e.g.

m	ɔ	ə	l	k	ə					
						m	ɛ	l	ə	k
X	X	X	X	X	X	Y	Y	Y	Y	Y

The model is described by the transition probability η and is displayed in Figure 3. The emission probabilities can be either set equal to the insertion and deletion probabilities of the word similarity model (Durbin et al., 1998) or can be specified separately based on the token frequencies in the data set (Mackay and Kondrak, 2005).

The final log-odds similarity score of a word pair is calculated by dividing the Viterbi or Forward probability by the probability generated by the random model, and subsequently taking the logarithm of this value. When using the Viterbi algorithm the regular log-odds score is obtained, while using the Forward algorithm yields the Forward log-odds score (Mackay, 2004). Note that there is no need for additional normalisation; by dividing two models we are already implicitly normalising.

Before we are able to use the algorithms described above, we have to estimate the emission probabilities (i.e. insertion, substitution and deletion probabilities) and transition probabilities of the model. These probabilities can be estimated by using the Baum-Welch expectation maximisation algorithm (Baum et al., 1970). The Baum-Welch algo-

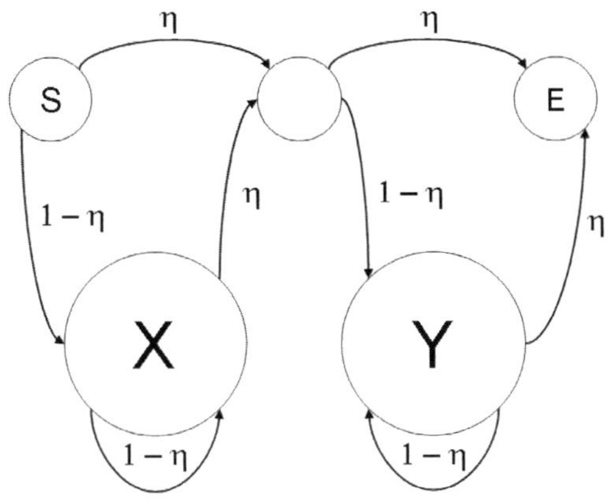

Figure 3. Random Pair Hidden Markov Model. Image courtesy of Mackay and Kondrak (2005).

rithm iteratively reestimates the transition and emission probabilities until a local optimum is found and has time complexity $\mathcal{O}(TN^2)$, where N is the number of states and T is the length of the observation sequence. The Baum-Welch algorithm for the PairHMM is described in detail in Mackay (2004).

3.1 Calculating dialect distances

When the parameters of the complete model have been determined, the model can be used to calculate the alignment probability for every word pair. As in Mackay and Kondrak (2005) and described above, we use the Forward and Viterbi algorithms in both their regular (normalised for length) and log-odds form to calculate similarity scores for every word pair. Subsequently, the distance between two dialectal varieties can be obtained by calculating all word pair scores and averaging them.

4 The Levenshtein distance

The Levenshtein distance was introduced by Kessler (1995) as a tool for measuring linguistic distances between language varieties and has been successfully applied in dialect comparison (Nerbonne et al., 1996; Heeringa, 2004). For this comparison we use a slightly modified version of the Levenshtein distance algorithm, which enforces a linguistic syllabicity constraint: only vowels may match with vowels, and consonants with consonants. The specific details of this modification are described in more detail in Wieling et al. (2007).

We do not normalise the Levenshtein distance measurement for length, because Heeringa et al. (2006) showed that results based on raw Levenshtein distances are a better approximation of dialect differences as perceived by the dialect speakers than results based on the normalised Levenshtein distances. Finally, all substitutions, insertions and deletions have the same weight.

5 Results

To obtain the best model probabilities, we trained the PairHMM with all data available from the 424 Netherlandic localities. For every locality there were on average 540 words with an average length of 5 tokens. To prevent order effects in training, every word pair was considered twice (e.g., $w_a - w_b$ and $w_b - w_a$). Therefore, in one training iteration almost 100 million word pairs had to be considered. To be able to train with these large amounts of data, a parallel implementation of the PairHMM software was implemented. After starting with more than 6700 uniform initial substitution probabilities, 82 insertion and deletion probabilities and 5 transition probabilities, convergence was reached after nearly 1500 iterations, taking 10 parallel processors each more than 10 hours of computation time.

In the following paragraphs we will discuss the quality of the trained substitution probabilities as well as comment on the dialectological results obtained with the trained model.

5.1 Trained substitution probabilities

We are interested both in how well the overall sequence distances assigned by the trained PairHMMs reveal the dialectological landscape of the Netherlands, and also in how well segment distances induced by the Baum-Welch training (i.e. based on the substitution probabilities) reflect linguistic reality. A first inspection of the latter is a simple check on how well standard classifications are respected by the segment distances induced.

Intuitively, the probabilities of substituting a vowel with a vowel or a consonant with a consonant (i.e. same-type substitution) should be higher than the probabilities of substituting a vowel with a consonant or vice versa (i.e. different-type substitution). Also the probability of substituting a phonetic symbol with itself (i.e. identity substitution) should be higher than the probability of a substitution with any other phonetic symbol. To test this assumption, we compared the means of the above three substitution groups for vowels, consonants and both types together.

In line with our intuition, we found a higher probability for an identity substitution as opposed to same-type and different-type non-identity substitutions, as well as a higher probability for a same-type substitution as compared to a different-type substitution. This result was highly significant in all cases: vowels (all $p's \leq 0.020$), consonants (all $p's < 0.001$) and both types together (all $p's < 0.001$).

5.2 Vowel substitution scores compared to acoustic distances

PairHMMs assign high probabilities (and scores) to the emission of segment pairs that are more likely to be found in training data. Thus we expect frequent dialect correspondences to acquire high scores. Since phonetic similarity effects alignment and segment correspondences, we hypothesise that phonetically similar segment correspondences will be more usual than phonetically remote ones, more specifically that there should be a negative correlation between PairHMM-induced segment substitution probabilities presented above and phonetic distances.

We focus on segment distances among vowels, because it is straightforward to suggest a measure of distance for these (but not for consonants). Phoneticians and dialectologists use the two first formants (the resonant frequencies created by different forms of the vocal cavity during pronunciation) as the defining physical characteristics of vowel quality. The first two formants correspond to the articulatory vowel features height and advancement. We follow variationist practice in ignoring third and higher formants. Using formant frequencies we can calculate the acoustic distances between vowels.

Because the occurrence frequency of the phonetic symbols influences substitution probability, we do not compare substitution probabilities directly to acoustic distances. To obtain comparable scores, the substitution probabilities are divided by the product of the relative frequencies of the two phonetic symbols used in the substitution. Since substitutions involving similar infrequent segments now get a much higher score than substitutions involving similar, but frequent segments, the logarithm of the score is used to bring the respective scores into a comparable scale.

In the program PRAAT we find Hertz values of the first three formants for Dutch vowels pronounced by 50 male (Pols et al., 1973) and 25 female (Van Nierop et al., 1973) speakers of standard Dutch. The vowels were pronounced in a /hVt/ context, and the quality of the phonemes for which we have formant information should be close to the vowel quality used in the GTRP transcriptions. By averaging over 75 speakers we reduce the effect of personal variation. For comparison we chose only vowels that are pronounced as monophthongs in standard Dutch, in order to exclude interference of changing diphthong vowel quality with the results. Nine vowels were used: /i, ɪ, y, ʏ, ɛ, a, ɑ, ɔ, u/.

We calculated the acoustic distances between all vowel pairs as a Euclidean distance of the formant values. Since our perception of frequency is non-linear, using Hertz values of the formants when calculating the Euclidean distances would not weigh $F1$ heavily enough. We therefore transform frequencies to Bark scale, in better keeping with human perception. The correlation between the acoustic vowel distances based on two formants in Bark and the logarithmical and frequency corrected PairHMM substitution scores is $r = -0.65$ ($p < 0.01$). But Lobanov (1971) and Adank (2003) suggested using standardised z-scores, where the normalisation is applied over the entire vowel set produced by a given speaker (one normalisation per speaker). This helps in smoothing the voice differences between men and women. Normalising frequencies in this way resulted in a correlation of $r = -0.72$ ($p < 0.001$) with the PairHMM substitution scores. Figure 4 visualises this result. Both Bark scale and z-values gave somewhat lower correlations when the third formant was included in the measures.

The strong correlation demonstrates that the PairHMM scores reflect phonetic (dis)similarity. The higher the probability that vowels are aligned in PairHMM training, the smaller the acoustic distance between two segments. We conclude therefore that the PairHMM indeed aligns linguistically corresponding segments in accord with phonetic similar-

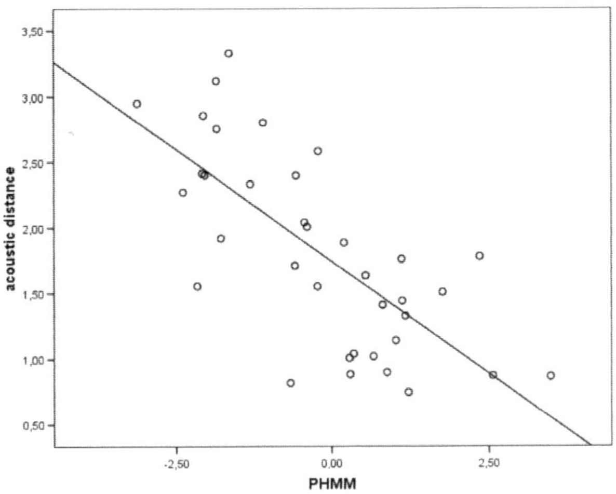

Figure 4. Predicting acoustic distances based on PairHMM scores. Acoustic vowel distances are calculated via Euclidean distance based on the first two formants measured in Hertz, normalised for speaker. $r = -0.72$

ity. This likewise confirms that dialect differences tend to be acoustically slight rather than large, and suggests that PairHMMs are attuned to the slight differences which accumulate locally during language change. Also we can be more optimistic about combining segment distances and sequence distance techniques, in spite of Heeringa (2004, Ch. 4) who combined formant track segment distances with Levenshtein distances without obtaining improved results.

5.3 Dialectological results

To see how well the PairHMM results reveal the dialectological landscape of the Netherlands, we calculated the dialect distances with the Viterbi and Forward algorithms (in both their normalised and log-odds version) using the trained model parameters.

To assess the quality of the PairHMM results, we used the LOCAL INCOHERENCE measurement which measures the degree to which geographically close varieties also represent linguistically similar varieties (Nerbonne and Kleiweg, 2005). Just as Mackay and Kondrak (2005), we found the overall best performance was obtained using the log-odds version of Viterbi algorithm (with insertion and deletion probabilities based on the token frequencies).

Following Mackay and Kondrak (2005), we also experimented with a modified PairHMM obtained by setting non-substitution parameters constant. Rather than using the transition, insertion and deletion parameters (see Figure 2) of the trained model, we set these to a constant value as we are most interested in the effects of the substitution parameters. We indeed found slightly increased performance (in terms of LOCAL INCOHERENCE) for the simplified model with constant transition parameters. However, since there was a very high correlation ($r = 0.98$) between the full and the simplified model and the resulting clustering was also highly similar, we will use the Viterbi log-odds algorithm using all trained parameters to represent the results obtained with the PairHMM method.

5.4 PairHMM vs. Levenshtein results

The PairHMM yielded dialectological results quite similar to those of Levenshtein distance. The LOCAL INCOHERENCE of the two methods was similar, and the dialect distance matrices obtained from the two techniques correlated highly ($r = 0.89$). Given that the Levenshtein distance has been shown to yield results that are consistent (Cronbach's $\alpha = 0.99$) and valid when compared to dialect speakers judgements of similarity ($r \approx 0.7$), this means in particular that the PairHMMs are detecting dialectal variation quite well.

Figure 5 shows the dialectal maps for the results obtained using the Levenshtein algorithm (top) and the PairHMM algorithm (bottom). The maps on the left show a clustering in ten groups based on UPGMA (Unweighted Pair Group Method with Arithmetic mean; see Heeringa, 2004 for a detailed explanation). In these maps phonetically close dialectal varieties are marked with the same symbol. However note that the symbols can only be compared within a map, not between the two maps (e.g., a dialectal variety indicated by a square in the top map does not need to have a relationship with a dialectal variety indicated by a square in the bottom map). Because clustering is unstable, in that small differences in input data can lead to large differences in the classifications derived, we repeatedly added random small amounts of noise to the data and iteratively generated the cluster borders based on the

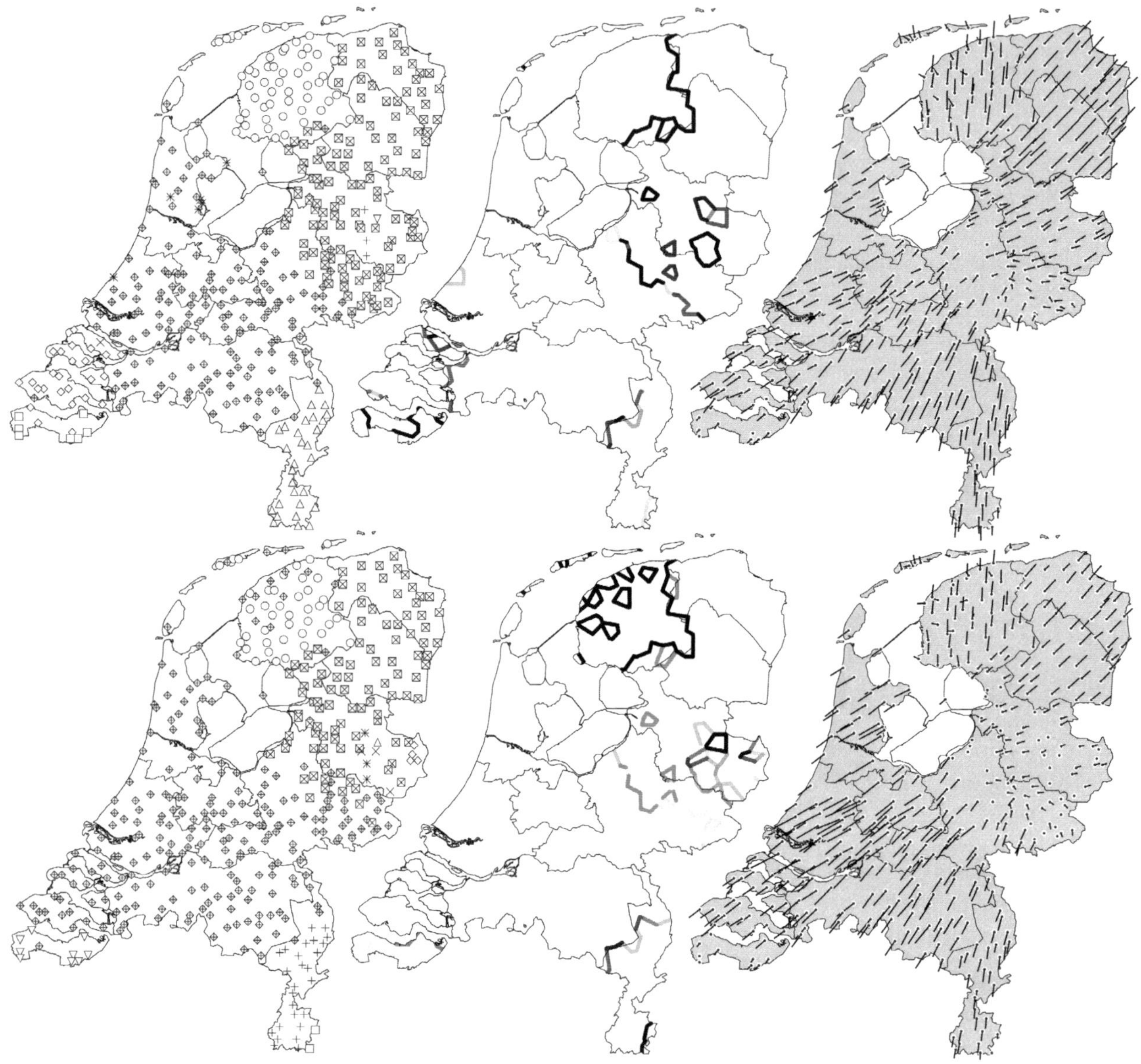

Figure 5. Dialect distances for Levenshtein method (top) and PairHMM method (bottom). The maps on the left show the ten main clusters for both methods, indicated by distinct symbols. Note that the shape of these symbols can only be compared within a map, not between the top and bottom maps. The maps in the middle show robust cluster borders (darker lines indicate more robust cluster borders) obtained by repeated clustering using random small amounts of noise. The maps on the right show for each locality a vector towards the region which is phonetically most similar. See section 5.4 for further explanation.

noisy input data. Only borders which showed up during most of the 100 iterations are shown in the map. The maps in the middle show the most robust cluster borders; darker lines indicate more robust borders. The maps on the right show a vector at each locality pointing in the direction of the region it is phonetically most similar to.

A number of observations can be made on the basis of these maps. The most important observation is that the maps show very similar results. For instance, in both methods a clear distinction can be seen between the Frisian varieties (north) and their surroundings as well as the Limburg varieties (south) and their surroundings. Some differences can also be observed. For instance, at first glance the Frisian cities among the Frisian varieties are separate clusters in the PairHMM method, while this is not the case for the Levenshtein method. Since the Frisian cities differ from their surroundings a great deal, this point favours the PairHMM. However, when looking at the deviating vectors for the Frisian cities in the two vector maps, it is clear that the techniques again yield similar results. Note that a more detailed description of the results using the Levenshtein distance on the GTRP data can be found in Wieling et al. (2007).

Although the PairHMM method is much more sophisticated than the Levenshtein method, it yields very similar results. This may be due to the fact that the data sets are large enough to compensate for the lack of sensitivity in the Levenshtein technique, and the fact that we are evaluating the techniques at a high level of aggregation (average differences in 540-word samples).

6 Discussion

The present study confirms Mackay and Kondrak's (2004) work showing that PairHMMs align linguistic material well and that they induce reasonable segment distances at the same time. We have extended that work by applying PairHMMs to dialectal data, and by evaluating the induced segment distances via their correlation with acoustic differences. We noted above that it is not clear whether the dialectological results improve on the simple Levenshtein measures, and that this may be due to the level of aggregation and the large sample sizes. But we would also like to test PairHMMs on a data set for which more sensitive validation is possible, e.g. the Norwegian set for which dialect speakers judgements of proximity is available (Heeringa et al., 2006); this is clearly a point at which further work would be rewarding.

At a more abstract level, we emphasise that the correlation between acoustic distances on the one hand and the segment distances induced by the PairHMMs on the other confirm both that alignments created by the PairHMMs are linguistically responsible, and also that this linguistic structure influences the range of variation. The segment distances induced by the PairHMMs reflect the frequency with which such segments need to be aligned in Baum-Welch training. It would be conceivable that dialect speakers used all sorts of correspondences to signal their linguistic provenance, but they do not. Instead, they tend to use variants which are linguistically close at the segment level.

Finally, we note that the view of diachronic change as on the one hand the accumulation of changes propagating geographically, and on the other hand as the result of a tendency toward local convergence suggests that we should find linguistically similar varieties nearby rather than further away. The segment correspondences PairHMMs induce correspond to those found closer geographically.

We have assumed a dialectological perspective here, focusing on local variation (Dutch), and using similarity of pronunciation as the organising variationist principle. For the analysis of relations among languages that are further away from each other—temporally and spatially—there is substantial consensus that one needs to go beyond similarity as a basis for postulating grouping. Thus phylogenetic techniques often use a model of relatedness aimed not at similarity-based grouping, but rather at creating a minimal genealogical tree. Nonetheless similarity *is* a satisfying basis of comparison at more local levels.

Acknowledgements

We are thankful to Greg Kondrak for providing the source code of the PairHMM training and testing algorithms. We thank the Meertens Instituut for making the GTRP data available for research and especially Boudewijn van den Berg for answering our questions regarding this data. We would also like to thank Vincent van Heuven for phonetic advice and Peter Kleiweg for providing support and the software we used to create the maps.

References

Patti Adank. 2003. *Vowel normalization - a perceptual-acoustic study of Dutch vowels*. Wageningen: Ponsen & Looijen.

Leonard E. Baum, Ted Petrie, George Soules, and Norman Weiss. 1970. A maximization technique occurring in the statistical analysis of probabilistic functions of Markov Chains. *The Annals of Mathematical Statistics*, 41(1):164–171.

Georges De Schutter, Boudewijn van den Berg, Ton Goeman, and Thera de Jong. 2005. *Morfologische atlas van de Nederlandse dialecten - deel 1*. Amsterdam University Press, Meertens Instituut - KNAW, Koninklijke Academie voor Nederlandse Taal- en Letterkunde.

Richard Durbin, Sean R. Eddy, Anders Krogh, and Graeme Mitchison. 1998. *Biological Sequence Analysis : Probabilistic Models of Proteins and Nucleic Acids*. Cambridge University Press, July.

Ton Goeman and Johan Taeldeman. 1996. Fonologie en morfologie van de Nederlandse dialecten. een nieuwe materiaalverzameling en twee nieuwe atlasprojecten. *Taal en Tongval*, 48:38–59.

Wilbert Heeringa, Peter Kleiweg, Charlotte Gooskens, and John Nerbonne. 2006. Evaluation of string distance algorithms for dialectology. In John Nerbonne and Erhard Hinrichs, editors, *Linguistic Distances*, pages 51–62, Shroudsburg, PA. ACL.

Wilbert Heeringa. 2004. *Measuring Dialect Pronunciation Differences using Levenshtein Distance*. Ph.D. thesis, Rijksuniversiteit Groningen.

Brett Kessler. 1995. Computational dialectology in Irish Gaelic. In *Proceedings of the seventh conference on European chapter of the Association for Computational Linguistics*, pages 60–66, San Francisco, CA, USA. Morgan Kaufmann Publishers Inc.

William Labov. 2001. *Principles of Linguistic Change. Vol.2: Social Factors*. Blackwell, Malden, Mass.

Boris M. Lobanov. 1971. Classification of Russian vowels spoken by different speakers. *Journal of the Acoustical Society of America*, 49:606–608.

Wesley Mackay and Grzegorz Kondrak. 2005. Computing word similarity and identifying cognates with Pair Hidden Markov Models. In *Proceedings of the 9th Conference on Computational Natural Language Learning (CoNLL)*, pages 40–47, Morristown, NJ, USA. Association for Computational Linguistics.

Wesley Mackay. 2004. Word similarity using Pair Hidden Markov Models. Master's thesis, University of Alberta.

John Nerbonne and Peter Kleiweg. 2005. Toward a dialectological yardstick. *Accepted for publication in Journal of Quantitative Linguistics*.

John Nerbonne, Wilbert Heeringa, Erik van den Hout, Peter van der Kooi, Simone Otten, and Willem van de Vis. 1996. Phonetic distance between Dutch dialects. In Gert Durieux, Walter Daelemans, and Steven Gillis, editors, *CLIN VI: Proc. from the Sixth CLIN Meeting*, pages 185–202. Center for Dutch Language and Speech, University of Antwerpen (UIA), Antwerpen.

Louis C. W. Pols, H. R. C. Tromp, and R. Plomp. 1973. Frequency analysis of Dutch vowels from 50 male speakers. *The Journal of the Acoustical Society of America*, 43:1093–1101.

Lawrence R. Rabiner. 1989. A tutorial on Hidden Markov Models and selected applications in speech recognition. *Proceedings of the IEEE*, 77(2):257–286.

Johan Taeldeman and Geert Verleyen. 1999. De FAND: een kind van zijn tijd. *Taal en Tongval*, 51:217–240.

D. J. P. J. Van Nierop, Louis C. W. Pols, and R. Plomp. 1973. Frequency analysis of Dutch vowels from 25 female speakers. *Acoustica*, 29:110–118.

Martijn Wieling, Wilbert Heeringa, and John Nerbonne. 2007. An aggregate analysis of pronunciation in the Goeman-Taeldeman-Van Reenen-Project data. *Taal en Tongval*. submitted, 12/2006.

Walt Wolfram and Natalie Schilling-Estes. 2003. Dialectology and linguistic diffusion. In Brian D. Joseph and Richard D. Janda, editors, *The Handbook of Historical Linguistics*, pages 713–735. Blackwell, Malden, Massachusetts.

Phonological Reconstruction of a Dead Language Using the Gradual Learning Algorithm

Eric J. M. Smith
Department of Linguistics
University of Toronto
130 St. George Street, Room 6076
Toronto, Ont. M5S 3H1
Canada
eric.smith@utoronto.ca

Abstract

This paper discusses the reconstruction of the Elamite language's phonology from its orthography using the Gradual Learning Algorithm, which was re-purposed to "learn" underlying phonological forms from surface orthography. Practical issues are raised regarding the difficulty of mapping between orthography and phonology, and Optimality Theory's neglected Lexicon Optimization module is highlighted.

1 Introduction

The purpose of this paper is to reconstruct the phonology of Elamite, an extinct language known only from written sources, whose phonology is currently poorly understood. Given that the mechanisms provided by Optimality Theory are powerful enough for a language learner to acquire a natural language given only overt forms, it should be possible to apply the same mechanisms to "learn" Elamite phonology given only its orthography.

The research described here was carried out with the aid of a piece of software, nicknamed *Grotefend*, which was developed as part of a larger research project into Elamite.[1] The data used in this paper consisted of the contents of the *Elamisches Wörterbuch* (Hinz and Koch, 1987) marked up as XML with attributes such as morphology, cognates, semantics, corpus frequency, and chronology. The *Wörterbuch* was used because it is the only source that incorporates Elamite data from all historical periods. It also has the virtue of containing every single attested form known to the authors, which is particularly useful for this project, since we have special interest in alternative spellings of given words.

2 Elamite Language

2.1 Historical and geographical context

Elamite is an extinct language spoken in what is now southwestern and central Iran. Elamite-language texts dating from 2400 BCE until 360 BCE are attested, written in the cuneiform script borrowed from the Sumerians and Akkadians.[2] Elamite has no known linguistic affiliations, although a connection to the Dravidian family has been proposed by McAlpin (1982) and others.

Since both the language and scribal practices are certain to have changed over such a long time-span, this study will restrict itself to text from a single era. The Achæmenid Elamite period (539 BCE to 360 BCE) was chosen, because this period contains the largest volume of texts, and also because those texts are particularly rich in Old Persian names and loanwords that provide a useful starting point for estimating the phonology.

2.2 The cuneiform writing system

As part of their adaptation of cuneiform, the Elamites abandoned most of the logographic ele-

[1] *Grotefend* was written in C++ using Trolltech's Qt toolkit, and runs under Mac OS X. The portions that implement the Gradual Learning Algorithm (§4.3) were adapted from Paul Boersma's Visual Basic source code for the *OTSoft* program, which was kindly provided by Bruce Hayes.

[2] Early texts from Elam using two other indigenous writing systems are not well-enough understood to provide useful linguistic information.

Proceedings of Ninth Meeting of the ACL Special Interest Group in Computational Morphology and Phonology, pages 57–64,
Prague, June 2007.

ments found in Sumerian and Akkadian usage, moving to an almost completely phonetic system, which would be a "core syllabary" in Sproat's (2000) typology. That is, each grapheme represents a syllable, but the system lacks graphemes to represent all of the language's syllables. This is particularly the case for many ⟨CVC⟩ graphemes, which must be written using "syllable telescoping", where a ⟨CV-VC⟩ combination is written, with the internal vowel being repeated. For example, lacking a ⟨lan⟩ grapheme, the syllable /lan/ would have to be written ⟨la-an⟩[3]. Even when the ⟨CVC⟩ grapheme does exist, the ⟨CV-VC⟩ writing is often preferred.

2.3 Hypotheses to be tested

The strategy of this research is to use the techniques of Optimality Theory to reconstruct the language's phonology. We will take the various hypotheses presented by earlier authors and attempt to encapsulate each in the form of an OT constraint.

Altogether 30 separate hypotheses were evaluated, arranged into 11 major groupings. Within each grouping, the sub-hypotheses (which may or may not be mutually exclusive) refer to a related context or related orthographic phenomenon. This paper will largely restrict its discussion to only two of the groupings: H3 (Geminate consonants) and H4 (Nasal vowels).[4]

H3 Geminate consonants
H3a Geminate orthographies represent underlying geminate phonologies.
H3b Geminate orthographies indicate voicelessness (Reiner, 1969).
H3c Certain geminate spellings indicate a distinction other than voicing, such as retroflex/alveolar (McAlpin, 1982).

H4 Nasal vowels
H4a Alternations in the writing of nasals indicate the presence of nasal vowels (e.g. /hũban/ → ⟨hu-um-ban⟩, ⟨hu-ban⟩).
H4b Alternations in the writing of nasals can be explained by underlying nasal consonants (e.g. /humban/ → ⟨hu-um-ban⟩, ⟨hu-ban⟩).

3 Theory of Writing Systems

The discussion of Elamite orthography will be framed within the theory of writing systems proposed by Sproat (2000), whose core claim that "particular (sets of) linguistic elements *license* the occurrence of (sets of) orthographic elements". The details of which linguistic elements license which orthographic ones are specific to any given combination of spoken language and writing system.

The licensing is implemented by a mapping function, $M_{ORL \to \Gamma}$, whose input is the Orthographically Relevant Level (ORL), and whose output is the orthography(Γ). In the case of Elamite, the relevant level is the surface phonology after the application of phonological processes such as assimilation and cluster simplification, so in Sproat's schema, Elamite is classified as having a "shallow" ORL.[5]

4 Applying OT to Orthography

In the normal application of Optimality Theory, the input and the output are both the same type of linguistic entity. However, in the problem dealt with here, the relationship is between an input that is phonological and an output that is orthographic. The comparison of phonological apples to orthographic oranges leads to complications that will be discussed in §6.1. All the modules of Optimality Theory must be adapted for use with orthography.

4.1 Background

As originally formulated, Optimality Theory can be considered as a set of three interconnected modules: GEN, H-EVAL, and Lexicon Optimization (Prince and Smolensky, 1993). Together GEN and H-EVAL comprise the grammar proper. For any given input, GEN generates a set of output candidates, and these candidates are then evaluated against a set of constraints by the H-EVAL module. Lexicon Optimization is not part of the grammar, but it provides

[3]Or ⟨ 𒆷 𒀭 ⟩, but since the readership of this paper is unlikely to be familiar with cuneiform, all graphemes will be presented in the traditional transliterated form used in Assyriology.

[4]The full list of hypothesis groups also includes: H1 (Interpretation of broken ⟨CV_1-V_2C⟩ writings), H2 (Voicing of stops), H5 (Word-final vowels), H6 (Sibilants), H7 (Existence of an /h/ phoneme), H8 (Existence of an /f/ or /v/ phoneme), H9 (Existence of a /j/ phoneme), H10 (Existence of a /w/ phoneme), and H11 (Existence of an /e/ phoneme). Full discussion of the results for these hypotheses can be found in Smith (2004).

[5]For instance, the noun *kittin* 'length' is spelled ⟨ki-it-ti-imma⟩ when followed by the locative suffix *-ma*, while the 3SG object prefix *in-* is written ⟨id⟩ before a verb like *dunih* 'I gave'.

a mechanism by which language learners can use that grammar to determine underlying forms based on the overt forms that are presented to them.

Optimality Theory can be seen as a model for how a language learner acquires a natural language, presented only with overt forms (Tesar and Smolensky, 2000). At first, the learner's constraint rankings and underlying forms will be inaccurate, but as more information is presented the estimates of the underlying forms become more accurate, which in turn improves the constraint rankings, which further improves the estimates of the underlying forms, and so on. In this study, the "learner" is the *Grotefend* software, which is presented with surface orthography and attempts to deduce the phonology.

4.2 Adaptation for orthography

The GEN module must be adapted to generate plausible overt forms (i.e. rival orthographies). The general strategy for GEN is described in §5, with the specific details given in §5.2.

The constraints are used by a ranking algorithm (§4.3) that compares the rival orthographies from GEN against underlying phonological forms in order to determine the number of constraint violations. In order to start the process, those underlying forms have to be seeded with reasonable initial estimates. If the word is a loanword, the initial estimate is based on the Old Persian or Akkadian phonology. If there is no available loanword phonology, the initial estimate is a direct transcription of the grapheme values as if the word were being read in Akkadian.

Once the constraints have been ranked, Lexical Optimization takes the orthographic forms and the newly-ranked constraints, and calculates an estimated phonology for each of the forms. At this point, the process can stop, or else it can proceed through another iteration of the ranking algorithm, using the new improved estimated phonologies as underlying forms.

4.3 Gradual Learning Algorithm

The Gradual Learning Algorithm (Boersma, 1997; Boersma and Hayes, 2001) is an evolution of the Constraint Demotion algorithm (Tesar, 1995), but avoids the infinite-looping which can arise in Constraint Demotion if underlying forms have more than one overt form. This limitation of Constraint Demotion is a serious one given the data from Elamite orthography; not only are the orthographic forms subject to considerable variation, but also this variation is a key piece of information in attempting to reconstruct the phonology.

In the GLA, constraints each have a numeric ranking value associated with them. It is no longer the case that Constraint A consistently outranks Constraint B; whenever a constraint is evaluated, a random "noise" factor is added to each of the ranking values, and an instantaneous constraint ordering is determined based on these adjusted values. If the ranking values for two constraints are far apart, the noise is unlikely to alter the ordering, and the results will be effectively the same as ordinary OT. If the ranking values for two constraints are close together, the noise could put either constraint on top, but ties are avoided.

In the GLA implementation within *Grotefend*, all constraints start with ranking values of 100.00. With each iteration of the algorithm, one of the observed forms is selected as an exemplar, and rivals (produced by GEN) are compared against the observed exemplar form. Whenever a rival beats the exemplar form, the constraint ranking values must be adjusted: all constraints that picked the wrong winner are penalized (adjusted downwards), and all constraints that picked the right winner are rewarded (adjusted upwards). The size of this adjustment is determined by a variable called "plasticity", which starts at 2.00 and is reduced gradually to 0.002 as the algorithm proceeds through its iterations.

5 Implementation of GEN

The purpose of GEN is to generate a set of plausible overt forms consisting of the real form and a set of rivals which will lose out to the real form. In this problem the overt forms are orthographies, so for any underlying form the challenge is to generate orthographic strings that compete with the real orthography, but which are "wrong" with respect to one or more of the constraints.

5.1 Background

There have been a number of computational implementations of GEN, but the most promising one for our purposes was that of Heiberg (1999). Heiberg's algorithm proceeds by choosing a starting point and then adding constraints to the system. As each constraint is added, new candidates are generated using what she calls "relevant" GEN operations. A GEN operation is considered to be relevant for the current constraint if the operation could affect a candidate's harmony relative to that constraint. So for instance, if the constraint being added evaluates the [+back] feature, the only GEN operations that are relevant are those which affect [+back] or its associations.

The candidates at each stage of the algorithm are not fully formed, and are slowly refined as the constraints are added to the system. One advantage of Heiberg's algorithm is that it functions even if the relative rankings of the constraints are not known. If the constraint rankings are known, the algorithm can operate more efficiently, by culling known losers, but knowing the rankings is not essential.

5.2 Adaptation of GEN for orthography

Generating all "plausible" orthographic candidates for a given form is computationally prohibitive.[6] So, borrowing Heiberg's notion of "relevant" operations, our approach is to generate candidates that specifically exercise one of the constraints in the constraint system.

Each of the hypothesis groups described in §2.3 refers to a particular orthographic context, and each context has a miniature version of GEN to generate appropriately test-worthy rivals. For example, the mini-GEN function for context H3 is as follows:

GEN **H3** (Geminate consonants)
Rule Whenever a geminate consonant is found in the orthography, generate a rival with the non-geminate equivalent.
Example ⟨hu-ut-ta⟩ → { ⟨hu-ta⟩ }

6 Implementation of H-EVAL

The H-EVAL module is responsible for the actual evaluations of the various candidates. It takes any output candidate produced by GEN, and counts the violation marks for each of the constraints.

[6]Initial experiments indicated that a moderately long string of four graphemes would generate in the neighbourhood of 18000 rivals. It seemed unrealistic to evaluate tens of thousands of rivals for each of the 8000+ forms in the database.

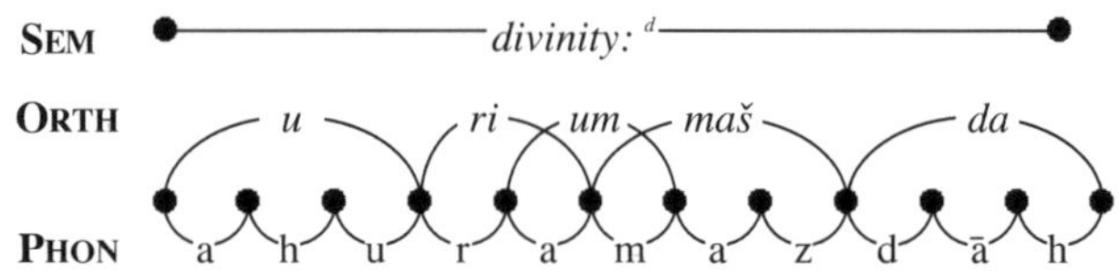

Figure 1: Annotation graph for Ahuramazdāh → ⟨^{d}u-ri-um-maš-da⟩

Each constraint is implemented as a function which takes two inputs (an underlying form and a surface form), and produces as an output the number of violations incurred by the comparing the two inputs. For full generality, both inputs are annotation graphs (Bird and Liberman, 1999; Sproat, 2000) such as the one shown in Figure 1. As implemented in *Grotefend*, the comparison involves only the PHON tier of the underlying form's graph and the ORTH tier of the surface form's graph.

Constraints were written to test each of the hypotheses described in §2.3. Since there is no prior art in the area of constraints involving orthography and phonology, they were developed in the most straightforward way possible. The implementation of these functions is described in §6.2.

6.1 Implementation of alignment

In order to count violations, the two inputs must be properly aligned. For an annotation graph to be "aligned", every grapheme must be licensed by some part of the phonology, and every phoneme must be represented in the orthography. Without such a licensing relationship, it is impossible to make the comparisons needed to count constraint violations.

There is considerable previous work in the area of alignment, most recently summarized by Kondrak and Sherif (2006). The algorithm used in this study is a similarity-based approach, not unlike ALINE (Kondrak, 2000). It differs in some significant respects, notably the use of binary features.

Determining the eligibility of two phonemes for matching requires a distance function. The approach taken was to assign a weight to each phonological feature, and to calculate the distance as the sum of the weights of all features that differ between the two phonemes. The full listing of feature weights is shown in Table 1. The weighting values were deter-

Table 1: Feature weights for computing distance

Phonological Feature	Weight
delayed release, voice, labio-dental, anterior, distributed, strident	1
approximant, continuant, nasal, lateral, round, low, pharyngeal	2
syllabic, consonantal, constricted glottis, spread glottis, high, front, back	4
sonorant, place of articulation	8

mined empirically, selecting the weightings that did the best job of aligning the orthography for the Old Persian loanwords given by Hinz and Koch (1987).

For the actual alignment, several approaches were tried, but the most effective one was simply to line up the consonants and let the vowels fall where they may. For instance, the licensing of ⟨^{d}u-ri-um-maš-da⟩ in Figure 1 used the Old Persian phonology as the best available initial estimate for the Elamite phonology, and proceeded as follows:

⟨**d**⟩ is the divine determinative, and is licensed by the semantic tier of the annotation graph, so it does not need to be anchored to the phonology.
⟨**u**⟩ is anchored at the left edge of the phonology.
⟨**ri**⟩ starts at /r/, but has no clear right edge. The anchoring of /r/ sets a right boundary on the ⟨u⟩, which must therefore be licensed by the initial /ahu/ of /ahuramazdāh/.
⟨**um**⟩ right edge at phoneme /m/; since the ⟨um⟩ has no clear left edge, the second /a/ of /ahuramazdāh/ is left floating between the ⟨ri⟩ and the ⟨um⟩. Since there is no clear choice between the two locations, the /a/ will be shared by ⟨ri⟩ and ⟨um⟩.
⟨**maš**⟩ starts at /m/ and ends at /z/, which is sufficiently similar to match *š*. The /m/ will be shared by ⟨um⟩ and ⟨maš⟩.
⟨**da**⟩ starts at /d/; since ⟨da⟩ is the last grapheme, it must be licensed by the remainder of the phonology.

The general strategy of aligning consonants proved to be an effective one. In the working dataset of Achæmenid Elamite words, there were 3045 that used Old Persian or Akkadian data to provide an initial estimate of the underlying phonology. The algorithm successfully aligned 2902 of those words, for a success rate of over 95%.

6.2 Implementation of constraints

Once the orthography has been successfully aligned with the underlying phonology, it is possible to evaluate the forms for violations against all the constraints in the system. In terms of the tiers shown in annotation graphs like Figure 1, the constraints are performing comparisons between the underlying forms in the PHON tier and overt forms in the ORTH tier. For example, the rules for calculating constraint violations for H3 are as follows:

H3a Geminate spellings indicate geminate pronunciations.
Rule Count a violation if the orthography contains a geminate consonant not matched by a geminate in the phonology.[7]
Violation /a**t**a/ → ⟨a**t-t**a⟩
Non-violations /a**tt**a/ → ⟨a**t-t**a⟩, /a**tt**a/ → ⟨a-**t**a⟩

H3b Geminate spellings indicate voicelessness.
Rule Count a violation if 1) the orthography contains an intervocalic geminate stop not matched by a voiceless stop in the phonology, or 2) the orthography contains an intervocalic non-geminate stop not matched by a voiced stop in the phonology, or 3) the phonology contains an intervocalic voiceless stop not matched by a geminate in the orthography, or 4) the phonology contains an intervocalic voiced stop not matched by a non-geminate in the orthography.[8]
Violations /du**b**a:la/ → ⟨du-i**b-b**a-la⟩, /garma**p**ada/ → ⟨^{d}kar-ma-**b**a-taš⟩
Non-violations /gauma:**t**a/ → ⟨kam-ma-a**d-d**a⟩, /ba**b**ili/ → ⟨ba-**p**i-li⟩

H3c Certain geminate spellings indicate a distinction other than voicing, such as retroflex/alveolar.
Rule Count a violation if 1) the orthography contains a ⟨Vl-lV⟩ or ⟨Vr-rV⟩ sequence not matched by a retroflex in the phonology, or 2) the phonology contains a /ɭ/ or /ɽ/ not matched by a ⟨Vl-lV⟩ or

[7] The claim made by Grillot-Susini and Roche (1988) was only that a geminate orthography represents a geminate phonology; a non-geminate orthography could still conceal a geminate phonology.

[8] Reiner (1969) restricted her claim about gemination representing voicelessness to intervocalic stops. Word-initial stops and intervocalic non-stops were not relevant here.

⟨Vr-rV⟩ in the orthography.
Violations /talu/ → ⟨ta-**al**-**lu**⟩, /taɭu/ → ⟨ta-**lu**⟩
Non-violation /taɭu/ → ⟨ta-**al**-**lu**⟩

7 Implementation of Lexicon Optimization

Given the set of constraints provided in §6.2 and rankings determined by the Gradual Learning Algorithm (§4.3), it is now possible to move on to the final stage of the "learning" process: Lexicon Optimization, which is responsible for choosing the most harmonic input form for any given output form.

There has been surprisingly little literature devoted to Lexicon Optimization, and discussions of how it might be implemented have been restricted to toy algorithms such as Itô et al's (1995) "tableau des tableaux". Hence, a novel approach was devised, based on the observation that Lexicon Optimization is a sort of mirror image of H-EVAL. For H-EVAL, there exists a separate GEN module whose task is to generate the possible output candidates. Clearly, Lexicon Optimization needs an equivalent module, but one that would generate a range of rival input forms. Since the GEN algorithm described in §5.2 uses a constraint-driven technique for generating output candidates, it seems appropriate to also use a constraint-driven technique for generating input candidates. Accordingly, this anti-GEN is implemented as a set of miniature anti-GENs, each of which is responsible for generating "relevant" input candidates for one of the hypothesis groupings. For example, the anti-GEN function for H3 is as follows:

Anti-GEN H3 (Geminate consonants)
Rule Whenever a geminate consonant is found in the orthography, create input candidates with the geminate phonology and the equivalent non-geminate phonology. If the geminate orthography is a ⟨Vl-lV⟩ or ⟨Vr-rV⟩, also create an input candidate with a "retroflex" phonology.[9]
Example ⟨ta-al-lu⟩ → { /tallu/, /talu/, /taɭu/ }

8 Results and Discussion

We ran 40000 iterations of the Gradual Learning Algorithm against the Achæmenid Elamite forms

[9]McAlpin (1982) hedges on whether the phonology represented by these geminates actually represents retroflexion, but he then proceeds to discuss Proto-Elamo-Dravidian cognates as if this orthography actually did represent a retroflex articulation.

Table 2: Final constraint rankings for H3 and H4

Hypothesis	Constraint	Ranking Value
H4b	NasalConsonants	−136.93
H3b	⟨Geminate⟩=/Voiceless/	−283.70
H4a	NasalVowels	−1434.77
H3c	⟨Geminate⟩=/Retroflex/	−1629.74
H3a	⟨Geminate⟩=/Geminate/	−3189.11

found in the *Elamisches Wörterbuch*. The final constraint rankings for hypothesis groups H3 and H4 are shown in Table 2.[10] The combination of constraints, GEN, and anti-GEN functions used by *Grotefend* tends to penalize constraints much more often than it rewards them. The absolute ranking values are not significant; what matters is their relative values.

8.1 Results for H3 (Geminate consonants)

The results for H3 strongly support the hypothesis (Reiner, 1969) that geminate orthographies are an attempt to indicate voicelessness; the opposing hypothesis (Grillot-Susini and Roche, 1988) that geminate orthographies represent geminate phonologies ended up being very heavily penalized.

What was surprising was that hypothesis H3c, that ⟨Vl-lV⟩ and ⟨Vr-rV⟩ geminates represent a separate phoneme from the non-geminate orthographies, ranked so poorly. The problem here is a side-effect of the process for generating input candidates.

Consider the Akkadian name *Nabû-kudurri-uṣur*; the ⟨ur-ri⟩ sequence that occurs in the various spellings of this name would appear to be an ideal context for evaluating H3c. However, when generating input candidates for *Nabû-kudurri-uṣur*, the various anti-GEN functions create 238 permutations (mostly permutations of voicing), but only four of those input candidates contain an /ɽ/ phoneme, with the rest having an /rr/ or an /r/. Since the anti-GEN function produces so few /ɽ/ input candidates for the ⟨ur-ri⟩ orthography, it is likely that the software will find an /r/ in the underlying phonology, and will count a violation against this constraint.

The prejudice against /ɭ/ and /ɽ/ highlights the importance of having a fair and balanced anti-GEN

[10]Results for the other nine groups are in Smith (2004).

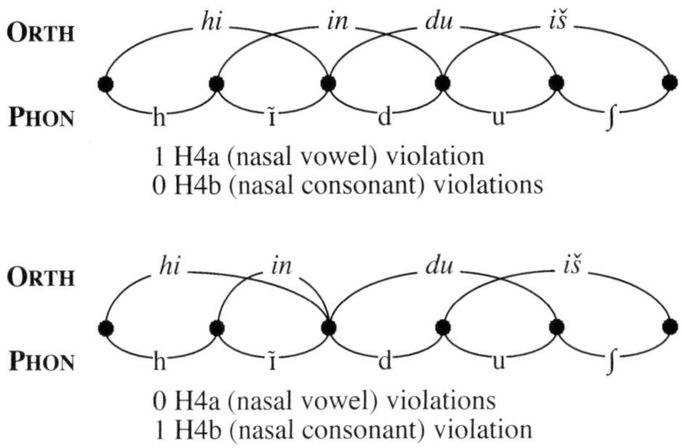

Figure 2: Licensing of ⟨hi-in-du-iš⟩ 'Indian'

function. The proposal to be discussed in §8.3 for cross-permuting the results of the constraint-specific anti-GEN functions would probably also improve the results for this hypothesis.

8.2 Results for H4 (Nasal vowels)

The effectiveness of the constraints for evaluating nasals was undermined by choices made in the alignment algorithm. Although constraint H4b (NasalConsonants) is ranked significantly higher than H4a (NasalVowels), this may be merely a side-effect of the alignment algorithm.

Consider the word for 'Indian', which shows up as ⟨hi-du-iš⟩, ⟨hi-in-du-iš⟩, or ⟨in-du-iš⟩. It is not unreasonable to postulate an underlying phonology of /hĩduʃ/, based both on the range of written forms, and on the Old Persian phonology. However, when the alignment algorithm attempts to determine which phoneme sequences are licensing which graphemes, it has a difficult choice to make for the ⟨in⟩ grapheme. Licensing the vowel portion of ⟨in⟩ is straightforward, but what should be done for the consonant? If the software assumes that the most salient features are [+consonantal] and [−syllabic], we get the first annotation graph shown in Figure 2, but if the most salient features are [+nasal] and [+sonorant], we get the second graph.

The choice of how to license the ⟨in⟩ grapheme makes a difference for how the H4a and H4b constraints are evaluated. Using the weightings given in Table 1, the software will align ⟨in⟩ with /ĩd/, because the distance between /n/ and /d/ is less than that between /n/ and /ĩ/. Hence, the alignment algorithm chooses the first of the two annotation graphs given in Figure 2. This has the result of prejudicing the learning algorithm in favour of H4b instead of H4a. Ideally, the alignment algorithm should be neutral with respect to the various constraints.

The licensing of the ⟨in⟩ sign in this example is one case of several where it appears that using phonological segments as the basis for licensing may be the wrong thing to do. It would be better to think of the second portion of the ⟨in⟩ sign in ⟨hi-in-du-iš⟩ as being licensed by a [+nasal] feature, without attempting to tie the feature down to either the /i/ or the /d/ segment.[11]

8.3 Discussion of Lexicon Optimization

The generation of useful input candidates is limited by the information that is available to us. For all we know, Elamite had an /ɯ/ vowel, and *Grotefend* could even generate input candidates that contained an /ɯ/. However, none of the constraints would weigh either for or against it, so there is no point in generating such an input candidate. Consequently, the correct underlying form may well be inaccessible to Lexicon Optimization. At best, Lexicon Optimization can produce an estimated underlying form that leaves as underspecified any features that cannot be verified by a corresponding constraint. This is a limitation of Lexicon Optimization in general, not just of the implementation in *Grotefend*.

One problem specific to our constraint-based generation of input candidates is that the anti-GEN functions work in isolation from each other. For example, when processing ⟨da-iš⟩, the H1 (broken-vowel) anti-GEN produces /daiʃ/, /dajʃ/, /dɛʃ/, and /daʃ/. Separately, the H6 (sibilant) anti-GEN will produce /dais/, /daiʃ/, /daiz/, /daitʃ/, and /daits/. Since the two functions operate independently, the software fails to generate a whole range of candidates. If the actual underlying phonology were /dɛtʃ/, *Grotefend* would never find it, since that particular phonology will never be generated and presented to Lexicon Optimization as a possible input candidate. A more sophisticated anti-GEN implementation would allow for the input candidates produced by one constraint's anti-GEN function to be further permuted

[11] Sproat (2000) uses phonological segments to describe licensing, but there is nothing in his theory that requires this; in fact, he says that his use of segments is merely a "shorthand" for a set of overlapping gestures.

by the anti-GEN function of another constraint.

9 Conclusions

This project represented an expedition into three largely unexplored territories: the application of Optimality Theory to orthography, the implementation of Lexicon Optimization in software, and the mass analysis of Elamite phonology. All three presented unanticipated challenges.

The problem of implementing GEN algorithmically appears to be at an early stage even in the processing of phonological data. The constraint-driven GEN adopted from Heiberg (1999) does appear to be a useful starting point for working with orthography.

The determination of the mapping between phonology and orthography can have unexpected consequences for the evaluation of constraints. Even when properly aligned, implementing meaningful constraints to evaluate the mismatches between phonology and orthography proved to be surprisingly complex. An alternative representation, licensing graphemes based on bundles of features rather than phonemes, might be more effective.

The whole area of Lexicon Optimization has received surprisingly little mention in the literature of Optimality Theory. The notion that there must be some form of anti-GEN module to produce suitable input candidates appears never to have been raised at all. The existence of anti-GEN is hardly specific to the study of orthography, but would seem to be an omission from Optimality Theory in general.

The constraint-driven implementation of the anti-GEN function does seem like a promising strategy, although the details need work. In particular, there is a need for the outputs of the various constraint-specific anti-GENs to be permuted together in order to produce all plausible input candidates.

Elamite has always been problematic both due to its status as an isolate and because the available clues end up being obscured by the writing system. So far, we can claim that this computational analysis of the body of Elamite vocabulary has succeeded in duplicating some of the tentative conclusions drawn from a century of hard work "by hand".

References

Steven Bird and Mark Liberman. 1999. A formal framework for linguistic annotation. Technical Report Technical Report MS-CIS-99-01, Department of Computer and Information Science, University of Pennsylvania.

Paul Boersma and Bruce Hayes. 2001. Empirical tests of the gradual learning algorithm. *Linguistic Inquiry*, 32:45–86.

Paul Boersma. 1997. How we learn variation, optionality, and probability. *Proceedings of the Institute of Phonetic Sciences of the University of Amsterdam*, 21:43–58.

Françoise Grillot-Susini and Claude Roche. 1988. *Eléments de grammaire élamite*. Etudes elamites. Editions Recherche sur les civilisations, Paris.

Andrea Heiberg. 1999. *Features in Optimality Theory: A computational model*. Ph.D. thesis, University of Arizona.

Walther Hinz and Heidemarie Koch. 1987. *Elamisches Wörterbuch*. D. Reimer, Berlin.

Junko Itô, Armin Mester, and Jaye Padgett. 1995. NC: Licensing and underspecification in optimality theory. *Linguistic Inquiry*, 26(4):571–613.

Grzegorz Kondrak and Tarek Sherif. 2006. Evaluation of several phonetic similarity algorithms on the task of cognate identification. In *Proceedings of the Workshop on Linguistic Distances*, pages 43–50.

Grzegorz Kondrak. 2000. A new algorithm for the alignment of phonetic sequences. In *Proceedings of the First Meeting of the NAACL*, pages 288–295.

David W. McAlpin. 1982. Proto-Elamo-Dravidian: The evidence and its implications. *Transactions of the American Philosophical Society*, 71(3):1–155.

Alan Prince and Paul Smolensky. 1993. Optimality theory. *Rutgers Optimality Archive*, #537.

Erica Reiner. 1969. The Elamite language. *Handbuch der Orientalistik I/II/1/2/2*, pages 54–118.

Eric J. M. Smith. 2004. *Optimality Theory and Orthography: Using OT to Reconstruct Elamite Phonology*. M.A. forum paper, University of Toronto.

Richard Sproat. 2000. *A Computational Theory of Writing Systems*. Cambridge University Press.

Bruce Tesar and Paul Smolensky. 2000. *Learnability in Optimality Theory*. MIT Press, Cambridge, Mass.

Bruce Tesar. 1995. *Computational Optimality Theory*. Ph.D. thesis, University of Colorado.

Evolution, Optimization, and Language Change: The Case of Bengali Verb Inflections

Monojit Choudhury[1], **Vaibhav Jalan**[2], **Sudeshna Sarkar**[1], **Anupam Basu**[1]
[1] Department of Computer Science and Engineering
Indian Institute of Technology, Kharagpur, India
{monojit,sudeshna,anupam}@cse.iitkgp.ernet.in
[2] Department of Computer Engineering
Malaviya National Institute of Technology, Jaipur, India
vaibhavjalan.mnit@gmail.com

Abstract

The verb inflections of Bengali underwent a series of phonological change between 10th and 18th centuries, which gave rise to several modern dialects of the language. In this paper, we offer a functional explanation for this change by quantifying the functional pressures of ease of articulation, perceptual contrast and learnability through objective functions or constraints, or both. The multi-objective and multi-constraint optimization problem has been solved through genetic algorithm, whereby we have observed the emergence of Pareto-optimal dialects in the system that closely resemble some of the real ones.

1 Introduction

Numerous theories have been proposed to explain the phenomenon of *linguistic change*, which, of late, are also being supported by allied mathematical or computational models. See (Steels, 1997; Perfors, 2002) for surveys on computational models of language evolution, and (Wang et al., 2005; Niyogi, 2006) for reviews of works on language change. The aim of these models is to explain why and how languages change under specific socio-cognitive assumptions. Although computational modeling is a useful tool in exploring linguistic change (Cangelosi and Parisi, 2002), due to the inherent complexities of our linguistic and social structures, modeling of real language change turns out to be extremely hard. Consequently, with the exception of a few (e.g., Hare and Elman (1995); Dras et al. (2003); Ke et al. (2003); Choudhury et al. (2006b)), all the mathematical and computational models developed for explaining language change are built for artificial toy languages. This has led several researchers to cast a doubt on the validity of the current computational models as well as the general applicability of computational techniques in diachronic explanations (Hauser et al., 2002; Poibeau, 2006).

In this paper, we offer a *functional explanation*[1] of a real world language change – the morpho-phonological change affecting the Bengali verb inflections (BVI). We model the problem as a multi-objective and multi-constraint optimization and solve the same using Multi-Objective Genetic Algorithm[2] (MOGA). We show that the different forms of the BVIs, as found in the several modern dialects, automatically emerge in the MOGA framework under suitable modeling of the objective and constraint functions. The model also predicts several

[1] Functionalist accounts of language change invoke the basic function of language, i.e. communication, as the driving force behind linguistic change (Boersma, 1998). Stated differently, languages change in a way to optimize their function, such that speakers can communicate maximum information with minimum effort (ease of articulation) and ambiguity (perceptual contrast). Often, ease of learnability is also considered a functional benefit. For an overview of different explanations in diachronic linguistics see (Kroch, 2001) and Ch. 3 of (Blevins, 2004).

[2] Genetic algorithm was initially proposed by Holland (1975) as a self-organizing adaptation process mimicking the biological evolution. They are also used for optimization and machine learning purposes, especially when the nature of the solution space is unknown or there are more than one objective functions. See Goldberg (1989) for an accessible introduction to single and multi-objective Genetic algorithms. Note that in case of a multi-objective optimization problem, MOGA gives a set of Pareto-optimal solutions rather than a single optimum. The concept of Pareto-optimality is defined later.

Proceedings of Ninth Meeting of the ACL Special Interest Group in Computational Morphology and Phonology, pages 65–74, Prague, June 2007.

other possible dialectal forms of Bengali that seems linguistically plausible and might exist or have existed in the past, present or future. Note that the evolutionary algorithm (i.e., MOGA) has been used here as a tool for optimization, and has no relevance to the evolution of the dialects as such.

Previously, Redford et al. (2001) has modeled the emergence of syllable systems in a multi-constraint and multi-objective framework using Genetic algorithms. Since the model fuses the individual objectives into a single objective function through a weighted linear combination, it is not a multi-objective optimization in its true sense and neither does it use MOGA for the optimization process. Nevertheless, the present work draws heavily from the quantitative formulation of the objectives and constraints described in (Redford, 1999; Redford and Diehl, 1999; Redford et al., 2001). Ke et al. (2003) has demonstrated the applicability and advantages of MOGA in the context of the vowel and tonal systems, but the model is not explicit about the process of change that could give rise to the optimal vowel systems. As we shall see that the conception of the *genotype*, which is arguably the most important part of any MOGA model, is a novel and significant contribution of this work. The present formulation of the genotype not only captures a snapshot of the linguistic system, but also explicitly models the course of change that has given rise to the particular system. Thus, we believe that the current model is more suitable in explaining a case of linguistic change.

The paper is organized as follows: Sec. 2 introduces the problem of historical change affecting the BVIs and presents a mathematical formulation of the same; Sec. 3 describes the MOGA model; Sec. 4 reports the experiments, observations and their interpretations; Sec. 5 concludes the paper by summarizing the contributions. In this paper, Bengali graphemes are represented in Roman script following the ITRANS notation (Chopde, 2001). Since Bengali uses a phonemic orthography, the phonemes are also transcribed using ITRANS within two /s.

2 The Problem

Bengali is an *agglutinative language*. There are more than 150 different inflected forms of a single verb root in Bengali, which are obtained through affixation of one of the 52 inflectional suffixes, optionally followed by the emphasizers. The suffixes mark for the tense, aspect, modality, person and polarity information (Bhattacharya et al., 2005). The origin of modern Bengali can be traced back to Vedic Sanskrit (circa 1500 BC 600 BC), which during the middle Indo-Aryan period gave rise to the dialects like $M\bar{a}gadh\bar{i}$, and $Ardham\bar{a}gadh\bar{i}$ (circa 600 BC 200 AD), followed by the $M\bar{a}gadh\bar{i} - apabhramsha$, and finally crystallizing to Bengali (circa 10th century AD) (Chatterji, 1926). The verbal inflections underwent a series of phonological changes during the middle Bengali period (1200 - 1800 AD), which gave rise to the several dialectal forms of Bengali, including the standard form – the Standard Colloquial Bengali (SCB).

Attributes	Classical (Λ_0)	SCB	ACB	Sylheti
PrS1	*kari*	*kori*	*kori*	*kori*
PrS2	*kara*	*karo*	*kara*	*kara*
PrS3	*kare*	*kare*	*kare*	*kare*
PrSF	*karen*	*karen*	*karen*	*karoin*
PrC1	*kariteChi*	*korChi*	*kartAsi*	*koirtAsi*
PrC2	*kariteCha*	*korCho*	*kartAsa*	*koirtAsae*
PrC3	*kariteChe*	*korChe*	*kartAse*	*koirtAse*
PrCF	*kariteChen*	*korChen*	*kartAsen*	*kortAsoin*
PrP1	*kariAChi*	*koreChi*	*korsi*	*koirsi*
PrP2	*kariACha*	*koreCho*	*karsa*	*koirsae*
PrP3	*kariAChe*	*koreChe*	*karse*	*koirse*
PrPF	*kariAChen*	*koreChen*	*karsen*	*korsoin*

Table 1: The different inflected verb forms of Classical Bengali and three other modern dialects. All the forms are in the phonetic forms and for the verb root kar. Legend: (tense) Pr – present; (aspects) S – simple, C – continuous, P – perfect, ; (person) 1 – first, 2 – second normal, 3 – third, F – formal in second and third persons. See (Bhattacharya et al., 2005) for list of all the forms.

The Bengali literature of the 19th century was written in the Classical Bengali dialect or the $s\bar{a}dhubh\bar{a}sh\bar{a}$ that used the older verb forms and drew heavily from the Sanskrit vocabulary, even though the forms had disappeared from the spoken dialects by 17th century. Here, we shall take the liberty to use the terms "classical forms" and "Classical Bengali" to refer to the dialectal forms of middle Bengali and not Classical Bengali of the 19th century literature. Table 1 enlists some of the corresponding verb forms of classical Bengali and SCB. Table 3 shows the derivation of some of the current verb inflections of SCB from its classical counterparts as reported in (Chatterji, 1926).

2.1 Dialect Data

Presently, there are several dialects of Bengali that vary mainly in terms of the verb inflections and intonation, but rarely over syntax or semantics. We do not know of any previous study, during which the different dialectal forms for BVI were collected and systematically listed. Therefore, we have collected dialectal data for the following three modern dialects of Bengali by enquiring the näive informants.

- *Standard Colloquial Bengali* (SCB) spoken in a region around Kolkata, the capital of West Bengal,
- *Agartala Colloquial Bengali* (ACB) spoken in and around Agartala, the capital of Tripura, and
- *Sylheti*, the dialect of the Sylhet region of Bangladesh.

Some of the dialectal forms are listed in Table 1. The scope of the current study is restricted to 28 inflected forms (12 present tense forms + 12 past tense forms + 4 forms of habitual past) of a single verb root, i.e., kar.

2.2 Problem Formulation

Choudhury et al. (2006a) has shown that a sequence of simple phonological changes, which we shall call the *Atomic Phonological Operators* or APO for short, when applied to the classical Bengali lexicon, gives rise to the modern dialects. We conceive of four basic types of APOs, namely Del or deletion, Met or metathesis, Asm or assimilation, and Mut or mutation. The complete specification of an APO includes specification of its type, the phoneme(s) that is(are) affected by the operation and the left and right context of application of the operator specified as regular expressions on phonemes. The semantics of the basic APOs in terms of rewrite rules are shown in Table 2.2. Since Bengali features assimilation only with respect to vowel height, here we shall interpret $Asm(p, LC, RC)$ as the height assimilation of the vowel p in the context of LC or RC. Also, we do not consider *epenthesis* or insertion as an APO, because epenthesis is not observed for the case of the change affecting BVI.

APO	Semantics
$Del(p, LC, RC)$	$p \rightarrow \phi / LC—RC$
$Met(p_i p_j, LC, RC)$	$p_i p_j \rightarrow p_j p_i / LC—RC$
$Asm(p, LC, RC)$	$p \rightarrow p' / LC—RC$
$Mut(p, p', LC, RC)$	$p \rightarrow p' / LC—RC$

Table 2: Semantics of the basic APOs in terms of rewrite rules. LC and RC are regular expressions specifying the left and right contexts respectively. p, p', p_i and p_j represent phonemes.

Rule No.	APO	Example Derivations		
		$kar-iteChe$	$kar-iten$	$kar-iAChi$
1	$Del(e, \phi, Ch)$	$kar-itChe$	NA	NA
2	$Del(t, \phi, Ch)$	$kar-iChe$	NA	NA
3	$Met(ri, \phi, \phi)$	$kair-Che$	$kair-ten$	$kair-AChi$
5	$Mut(A, e, \phi, Ch)$	NA	NA	kair-eChi
6	$Asm(a, i, \phi, \phi)$	$koir-Che$	$koir-ten$	$koir-eChi$
7	$Del(i, o, \phi)$	$kor-Che$	$kor-ten$	$kor-eChi$

Table 3: Derivations of the verb forms of SCB from classical Bengali using APOs. "NA" means the rule is not applicable for the form. See (Choudhury et al., 2006a) for the complete list of APOs involved in the derivation of SCB and ACB forms

The motivation behind defining APOs rather than representing the change in terms of rewrite rules is as follows. Rewrite rules are quite expressive and therefore, it is possible to represent complex phonological changes using a single rewrite rule. On the other hand, APOs are simple phonological changes that can be explained independently in terms of phonetic factors (Ohala, 1993). In fact, there are also computational models satisfactorily accounting for cases of vowel deletion (Choudhury et al., 2004; Choudhury et al., 2006b) and assimilation (Dras et al., 2003).

Table 3 shows the derivation of the SCB verb forms from classical Bengali in terms of APOs. The derivations are constructed based on the data provided in (Chatterji, 1926).

2.3 Functional Explanation for Change of BVI

Let Λ_0 be the lexicon of classical Bengali verb forms. Let $\Theta : \theta_1, \theta_2, \cdots \theta_r$ be a sequence of r APOs. Application of an APO on a lexicon implies the application of the operator on every word of the lexicon. The sequence of operators Θ, thus, represent a dialect obtained through the process of change from Λ_0, which can be represented as follows.

$$\Theta(\Lambda_0) = \theta_r(\cdots\theta_2(\theta_1(\Lambda_0))\cdots) = \Lambda_d$$

The derivation of the dialect Λ_d from Λ_0 can be constructed by following the APOs in the sequence of their application.

We propose the following functional explanation for the change of BVI.

A sequence of APOs, Θ is preferred if $\Theta(\Lambda_0)$ has some functional benefit over Λ_0. Thus, the modern Bengali dialects are those, which have some functional advantage over the classical dialect.

We would like to emphasize the word "some" in the aforementioned statements, because the modern dialects are *not better* than the classical one (i.e., the ancestor language) in an absolute sense. Rather, the classical dialect is suboptimal compared to the modern dialects only with respect to "some" of the functional forces and is better than the them with respect to "some other" forces. Stated differently, we expect both the classical as well as the modern dialects of Bengali to be Pareto-optimal[3] with respect to the set of functional forces.

In order to validate the aforementioned hypothesis, we carry out a multi-objective and multi-constraint optimization over the possible dialectal forms of Bengali, thereby obtaining the Pareto-optimal set, which has been achieved through MOGA.

3 The MOGA Model

Specification of a problem within the MOGA framework requires the definition of the *genotype*, *phenotype* and genotype-to-phenotype mapping plus the objective functions and constraints. In this section, we discuss the design choices explored for the problem of BVI.

[3]Consider an optimization problem with n objective functions f_1 to f_n, where we want to minimize all the objectives. Let S be the solution space, representing the set of all possible solutions. A soulution $sinS$ is said to be Pareto-optimal with respect to the objective functions f_1 to f_n, if and only if there does not exist any other solution $s' \in S$ such that $f_i(s') \leq f_i(s)$ for all $1 \leq i \leq n$ and $f_i(s') < f_i(s)$ for at least one i.

3.1 Phenotype and Genotype

We define the *phenotype* of a dialect d to be the lexicon of the dialect, Λ_d, consisting of the 28 inflected forms of the root verb kar. This choice of phenotype is justified because, at the end of the optimization process, we would like to obtain the Pareto-optimal dialects of Bengali and compare them with their real counterparts.

The *genotype* of a dialect d could also be defined as Λ_d, where the word forms are the genes. However, for such a choice of genotype, crossover and mutation lead to counter-intuitive results. For example, mutation would affect only a single word in the lexicon, which is against the *regularity* principle of sound change (see Bhat (2001) for explanation). Similarly, exchanging a set of words between a pair of lexica, as crossover would lead to, seems insensible.

Therefore, considering the basic properties of sound change as well as the genetic operators used in MOGA, we define a chromosome (and thus the genotype) as a sequence of APOs. The salient features of the genotype are described below.

• *Gene*: A gene is defined as an APO. Since in order to implement the MOGA, every gene must be mapped to a number, we have chosen an 8-bit binary representation for a gene. This allows us to specify 256 distinct genes or APOs. However, for reasons described below, we use the first bit of a gene to denote whether the gene (i.e., the APO) is active (the bit is set to 1) or not. Thus, we are left with 128 distinct choices for APOs. Since the number of words in the lexicon is only 28, the APOs for Del, Asm and Met are limited, even after accounting for the various contexts in which an APO is applicable. Nevertheless, there are numerous choices for Mut. To restrain the possible repertoire of APOs to 128, we avoided any APO related to the mutation of consonants. This allowed us to design a comprehensive set of APOs that are applicable on the classical Bengali lexicon and its derivatives.

• *Chromosome*: A chromosome is a sequence of 15 genes. The number 15 has been arrived through experimentation, where we have observed that increasing the length of a chromosome beyond 15 does not yield richer results for the current choice of APOs and Λ_0. Since the probability of any gene

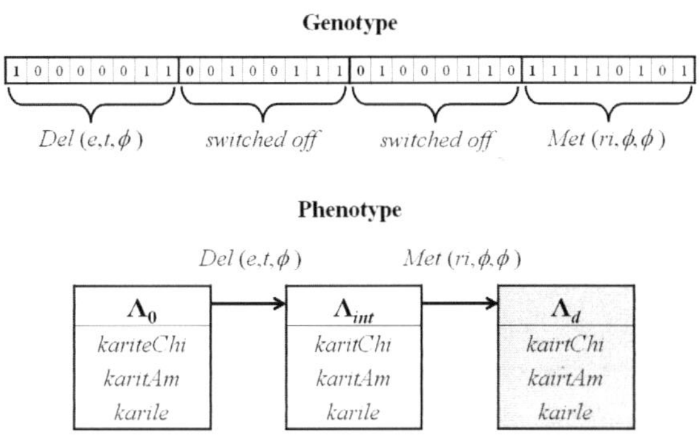

Figure 1: Schematic of genotype, phenotype and genotype-to-phenotype mapping.

being switched off (i.e., the first bit being 0) is 0.5, the expected number of active APOs on a chromosome with 15 genes is 7.5. It is interesting to note that this value is almost equal to the number of APOs required (7 to be precise) for derivation of the SCB verb forms.

• *Genotype to phenotype mapping*: Let for a given chromosome, the set of active APOs (whose first bit is 1) in sequence be $\theta_1, \theta_2, \cdots, \theta_r$. Then the phenotype corresponding to this chromosome is the lexicon $\Lambda_d = \theta_r(\cdots\theta_2(\theta_1(\Lambda_0))\cdots)$. In other words, the phenotype is the lexicon obtained by successive application of the active APOs on the chromosome on the lexicon of classical Bengali.

The concepts of gene, chromosome and the mapping from genotype to the phenotype are illustrated in Fig. 3.1. It is easy to see that the regularity hypothesis regarding the sound change holds good for the aforementioned choice of genotype. Furthermore, crossover in this context can be interpreted as a shift in the course of language change. Similarly, mutation of the first bit turns a gene on or off, and of the other bits changes the APO. Note that according to this formulation, a chromosome not only models a dialect, but also the steps of its evolution from the classical forms.

3.2 Objectives and Constraints

Formulation of the objective functions and constraints are crucial to the model, because the linguistic plausibility, computational tractability and the results of the model are overtly dependent on them. We shall define here three basic objectives of ease of articulation, perceptual contrast and learnability, which can be expressed as functions or constraints.

Several models have been proposed in the past for estimating the articulatory effort (Boersma (1998), Ch. 2, 5 and 7) and perceptual distance between phonemes and/or syllables (Boersma (1998), Ch. 3, 4 and 8). Nevertheless, as we are interested in modeling the effort and perceptual contrast of the whole lexicon rather than a syllable, we have chosen to work with simpler formulations of the objective functions. Due to paucity of space, we are not able to provide adequate details and justification for the choices made.

3.2.1 f_e: Articulatory Effort

Articulatory effort of a lexicon Λ is a positive real number that gives an estimate of the effort required to articulate the words in Λ in some unit. If f_e denotes the effort function, then

$$f_e(\Lambda) = \frac{1}{|\Lambda|} \sum_{w \in \Lambda} f_e(w) \quad (1)$$

The term $f_e(w)$ depends on three parameters: 1) the length of w in terms of phonemes, 2) the structure of the syllables, and 3) the features of adjacent phonemes, as they control the effort spent in co-articulation. We define $f_e(w)$ to be a weighted sum of these three.

$$f_e(w) = \alpha_1 f_{e1}(w) + \alpha_2 f_{e2}(w) + \alpha_3 f_{e3}(w) \quad (2)$$

where, $\alpha_1 = 1$, $\alpha_2 = 1$ and $\alpha_3 = 0.1$ are the relative weights.

The value of f_{e1} is simply the length of the word, that is

$$f_{e1}(w) = |w| \quad (3)$$

Suppose $\psi = \sigma_1\sigma_2\cdots\sigma_k$ is the usual syllabification of w, where the usual or optimal syllabification for Bengali is defined similar to that of Hindi as described in (Choudhury et al., 2004). Then, f_{e2} is defined as follows.

$$f_{e2}(w) = \sum_{i=1}^{k} hr(\sigma_i) \quad (4)$$

$hr(\sigma)$ measures the hardness of the syllable σ and is a function of the syllable structure (i.e. the CV pattern) of σ. The values of $hr(\sigma)$ for different syllable structures are taken from (Choudhury et al., 2004).

Since *vowel height assimilation* is the primary co-articulation phenomenon observed across the dialects of Bengali, we define f_{e3} so as to model only the effort required due to the difference in the heights of the adjacent vowels.

Let there be n vowels in w represented by V_i, where $1 \leq i \leq n$. Then f_{e3} is defined by the following equation.

$$f_{e3}(w) = \sum_{i=1}^{n-1} |ht(V_i) - ht(V_{i+1})| \quad (5)$$

The function $ht(V_i)$ is the tongue height associated with the vowel V_i. The value of the function $ht(V_i)$ for the vowels $/A/$, $/a/$, $/E/$ $/o/$, $/e/$, $/i/$ and /u/ are 0, 1, 1, 2, 2, 3, and 3 respectively. Note that the values are indicative of the ordering of the vowels with respect to tongue height, and do not reflect the absolute height of the tongue in any sense.

3.2.2 f_d and C_d: Acoustic Distinctiveness

We define the acoustic distinctiveness between two words w_i and w_j as the edit distance between them, which is denoted as $ed(w_i, w_j)$. The cost of insertion and deletion of any phoneme is assumed to be 1; the cost of substitution of a vowel (consonant) for a vowel (consonant) is also 1, whereas that of a vowel (consonant) for a consonant (vowel) is 2, irrespective of the phonemes being compared. Since languages are expected to increase the acoustic distinctiveness between the words, we define a minimizing objective function f_d over a lexicon Λ as the sum of the inverse of the edit distance between all pair of words in Λ.

$$f_d(\Lambda) = \frac{2}{|\Lambda|(|\Lambda| - 1)} \sum_{ij, i \neq j} ed(w_i, w_j)^{-1} \quad (6)$$

If for any pair of words w_i and w_j, $ed(w_i, w_j) = 0$, we redefine $ed(w_i, w_j)^{-1}$ as 20 (a large penalty).

We say that a lexicon Λ violates the acoustic distinctiveness constraint C_d, if there are more than two pairs of words in Λ, which are identical.

3.2.3 C_p: Phonotactic constraints

A lexicon Λ is said to violate the constraint C_p if any of the words in Λ violates the phonotactic constraints of Bengali. As described in (Choudhury et al., 2004), the PCs are defined at the level of syllable onsets and codas and therefore, syllabification is a preprocessing step before evaluation of C_p.

3.2.4 f_r and C_r: Regularity

Although learnability is a complex notion, one can safely equate the learnability of a system to the regularity of the patterns within the system. In fact, in the context of morphology, it has been observed that the so called *learning bottleneck* has a regularizing effect on the morphological structures, thereby leaving out only the most frequently used roots to behave irregularly (Hare and Elman, 1995; Kirby, 2001).

In the present context, we define the regularity of the verb forms in a lexicon as the predictability of the inflectional suffix on the basis of the morphological attributes. Brighton et al. (2005) discuss the use of Pearson correlation between phonological edit distance and semantic/morphological hamming distance measures as a metric for learnability. On a similar note, we define the regularity function f_r as follows. For two words $w_i, w_j \in \Lambda$, the (dis)similarity between them is given by $ed(w_i, w_j)$. Let $ma(w_i, w_j)$ be the number of morphological attributes shared by w_i and w_j. We define the regularity of Λ, $f_r(\Lambda)$, as the *Pearson correlation coefficient* between $ed(w_i, w_j)$ and $ma(w_i, w_j)$ for all pairs of words in Λ. Note that for a regular lexicon, $ed(w_i, w_j)$ decreases with an increase in $ma(w_i, w_j)$. Therefore, $f_r(\Lambda)$ is negative for a regular lexicon and 0 or positive for an irregular one. In other words, $f_r(\Lambda)$ is also a minimizing objective function.

We also define a regularity constraint C_r, such that a lexicon Λ violates C_r if $f_r(\Lambda) > -0.8$.

4 Experiments and Observations

In order to implement the MOGA model, we have used the Non-dominated Sorting GA-II or NSGA-II (Deb et al., 2002), which is a multi-objective, multi-constraint elitist GA. Different MOGA models have been incrementally constructed by introducing the different objectives and constraints. The motivation behind the incorporation of a new objective or constraint comes from the observations made on the emergent dialects of the previous models. For instance, with two objectives f_e and f_d, and no constraints, we obtain dialects that violate phonotactic constraints or/and are highly irregular. One such example of an emergent dialect[4] is Λ = { *kor, kara, kar, kore, korea, kore, karA, karAa, karA, *korAlm, *korl, korla, *koreAlm, korel, korela, *karAlm, karAl, karAla* }. The * marked forms violate the phonotactic constraints. Also note that the forms are quite indistinct or close to each other. These observations led to the formulation of the constraints C_p and C_d.

Through a series of similar experiments, finally we arrived at a model, where we could observe the emergence of dialects, some of which closely resemble the real dialects and others also seem linguistically plausible. In this final model, there are two objectives, f_e and f_d, and 3 constraints, C_p, C_d and C_r. Table 4 lists the corresponding forms of some of the emergent dialects, whose real counterparts are shown in Table 1.

Fig. 2 shows the Pareto-optimal front obtained for the aforementioned model after 500 generations, with a population size of 1000. Since the objectives are minimizing in nature, the area on the plot below and left of the Pareto-optimal front represents impossible languages, whereas the area to the right and top of the curve pertains to unstable or suboptimal languages. It is interesting to note that the four real dialects lie very close to the Pareto-optimal front. In fact, ACB and SCB lie on the front, whereas classical Bengali and Sylheti appears to be slightly suboptimal. Nevertheless, one should always be aware that *impossibility* and *suboptimality* are to be interpreted in the context of the model and any generalization or extrapolation of these concepts for the real languages is controversial and better avoided.

Several inferences can be drawn from the experiments with the MOGA models. We have observed that the Pareto-optimal fronts for all the MOGA Models look like rectangular hyperbola with a horizontal and vertical limb; the specific curve of Fig. 2 satisfies the equation:

$$f_d(\Lambda)^{0.3}(f_e(\Lambda) - 5.6) = 0.26 \quad (7)$$

Several interesting facts, can be inferred from the above equation. First, the minimum value of f_e under the constraints C_r and C_d, and for the given

[4]Due to space constraints, we intentionally omit the corresponding classical forms.

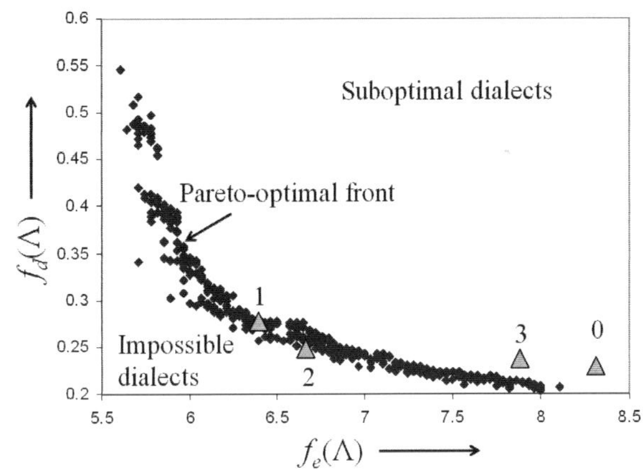

Figure 2: The Pareto-optimal front. The gray triangles (light blue in colored version available online) show the position of the real dialects: 0 – Classical Bengali, 1 – SCB, 2 – ACB, 3 – Sylheti. The top-most dot in the plot corresponds to the emergent dialect D0 shown in Table 4.

repertoire of APOs is 5.6. Second, at $f_e(\Lambda) = 6$, the slope of the front, i.e. df_d/df_e, is approximately -2, and the second derivative d^2f_d/df_e^2 is around 20. This implies that there is sharp transition between the vertical and horizontal limbs at around $f_e(\Lambda) = 6$.

Interestingly, all the real dialects studied here lie on the horizontal limb of the Pareto-optimal front (i.e., $f_e(\Lambda) \geq 6$), classical Bengali being placed at the extreme right. We also note the negative correlation between the value of f_e for the real dialects, and the number of APOs invoked during derivation of these dialects from classical Bengali. These facts together imply that the natural direction of language change in the case of BVIs has been along the horizontal limb of the Pareto-optimal front, leading to the formation of dialects with higher and higher articulatory ease. Among the four dialects, SCB has the minimum value for $f_e(\Lambda)$ and it is positioned on the horizontal limb of the front just before the beginning of the vertical limb.

Therefore, it is natural to ask whether there are any real dialects of modern Bengali that lie on the vertical limb of the Pareto-optimal front; and if not, what may be the possible reasons behind their inexistence? In the absence of any comprehensive collection of Bengali dialects, we do not have a clear answer to the above questions. Nevertheless, it may

Attributes	D0	D1	D2	D3
PrS1	*kar*	*kor*	*kori*	*kori*
PrS2	*kara*	*kora*	*kora*	*kora*
PrS3	*kare*	*kore*	*kore*	*korA*
PrSF	*karen*	*koren*	*koren*	*koren*
PrC1	*kartA*	*karChi*	*karteChi*	*kairteChi*
PrC2	*kartAa*	*karCha*	*karteCha*	*kairteCha*
PrC3	*kartAe*	*karChe*	*karteChe*	*kairteChA*
PrCF	*kartAen*	*karChen*	*karteChen*	*kairteChen*
PrP1	*karA*	*korChi*	*koriChi*	*koriChAi*
PrP2	*karAa*	*korCha*	*koriCha*	*koriACha*
PrP3	*karAe*	*korChe*	*koriChe*	*koriAChA*
PrPF	*karAen*	*korChen*	*koriChen*	*koriAChen*

Table 4: Examples of emergent dialects in the MOGA model. Note that the dialects D1, D2 and D3 resemble SCB, ACB and Sylheti, whereas D0 seems to be linguistically implausible. For legends, refer to Table 1

be worthwhile to analyze the emergent dialects of the MOGA models that lie on the vertical limb. We have observed that the vertical limb consists of dialects similar to D0 – the one shown in the first column of Table 4. Besides poor distinctiveness, D0 also features a large number of diphthongs that might result in poorer perception or higher effort of articulation of the forms. Thus, in order to eliminate the emergence of such seemingly implausible cases in the model, the formulations of the objectives f_e and f_d require further refinements.

Similarly, it can also be argued that the structure of the whole lexicon, which has not been modeled here, has also a strong effect on the BVIs. This is because even though we have measured the acoustic distinctiveness f_d with respect to the 28 inflected forms of a single verb root kar, ideally f_d should be computed with respect to the entire lexicon. Thus, change in other lexical items (borrowing or extinction of words or change in the phonological structures) can trigger or restrain an event of change in the BVIs.

Furthermore, merging, extinction or appearence of morphological attributes can also have significant effects on the phonological change of inflections. It is interesting to note that while Vedic Sanskrit had different morphological markers for three numbers (singular, dual and plural) and no gender markers for the verbs, Hindi makes a distinction between the genders (masculine and feminine) as well as numbers (but only singular and plural), and Bengali has markers for neither gender nor number. Since both Hindi and Bengali are offshoots of Vedic Sanskrit, presumably the differences between the phonological structure of the verb inflections of these two languages must have also been affected by the loss or addition of morphological attributes. It would be interesting to study the precise nature of the interaction between the inflections and attributes within the current computational framework, which we deem to be a future extension of this work.

5 Conclusions

In this paper, we have described a MOGA based model for the morpho-phonological change of BVIs. The salient contributions of the work include: (1) the conception of the genotype as a sequence of APOs, whereby we have been able to capture not only the emergent dialects, but also the path towards their emergence, and (2) a plausible functional explanation for the morpho-phonological changes affecting the BVIs. Nevertheless, the results of the experiments with the MOGA models must be interpreted with caution. This is because, the results are very much dependent on the formulation of the fitness functions and the choice of the constraints. The set of APOs in the repertoire also play a major role in shaping the Pareto-optimal front of the model.

Before we conclude, we would like to re-emphasize that the model proposed here is a functional one, and it does not tell us how the dialects of Bengali have self-organized themselves to strike a balance between the functional pressures, if at all this had been the case. The evolutionary algorithm (i.e., MOGA) has been used here as a tool for optimization, and has no relevance to the evolution of the dialects as such. Nevertheless, if it is possible to provide linguistically grounded accounts of the sources of *variation* and the process of *selection*, then the MOGA model could qualify as an evolutionary explanation of language change as well. Although such models have been proposed in the literature (Croft, 2000; Baxter et al., 2006), the fact, that global optimization can be an outcome of local interactions between the speakers (e.g., Kirby (1999), de

Boer (2001), Choudhury et al. (2006b)), alone provides sufficient ground to believe that there is also an underlying self-organizational model for the present functional explanation.

References

G. J. Baxter, R. A. Blythe, W. Croft, and A. J. McKane. 2006. Utterance selection model of language change. *Physical Review E*, 73(046118).

D.N.S. Bhat. 2001. *Sound Change*. Motilal Banarsidass, New Delhi.

S. Bhattacharya, M. Choudhury, S. Sarkar, and A. Basu. 2005. Inflectional morphology synthesis for bengali noun, pronoun and verb systems. In *Proc. of NCCPB*, pages 34–43, Dhaka.

Julia Blevins. 2004. *Evolutionary Phonology*. Cambridge University Press, Cambridge, MA.

P. Boersma. 1998. *Functional Phonology: Formalizing the interactions between articulatory and perceptual drives*. Uitgave van Holland Academic Graphics, Hague.

Henry Brighton, Kenny Smith, and Simon Kirby. 2005. Language as an evolutionary system. *Physics of Life Reviews*, 2(3):177–226, September.

A. Cangelosi and D. Parisi. 2002. Comuputer simulation: A new scientific approach to the study of language evolution. In *Simulating the Evolution of Language*, pages 3–28. Springer Verlag, London.

S. K. Chatterji. 1926. *The Origin and Development of the Bengali Language*. Rupa and Co., New Delhi.

A. Chopde. 2001. Itrans version 5.30: A package for printing text in indian languages using english-encoded input. *http://www.aczoom.com/itrans/*.

M. Choudhury, A. Basu, and S. Sarkar. 2004. A diachronic approach for schwa deletion in indo-aryan languages. In *Proc. of ACL SIGPHON-04*, pages 20–26, Barcelona.

M. Choudhury, M. Alam, S. Sarkar, and A. Basu. 2006a. A rewrite rule based model of bangla morpho-phonological change. In *Proc. of ICCPB*, pages 64–71, Dhaka.

M. Choudhury, A. Basu, and S. Sarkar. 2006b. Multi-agent simulation of emergence of the schwa deletion pattern in hindi. *JASSS*, 9(2).

W. Croft. 2000. *Explaining Language Change: An Evolutionary Approach*. Longman Linguistic Library.

B. de Boer. 2001. *The Origins of Vowel Systems*. Oxford University Press.

K. Deb, A. Pratap, S. Agarwal, and T. Meyarivan. 2002. A fast and elitist multi-objective genetic algorithm: NSGA-II. *IEEE Transactions on Evolutionary Computation*, 6:182–197.

M. Dras, D. Harrison, and B. Kapicioglu. 2003. Emergent behavior in phonological pattern change. In *Artificial Life VIII*. MIT Press.

David E. Goldberg. 1989. *Genetic Algorithms in Search, Optimization and Machine Learning*. Addison-Wesley.

M. Hare and J. L. Elman. 1995. Learning and morphological change. *Cognition*, 56(1):61–98, July.

M. D. Hauser, N. Chomsky, and W. T. Fitch. 2002. The faculty of language: What is it, who has it, and how did it evolve? *Science*, 298:1569–1579, 11.

John H. Holland. 1975. *Adaptation in Natural and Artificial Systems*. The University of Michigan Press, Ann Arbor.

Jinyun Ke, Mieko Ogura, and William S-Y. Wang. 2003. Modeling evolution of sound systems with genetic algorithm. *Computational Linguistics*, 29(1):1–18.

S. Kirby. 1999. *Function, Selection and Innateness: the Emergence of Language Universals*. Oxford University Press. The full-text is only a sample (chapter 1: A Puzzle of Fit).

S. Kirby. 2001. Spontaneous evolution of linguistic structure: an iterated learning model of the emergence of regularity and irregularity. *IEEE Transactions on Evolutionary Computation*, 5(2):102–110.

Anthony Kroch. 2001. Syntactic change. In Mark baltin and Chris Collins, editors, *Handbook of Syntax*, pages 699–729. Blackwell.

P. Niyogi. 2006. *The Computational Nature of Language Learning and Evolution*. MIT Press, Cambridge, MA.

J. Ohala. 1993. The phonetics of sound change. In C. Jones, editor, *Historical linguistics: Problems and perspectives*, page 237278. Longman, London.

A. Perfors. 2002. Simulated evolution of language: a review of the field. *Journal of Artificial Societies and Social Simulation*, 5(2).

T. Poibeau. 2006. Linguistically grounded models of language change. In *Proc. of CogSci 2006*, pages 255–276.

Melissa A. Redford and R. L. Diehl. 1999. The relative perceptibility of syllable-initial and syllable-final consonants. *Journal of Acoustic Society of America*, 106:1555–1565.

Melissa A. Redford, Chun Chi Chen, and Risto Miikkulainen. 2001. Constrained emergence of universals and variation in syllable systems. *Language and Speech*, 44:27–56.

Melissa A. Redford. 1999. *An Articulatory Basis for the Syllable*. Ph.D. thesis, Psychology, University of Texas, Austin.

L. Steels. 1997. The synthetic modeling of language origins. *Evolution of Communication*, 1(1):1–34.

W. S-Y. Wang, J. Ke, and J. W. Minett. 2005. Computational studies of language evolution. In *Computational Linguistics and Beyond: Perspectives at the beginning of the 21st Century, Frontiers in Linguistics 1. Language and Linguistics*.

On the geolinguistic change in Northern France between 1300 and 1900: a dialectometrical inquiry

Hans Goebl
Salzburg University
Department of Romance Philology
Akademiestrasse 24
A-5020 Salzburg
hans.goebl@sbg.ac.at

Abstract

With the supply of 8 closely interpreted dialectometrical maps, this paper analyses the linguistic change of the geolinguistic deep structures in Northern France (Domaine d'Oïl) between 1300 and 1900. As a matter of fact, the result will show – with one exception – the great stability of these deep structures.

1 Introduction to the issue

Through the comparison of two data sets of 1300 and of 1900, the present contribution discusses, if and in which way the basic geolinguistic structure of Northern France (Domaine d'Oïl) changed in the course of this period. In this investigation, a number of different methods of dialectometry (DM) will be applied. DM is a subdiscipline of quantitative linguistics which concentrates on the exploration of the actual deep geolinguistic structures of a given space, using as data source linguistic atlases or similarly structured data collections (consisting of N inquiry points and p atlas or working maps). Of course, it has to be assumed that these deep structures were generated by a genuine specific activity of man (i.e of of the *homo loquens*), that is to say: the « linguistic (or dialectal) management of space by the *homo loquens* ». Insofar as man has obviously many *other* opportunities of managing a given natural space besides the *linguistic* management, there result many opportunities for interdisciplinary cooperation with DM.

The Salzburg-based DM (Goebl 2006a) pursues the genuine principles of traditional (Romance) linguistic geography with quantitative means. It therefore defines its main aim in the empowering of the diagnostic virtue of traditional linguistic geography by introducing global or synthetic (quantitative) methods.

2 Data basis

It consists of two machine-readable data matrices, the first resuming the period around 1300, the other one resuming the period around 1900.

2.1 Corpus 1300 (drawn from Dees 1980)

The medieval corpus was borrowed from the scripta-atlas (1980) of the Amsterdam Romance linguist A. Dees. This atlas is based on the comprehensive interpretation of 3300 original charters of Northern France of the second half of the 13th century, which were analysed in that instance according to a list of ca. 300 written (or scripta-) attributes. These scripta-attributes are mainly of phonetic relevance, most of them referring to vocalism (189 attributes), but also to consonantism (87 attributes), and some of them even to morphology (22 attributes). As a result, the data matrix holds 298 attributes and 85 « inquiry points ». The latter correspond actually to *scripta-centres* (scriptoria, chanceries) which are distributed as evenly as possible all over the Domaine d'Oïl. For the measuring of the graphic variation in the 3300 charters, A. Dees developped a specific method. As a result, he was able to determine – for each single attribute – its relative occurrence (in percentage) in the charters of the 85

Proceedings of Ninth Meeting of the ACL Special Interest Group in Computational Morphology and Phonology, pages 75–83,
Prague, June 2007.

scripta-centres. The content of the data matrix lies therefore on a *metrical* scale.

In the ninetees, A. Dees and his collaborator Piet von Reenen handed me over this data matrix, as a basis which allowed me to realize many dialectometrical experiments. Its only disadvantage is that the machine-readable matrix holds less attributes (268) than the printed atlas (298). Nevertheless, by applying the « Average Euclidean Metric » (AEM), the « Average Manhattan Metric » (AMM) and the « Bravais-Pearson correlation coefficent » [r(BP)], the dialectometrical results are very profitable (see Goebl 2006b). The scripta-atlas published by Dees in 1980 shows quantitative visualisations of the spatial distribution of the 298 attributes, but does not encompass global data interpretation with dialectometrical (or similar) methods.

2.1.1 The Dees-data: one illustrative example

In his scripta-atlas (1980: carte 87, p. 93), A. Dees also investigated the regional variation in the spelling of the French possessive pronoun: *leur, leurs, leurz* etc. which are all derived from the Latin etymon ILLÓRU. Most probably they were created under the influence of a specific regional dialect pronunciation. At the end of the 13th century, the geographic contrast between these *eu*-spellings and the older equivalent forms *lor, lors, lors* etc. was quite sharp in the Domaine d'Oïl. Hence, Dees checked the number of all occurrences of *eu*-spellings (belonging to the possessive pronoun) in the 3300 above mentioned charters and listed, for each of the 85 scripta-centres of his atlas, the percentages of those charters which show at least one occurence of the spelling *-eu-*. As a result, 81 out of the 93 charters of the scripta-region 26 « Somme, Pas-de-Calais » (located in the medieval Artois: see the top of the figures 1, 3, 5 and 7) showed a considerable amount of *eu*-spellings, unlike the remaining 12 charters. In the 105 charters of the scripta-region 1 « Charente, Charente-Maritime » (South-western corner of the Domaine d'Oïl), no occurrences of the *eu*-spellings were found. Obviously, the different spellings of the possessive pronoun in that region were still on *-o-*. Thus, Dees registered the value 87% (= 81 : 93) for the scripta-region 26 in the North and the value 0% for the scripta-region 1 in the South-west.

As Dees analysed 298 scripta-features in the same way, he succeeded in covering the whole range of the stressed and unstressed vocalism and consonantism of Old French.

2.2 Corpus 1900 (drawn from ALF)

The second corpus, referring to 1900, was drawn from the data of the French linguistic atlas ALF, precisely: from a data matrix which had been established in the process of dialectometrization of the total ALF grid. The dimensions of this data matrix are: N = 641 inquiry points (distributed all over France), p = 1687 working maps, 1117 referring to phonetics (612 to vocalism, and 505 to consonantism), 417 referring to vocabulary, and 99 to morphology. 347 inquiry points (out of the 641 points on the total ALF grid) are located in Northern France : they represent therefore the Domaine d'Oïl. Among these 347 inquiry points, 85 points were selected in geographic correspondance to the 85 scripta-centres of the Dees-atlas, and subsequently reunited to a new grid (see the right halves of Maps 1-8).

Among the 1687 workings maps mentioned above, we took only into consideration those of phonetic relevance, thus: 1117 maps. They derived from 247 original maps of the ALF by phonetic typization, which is a common procedure in Romance linguistics. The units of this ALF data matrix are upon the *nominal* scale. With the supply of the « Weighted Identity Value (with the weight 1) » [WIV (1)], the dialectometrical interpretation of this data matrix proved to be very successful (see Goebl 1984, I: 83-86, and 2006a: 418-419).

2.2.1 The ALF-data : two illustrative examples

An example for two characteristic phonetic features is given in Map 812 of the ALF *le marché* « the market ». The 85 occurrences in the Domaine d'Oïl all derive from the Latin etymon MERCÁTU. The different dialectal followers of the stressed Á which is considered in this instance show the following results: a) pronunciation with *-i* (19 ALF-points), b) with (closed) *-é* (60 ALF-points), c) with (open) *-è* (1 ALF-point), d) with *-ö* (4 ALF-points), e) with (neutral) *-e* (1 ALF-point). From the metrological point of view, these five phonetic types represent what is called « (nominal) multistate characters ». As the corresponding working map contains five different (phonetic) types (or « taxates » in Salzburg terminology), it is called as well a « 5-nymic working map ».

Nevertheless, the data of the same ALF-map can also be analysed according to consonantal principles, which is realized by listing the dialectal results of the postconsonantal C before stressed Á in MERCÁTU. The results are as follows: a) *š* (72 ALF-points), b) *šy* (2), c) *ts* (1), d) *tšy* (3), e) *k* (2), f) *tš* (3), g) *ky* (1), h) *ty* (1). On the map, these eight consonantal types show a geographic distribution which is far from being similar to the former one of the five vocalic types. Actually, this experience is also valid for the great majority of our ALF-working maps.

The reduced data matrix drawn from the integral ALF-grid (with 1687 working maps) consists of 914 working maps: it starts with 2-nymic maps and has up to 23-nymic maps, embracing a total of 4263 phonetic types or « taxates ».

3 Establishement of the dialectometrical maps

DM is a map-based discipline: It visualises systematically all its results by using previously defined cartographic standards and by a very handsome computer program called VDM (« Visual DialectoMetry »), which supports and resets these visualisations perfectly. With VDM, choropleth maps and isarithmic maps, as well as trees can be generated. The results are always mapped in colours that are ranged according to the solar (or rainbow) spectrum, the warm colours lying above the arithmetic means of the respective frequency distribution, and the cold colours below it. The trees are all « spatialized » in principle, which means that their structural information is projected directly from the tree on the map.

The comparison between the medieval versus the modern data occurs basically in visual form, a methodically correct procedure, as the two corresponding iconic patterns are established according to the same cartographic norms. Further, the respective frequency distributions may also be correlated in order to gain a correlation map. For reasons of space, this procedure will not be demonstrated in this paper.

All the maps shown in section 4 are taken from two square similarity matrices (N x N) consisting of 85 items (N = 85), calculated by means of special similarity indexes – AEM and WIV(1) – on the basis of two data matrices (N = 85 ; p_{1300} = 268 metrical attributes, p_{1900} = 1117 nominal attributes). Hence, this demonstration includes two similarity maps, two parameter maps, two interpoint maps and two trees (with the respective spatializations). These four comparison planes are actually of special relevance, by allowing a global comparison which is also precise to the last detail of the medieval versus the modern data.

4 Four comparison planes between 1300 and 1900

4.1 Comparison plane 1 : two similarity maps

The most important instrument of DM is the similarity map. Each similarity map consists of a reference point and N-1 similarity values distributed in space, which values decrease proportionally with their geographical distance from the reference point. The geographic pattern of the progressive drop of these measurement values is clearly shown with the cartographic means of DM. In Maps 1 and 2, the reference point is located in the Poitou (South-west). The visual comparison of the two choropleth profiles shows their great similarity. The same effect occurs also from the remaining 84 reference points. This means that the linguistic management of the Domaine d'Oïl was very similar in the Middle Ages (through the linguistic activity of the scribes) and in modern times (through the linguistic activity of the dialect speakers). It must be added that, generally speaking, medieval non-Latin charters of the 13th and the 14th centuries (mainly) had a strong dialectal colouring, a phenomenon which was noted not in France only, they showed therefore a great number of local and/or regional written attributes. In the 19th century already, it was assumed that this graph(et)ic variation was generated or at least partly caused by the oral variation of the different medieval dialects. In Northern France, this regional colouring of the charters decreases rapidly after ca. 1400, and vanishes after 1450.

4.2 Comparison plane 2 : two parameter-maps : synopsis of the skewness values

Maps 3 and 4 reveal an entirely different question. The synopsis (or combination) of the N skewness values of a given similarity matrix indicates the degree of variation between different regions in regard to the so-called « linguistic compromise or exchange ». This phenomenon is defined as the degree of the intermixing of geolinguistic attributes with (respectively) regionally varying extension and/or intensity. Our DM-classification distinguishes therefore zones of high linguistic compromise (here : clear shadings) and zones of weak linguistic compromise (here : dark shadings). Where this linguistic exchange is high or great, a strong linguistic intermixing is prevailing. Where it is weak, the linguistic interaction is also low: these areas went on keeping a strong linguistic autonomy and were not yet seized by the general intermixing.

In Map 3 (left), the zones of high linguistic compromise or exchange form a kind of cross: they are located in the centre of the Domaine d'Oïl, whereas on its peripherical boarders the areas of different historical provinces (such as: Normandy, Picardy, Lorraine, etc.) are found. In Map 4 (right), the clear shaded zone occupies now the main part of the grid of the Domaine d'Oïl: in comparison with the left map it has virtually « exploded » (note the black circle), as a consequence of the continuous expansion of the language type of the Ile-de-France, which had been strongly supported by the French kings and after 1789 also by the Republic. Only on the Eastern peripherical boarders, some provinces (Picardy, the Walloons, Lorraine, etc.) could elude the general language compromise and thus the general linguistic intermixing.

Both maps consist of respectively 85 skewness values which were gained by respectively 85 similarity distributions. Since almost 20 years, it is well-known that the skewness value is an excellent instrument for measuring language compromise or exchange; in many instances, evidence of this fact has been given with different data sets (see Goebl 1984, I: 150-153, and 2006a: 419-420).

4.3 Comparison plane 3 : two interpoint or honeycomb maps

Actually, Maps 5 and 6 represent two honeycomb maps, each of them consisting of 225 polygon sides which vary according to thickness and darkness. Every one of these polygon sides lies between (= *inter*) contiguous inquiry points (hence the name *inter*point map), and indicates virtually the relative dialectal differences. Instead of the linguistic *similarities* (*sim*), the potential linguistic *differences* or *distances* (*dist*) were mapped. In quantitative regard, they are interrelated according to the formula: $dist + sim = 100$. Thus, the distance related counterpart of the above mentioned similarity index WIV(1) is the WDV (1) (« Weighted Distance Value (with the weight 1)) ».

The cartographic message of the two maps largely corresponds to the evidence of the traditional isogloss syntheses which were commonly established during the 20th century in Romance, German and English linguistics. The thick (and dark) polygon sides represent the so called « linguistic boundaries», a linguistic term which is rather colloquial and imprecise. One clearly recognizes that in Map 5 (left) in the North (Picardy) and the South-west (Poitou, Saintonge) there are very prominent and distinct « boundaries ». But it also shows very clearly in Map 6 (right) that in the period between 1300 and 1900 these « boundaries » were moved to the North (and East) as well as to the utmost borders of the South by an « invisible force » and that a zone with only very weak interpunctual demarcations emerged in the middle of the Domaine d'Oïl. Our knowledge of the history of the French language allows us to identify this « invisible force »: it is the irradiation of the linguistic type of the Ile-de-France, pushed by the politics.

4.4 Comparison plane 4: two dendrographic analyses (following Ward's method)

Moreover, the two similarity matrices can first be processed by dendrographic methods, in a next step, the two trees are compared. In this procedure, one has to pay attention to those bifurcations of the tree which are located near the trunk (or the root). Among the relevant « hierarchic agglomerative methods » applied for the generation of trees, Ward's method has proved to be most appropriate. In Maps 7 and 8, the tree and the map were drawn and visualised, isolating thereby (respectively) three distinct cartographic clusters. These clusters are called « dendremes » in the tree, and their correspondences on the map « choremes ». The heuristic comparison of Maps 7 and 8 concentrates on the position of the dendremes in the tree and simultaneously on the position of the choremes on the map. First, the perfect spatial coherence of all choremes is striking. Further, it clearly results that the three dendremes (No. 1-3) at the top seize the East, the North and the Centre (including the West) of the Domaine d'Oïl, though in such a way that the central dendreme-choreme (No. 1) expanded in the course of the six centuries between 1300 and 1900 at the expense of the Eastern (No. 3) and the Northern (No. 2) choreme-dendreme. Again, this is a consequence of the irradiation of the dialect of the Ile-de-France, supported by the French royal dynasty and the Republic.

5 Final remarks

By the visual comparison of four pairs of maps established with dialectometrical methods, evidence was given that the geolinguistic deep structures of the Domaine d'Oïl (Northern France) – in the period between 1300 and 1900 – maintained a large stability, that is to say : remained mostly identical in regard to their phonetics. Hence the question arises on determining the chronological development and elaboration *before 1300* of these phonetic deep structures. Nevertheless, the present investigation revealed the actual expansion of the linguistic type of the Ile-de-France between 1300 and 1900 which represents the typological basis for standard French. The dialectometrical techniques, which were again applied in this contribution, have proven many times their great diagnostic value in the last three decades.

References

ALF: Jules Gilliéron and Edmond Edmont. 1902-1910. *Atlas linguistique de la France*, 10 vol., Paris, Champion.

Anthonij Dees. 1980. *Atlas des formes et des constructions des chartes françaises du XIIIe siècle*, Tübingen, Niemeyer.

Hans Goebl. 1984. *Dialektometrische Studien. Anhand italoromanischer, rätoromanischer und galloromanischer Sprachmaterialien aus AIS und ALF*, Tübingen, Niemeyer.

Hans Goebl 2003. Regards dialectométriques sur les données de l'Atlas linguistique de la France (ALF): Relations quantitatives et structures de profondeur. *Estudis Romànics*, 25: 59-120.

Hans Goebl. 2006a. Recent Advances in Salzburg Dialectometry. *Literary and Linguistic Computing* 21 (4): 411-133.

Hans Goebl. 2006b. Sur le changement macrolinguistique survenu entre 1300 et 1900 dans le domaine d'Oïl. Une étude diachronique d'inspiration dialectométrique. *Linguistica* 46: 3-43.

Frequently used abbreviations (also in the legends of the Figures 1-8)

AEM: Average Euclidean Metric: see chapter 2.1.

ALF: Atlas linguistique de la France: see also the References

AMM: Average Manhattan Metric: see chapter 2.1.

DM: Dialectometry

r(BP): Bravais-Pearson correlation coefficent: see chapter 2.1.

VDM: Visual DialectoMetry

WDV(1): Weighted Distance Value (with the weight 1): see chapter 4.3.

WIV(1): Weighted Identity Value (with the weight 1): see chapter 2.2.

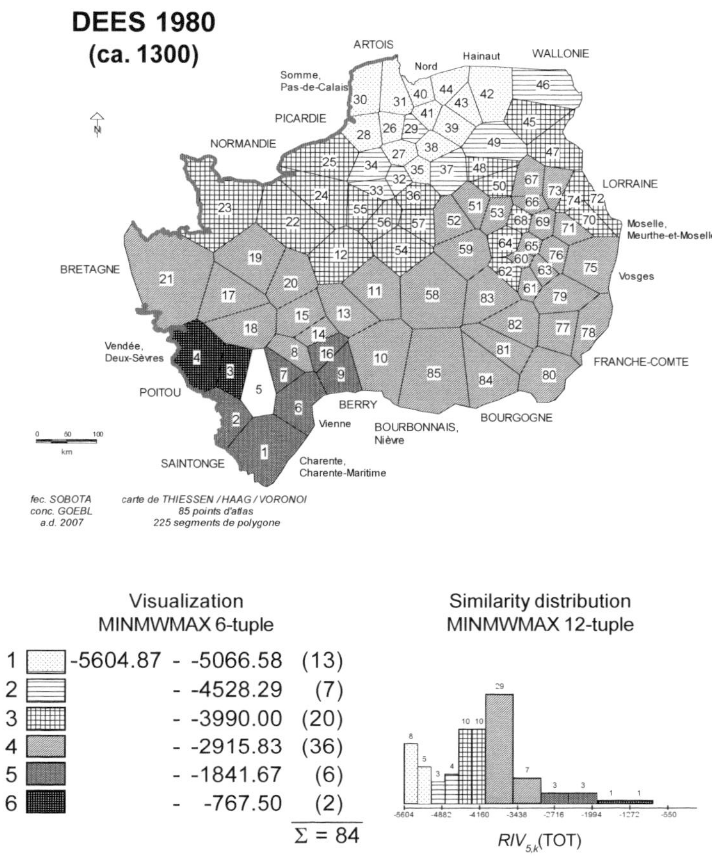

Figure 1: A similarity profile of the medieval Domaine d'Oïl: similarity map to the scripta-region 5 (Deux-Sèvres)
Similarity index: $AEM_{5,k}$
Corpus: 268 quantitative maps (from Dees 1980)
Algorithm of visualization: MINMWMAX (6-tuple)

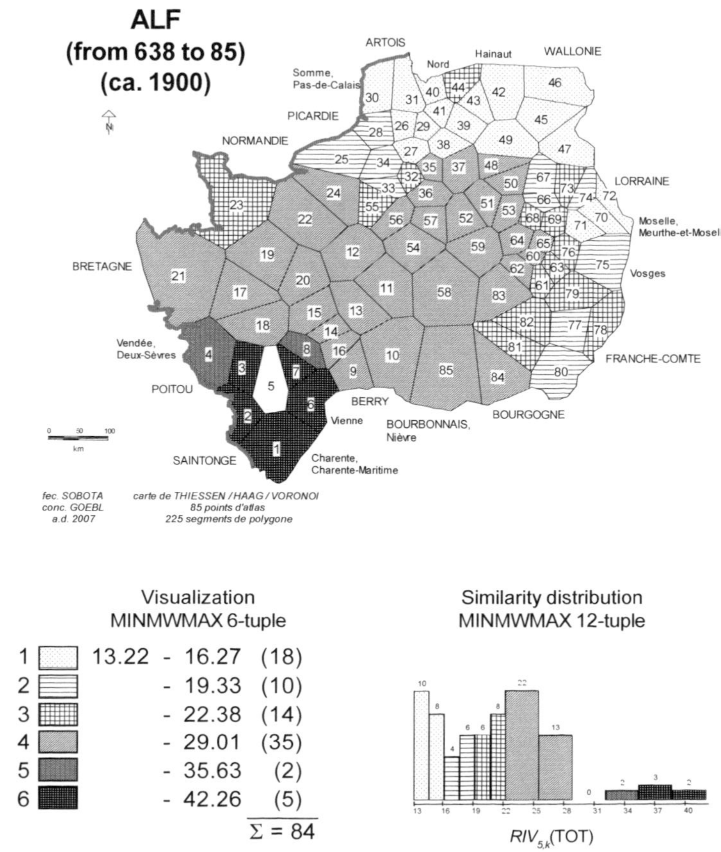

Figure 2: A similarity profile of the modern Domaine d'Oïl: similarity map to the ALF-point 510 (Echiré, Département Deux-Sèvres)
Similarity index: $WIV(1)_{510,k}$
Corpus: 914 phonetic working maps (from ALF)
Algorithm of visualization: MINMWMAX (6-tuple)

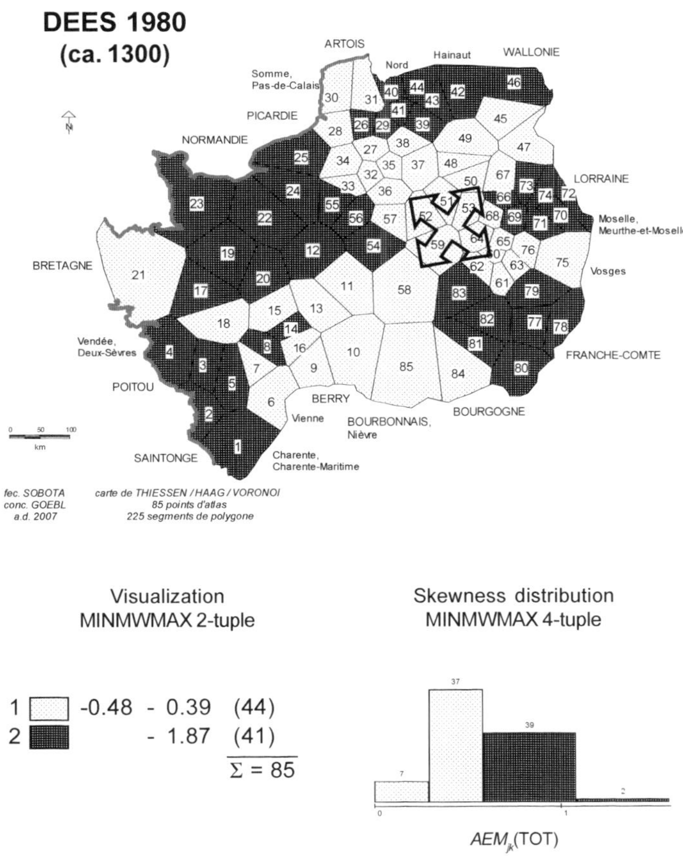

Figure 3: Choropleth map of the medieval Domaine d'Oïl: the synopsis of the skewness values of 85 similarity distributions
Similarity index: AEM_{jk}
Corpus: 268 quantitative maps (from Dees 1980)
Algorithm of visualization: MINMWMAX (2-tuple)

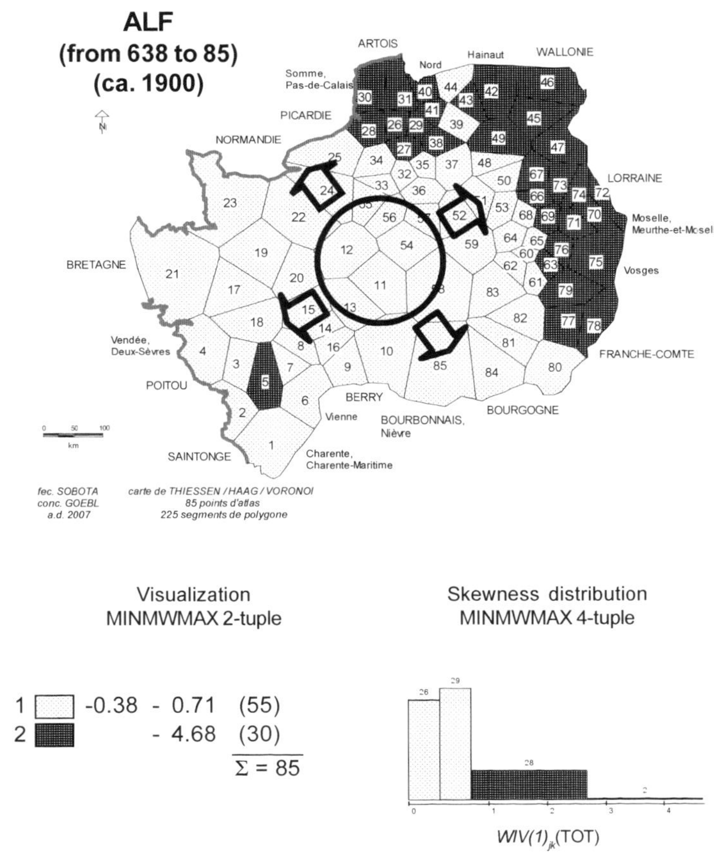

Figure 4: Choropleth map of the modern Domaine d'Oïl: the synopsis of the skewness values of 85 similarity distributions
Similarity index: $WIV(1)_{jk}$
Corpus: 914 phonetic working maps (from ALF)
Algorithm of visualization: MINMWMAX (2-tuple)

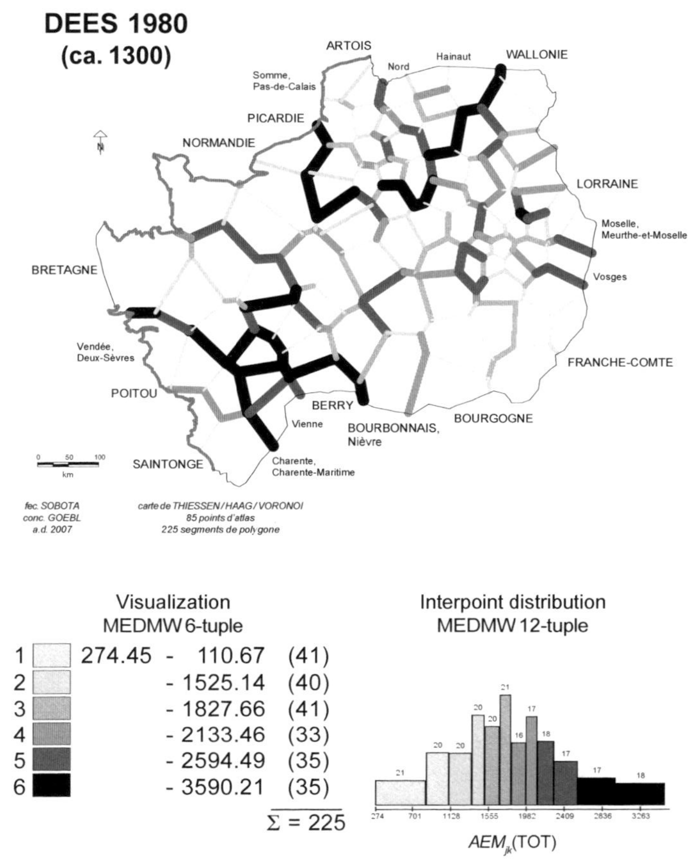

Figure 5: Honeycomb map of the medieval Domaine d'Oïl showing a synopsis of 225 interpoint distance values
Distance index: AEM_{jk}
Corpus: 268 quantitative maps (from Dees 1980)
Algorithm of visualization: MEDMW (6-tuple)

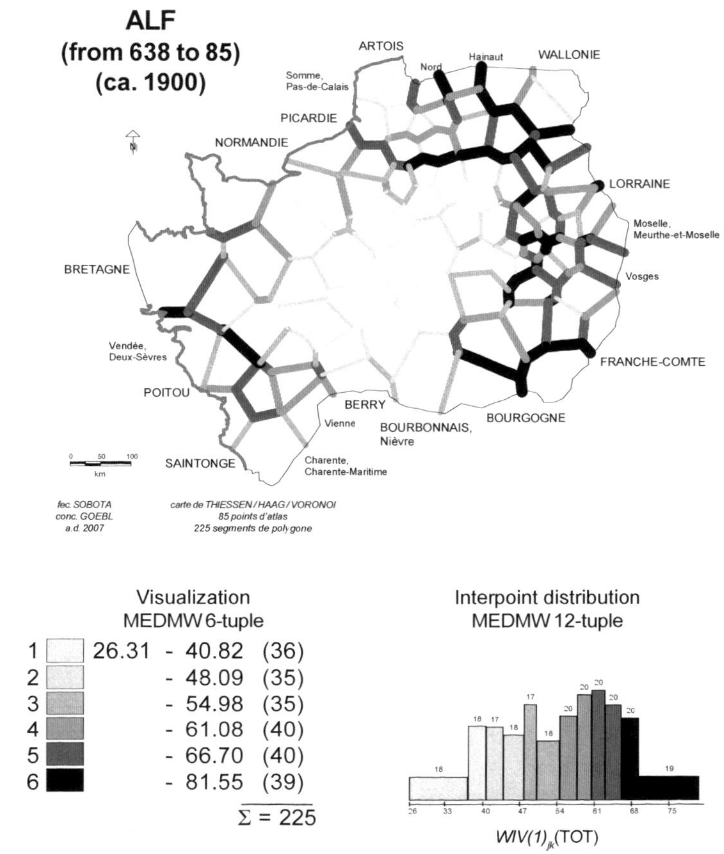

Figure 6: Honeycomb map of the modern Domaine d'Oïl showing a synopsis of 225 interpoint distance values
Distance index: $WDV(1)_{jk}$
Corpus: 914 phonetic working maps (from ALF)
Algorithm of visualization: MEDMW (6-tuple)

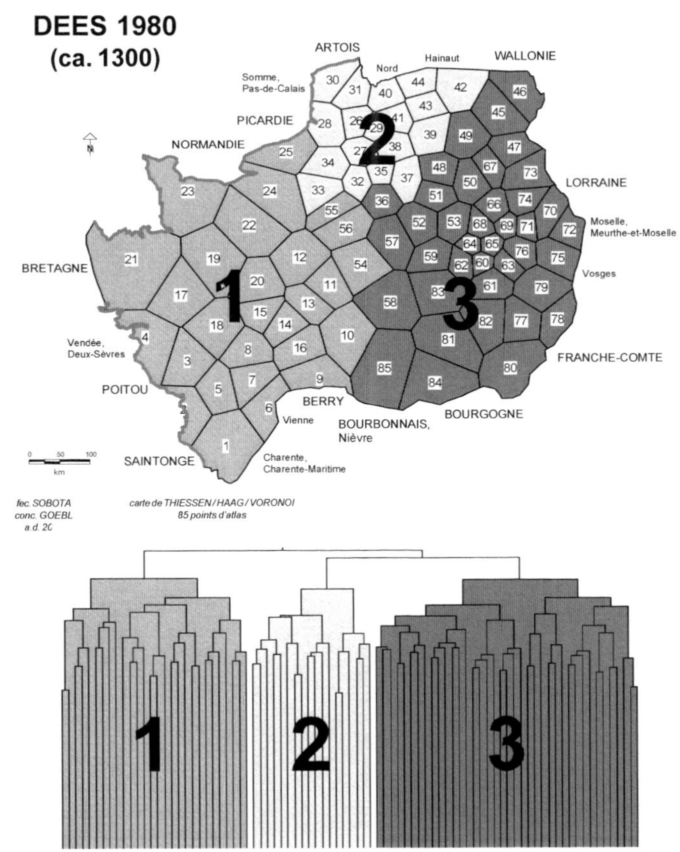

Figure 7: Dendrographic classification (and corresponding spatialization) of the medieval Domaine d'Oïl (85 scripta-regions according to Dees 1980)
Similarity index: AEM_{jk}
Dendrographic algorithm: hierarchical grouping method of Ward
Number of marked dendremes resp. choremes: 3

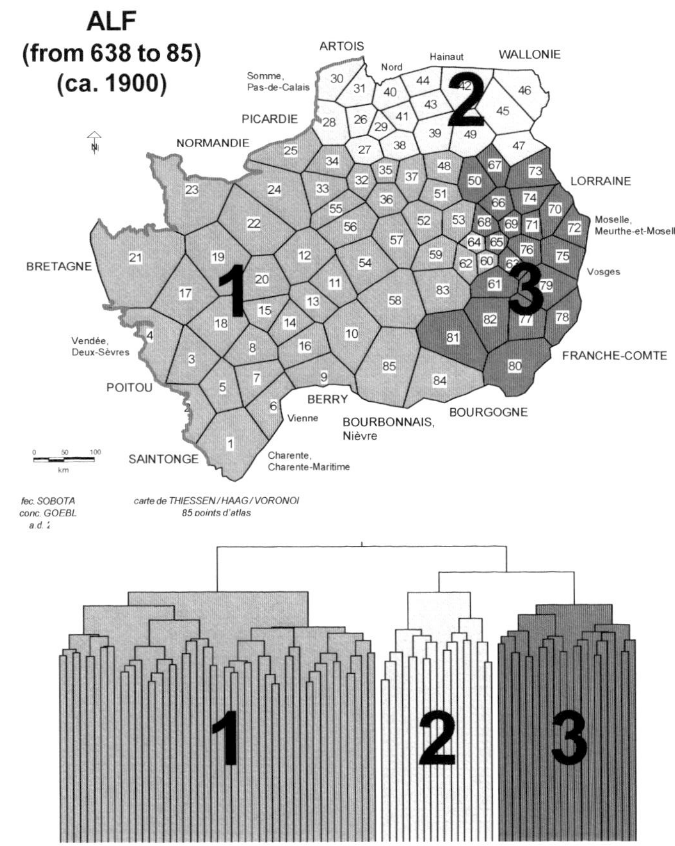

Figure 8: Dendrographic classification (and corresponding spatialization) of the modern Domaine d'Oïl (85 ALF-points)
Similarity index: $WIV(1)_{jk}$
Dendrographic algorithm: hierarchical grouping method of Ward
Number of marked dendremes resp. choremes: 3

Visualizing the evaluation of distance measures

Thomas Pilz

University of Duisburg-Essen
Faculty of Engineering
Department of Computer Science
pilz@inf.uni-due.de

Axel Philipsenburg

University of Duisburg-Essen
axel.philipsenburg@uni-due.de

Wolfram Luther

University of Duisburg-Essen
Faculty of Engineering
Department of Computer Science
luther@inf.uni-due.de

Abstract

This paper describes the development and use of an interface for visually evaluating distance measures. The combination of multidimensional scaling plots, histograms and tables allows for different stages of overview and detail. The interdisciplinary project Rule-based search in text databases with nonstandard orthography develops a fuzzy full text search engine and uses distance measures for historical text document retrieval. This engine should provide easier text access for experts as well as interested amateurs.

1 Introduction

In recent years interest in historical digitization projects has markedly increased, bearing witness to a growing desire to preserve cultural heritage through new media. All over Europe projects are arising digitizing not only monetary but also intellectually valuable text documents. While more and more documents are being digitized and often provided with well designed interfaces, they are not necessarily easy to work with, especially for nonlinguists. Spelling variants, faulty character recognition (OCR) and typing errors hamper if not circumvent sensible utilization of the data. One such example is the archive of Jewish periodicals in German language, Compact Memory (www.compactmemory.de). Even though of great cultural value and very well maintained, the operators of this project simply did not have the resources required to postprocess or annotate their automatically recognized text documents. A user for example searching for the word "Fruchtbarkeit" (=fertility) will not be able to find a certain periodical from 1904 even though it clearly contains the word. Worse, he will not even come to know that this text was missed. Because the full text aligned with the graphical representation of the text contains recognition errors, only the search for the misspelled word "Piuchtbaikeit" instead of "Fruchtbarkeit" finds the correct page (cf. Figure 1). The same problem arises when dealing with historical spelling variation. German texts prior to 1901 often contain historical spelling variants. Numerous projects are dealing with similar problems of optical character recognition or spelling variation.

To meet those problems linguistics and computer science are closing ranks. Fuzzy full-text search functions provide access to nonstandard text databases. Since the amount of data on the one hand and the divergence of users on the other increases day by day, search methods are continuously presented with new challenges. The project RSNSR (Rule-based search in text databases with

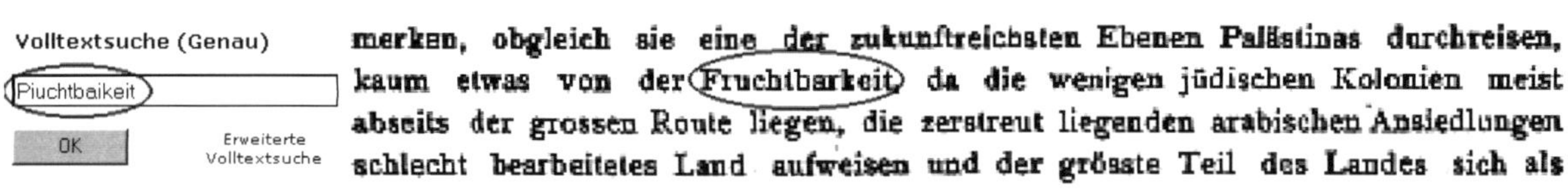

Figure 1. OCR errors prevent successful retrieval on digitized texts if misspelled variants are used for full text search.

Proceedings of Ninth Meeting of the ACL Special Interest Group in Computational Morphology and Phonology, pages 84–92, Prague, June 2007.

nonstandard orthography) seeks to improve the retrieval of nonstandard texts. Such texts might include historical documents, texts with regional/dialectal or phonetic variation, typos or OCR errors. The project's funding by the Deutsche Forschungsgemeinschaft (DFG [German Research Foundation]) was recently extended by two years.

2 Comparing similarity measures

One of the important issues in building a search engine for nonstandard spellings is a reliable way to allow the comparison of words, that is, to measure the similarity between the search expression and the results provided. Given the abundance of distance measures and edit-distances available, methods are needed for efficiently comparing different similarity measures. In (Kempken et al. 2006) we evaluated 13 different measures with the calculation of precision and recall to determine which were most qualified to deal with historical German spelling variants. We mainly used our own database of historical spellings, manually collected from the German text archives Bibliotheca Augustana, documentArchiv.de and Digitales Archiv Hessen-Darmstadt. Currently our database consists of 12,687 modern-historical word pairs (that we call *evidences*) originating between 1293 and 1919.

The algorithm that proved best for calculating the edit costs between the modern and the historical spellings is called *Stochastic distance* (SM) and was originally proposed in 1975 by Bahl and Jelinek. In 1997 Ristad and Yianilos (Ristad et al, 1997) took it up again and extended the approach to machine learning abilities. Due to the complexity of language, apparently similar scopes can obviously favor totally different mechanisms. The Variant Detector VARD developed by Rayson et al. to detect spelling variants in historical English texts uses the standard Soundex algorithm with convincing efficiency (Rayson et al, 2005). The same algorithm yields an error rate 6.7 times higher than the stochastic distance for the comparison of German spelling variants. Cases like these suggest that finding one "most suitable" distance measure for all data might not be possible. As soon as the inherent structures change, another measure can prove to be more efficient. Even though, with the SM, we already found a suitable measure, its dependency on the underlying training data forces us to evaluate the training results: what is the size of an optimal training set? Is the training set well chosen? Does 14th-century data appropriately represent 13th-century spellings? Answers to these and similar questions not only help to ensure better retrieval but can also give an insight into phonetic or graphematic changes of language. Since standard calculations of retrieval quality, as we did for the 13 measures, require not only extensive work but are also difficult to evaluate, we propose possibilities for visual evaluation means to speed up and ease this process. The prototype we developed is but one example for those possibilities and is meant to encourage scientists to benefit from visual information representation.

3 Development and functions of an interactive visual interface

Since our project already deals with different methods for calculating word distance, the definition of a generic interface was necessary. Priority was given to the development of a slim and easily accessible device that allows the connection of arbitrary concepts of word distance. Our SM, a rule based measure using regular expressions, Soundex (Knuth, 1973), Jaro(-Winkler) (Jaro, 1995) and a number of additional measures are already implemented in our system. It was built in Java and is embedded in our general environment for the processing of nonstandard spellings.

Information Visualization is a fairly new field of research that is rapidly evolving. A well established definition of information visualization is "the use of computer-supported, interactive, visual representations of abstract data to amplify cognition" (Card et al, 1999). While planning the prototype, we also kept Shneiderman's paradigm in mind: "Overview first, zoom and filter details on demand" (Shneiderman, 1996). In dealing with distance measures, our main task is to represent word distance. We employed multidimensional scaling (MDS) to display abstract distance in 2D space (see below). Interactivity is gained with the ability to select and remove spellings from the calculations, lower or raise cutoff frequencies and filters and even change replacement costs with instantaneous effect (see below). This led to a user interface separated into three main views:

- The **Histogram** allows an overview of thousands of data items. The selection of a certain portion of data triggers MDS and table views.

- **Multidimensional Scaling (MDS)** functions as a detail view. Such visualization is used to display sets of several dozen to a few hundred items.
- The **Table View** can display different levels of detail. In (Kempken et al, 2007) we presented a TreeMap approach, another way to display details of single word derivations as an add-on for table views.

3.1 Histograms

Histograms are a widely spread tool for display of statistical distribution of values. In favor of Shneiderman's paradigm, the histogram view represents a combination of overview and zoom functionality. This first stage allows for the reduction of the data set from up to several thousand items down to much more manageable sizes.

To get a first impression of how a spelling distance performs on a set of evidences, we calculate the distance between a spelling variant and the entries in a dictionary. It is ensured that the collection also contains the standard spelling related to the variant. The results are sorted in ascending order by their distance from the spelling variant. Afterwards, the rank of the corresponding spellings is determined. In the best case, the correct relation will appear as the first entry in this list, that is, at the smallest distance from the variant. Often, other spellings appear "closer" to the variant and thus have a higher rank, pushing the spelling we sought for further down the list (cf. Figure 2).

By applying this procedure to a collection of word pairs, we get a distribution of spelling ranks over the set of evidences based on the spelling collection. Good distance measures produce a histogram with most of its largest bars close to the first rank on the left. A good example is the evaluation in section 5 (cf. Figure 5).

	lieb	liebe	lebt
lebt	1.211	1.542	0.0
leib	0.728	1.060	1.243
leibt	1.301	1.632	0.676
lieb	0.0	0.331	1.243
liebe	0.397	0.0	1.641
liebd	0.903	0.991	1.246

Figure 2. The standard spelling "liebe" corresponding to variant "liebd" was pushed back by "lieb" because deletion of <d> is cheaper than the replacement of <d> with <e>.

The histogram provides a good representation of the overall performance of a spelling distance given for a set of test data. The user will quickly notice if a large number of spellings are found in the acceptable ranking range, if there are noticeable isolated outliers or if the values are spread widely over the whole interval. In addition, histograms can be useful as tools for comparing different spelling distances. Usually multiple histograms are viewed one after another or arranged next to each other. While this might be enough to perceive considerable differences in distributions, small-scale variations may pass unnoticed. An easy solution to this problem is to arrange the different histograms in a combined display area, where the relevant subinterval bars are lined up next to one another and made distinguishable by color or texture. Through this simple rearrangement, even small changes become noticeable to the user. Slight height differences between bars of the same value interval can be noticed as can shifts in peaks along the value range.

For more quantitative performance measurement mean value and standard deviation are calculated and presented in numerical form. A distance definition that performs well will have a low mean value as more spellings are found with a good ranking. However, a mean value that is not especially high or low by itself is usually not enough to characterize a distribution. For this reason, it is important to know the values' spread around the distribution's mean value measured by the standard deviation (SD). A distribution with only a few, tightly packed value peaks provides a small SD whereas a widely spread one will have a large SD. A spelling distance that performs well can be recognized by a low mean value accompanied by a low SD. Both key values can also be made visible in a histogram by drawing markers in its background. In this way, even the key values are easy to compare when comparing spelling distances.

3.2 Multidimensional scaling

The MDS view displays smaller subsets, thus allowing further refinement while providing additional information detail.

MDS is a class of statistical methods that has its roots in psychological research. The main application of such techniques is to assign the elements of an item set to a spatial configuration in such a way that it represents the elements' relationships with as little distortion as possible. In this context, MDS can be used to arrange spellings in a two-dimensional space according to their spelling distances from one another. Every available dimension reduces the need for distortion but increases the difficulty to interpret. Two or three dimensions are a good trade-off. This allows for an intuitive display of distances and clusters of spelling variants. It also makes it possible to discover distance anomalies. If this representation is provided with filtering features, it can be used to select subsets of elements quickly and comfortably. These subsets can then be displayed in detailed information views that would be too cluttered with greater numbers of items.

The "distortion" is evaluated by comparing the distances calculated by the spelling distances with the configuration's geometric distances (i.e. distances following geometric rules). A common calculation for this distortion is the so-called "raw stress" factor. Kruskal (Kruskal, 1964) defined raw stress as the sum of distance errors over a configuration. To calculate this error, we use the distance matrix *D*, where each entry holds the calculated distance δ_{ij} between the spellings of the relevant row and column. These values can be modified by $f(\delta_{ij})=a\ \delta_{ij}$ to achieve a scaling more fit for visual distances, thus reducing stress. Comparison with geometric distances also requires this matrix to be symmetric. Because spelling distances are not necessarily symmetric (distance A – B differs from B – A), we use the mean value of both distance directions to create symmetry, as Kruskal suggests. The second part of the error calculation requires the geometric distances d_{ij} between the spellings, which is determined by *i* and *j* of the current configuration *X*. The actual error is the difference between the two distances squared.

$$e_{ij} = \left[f(\delta_{ij}) - d_{ij}(X) \right]^2$$

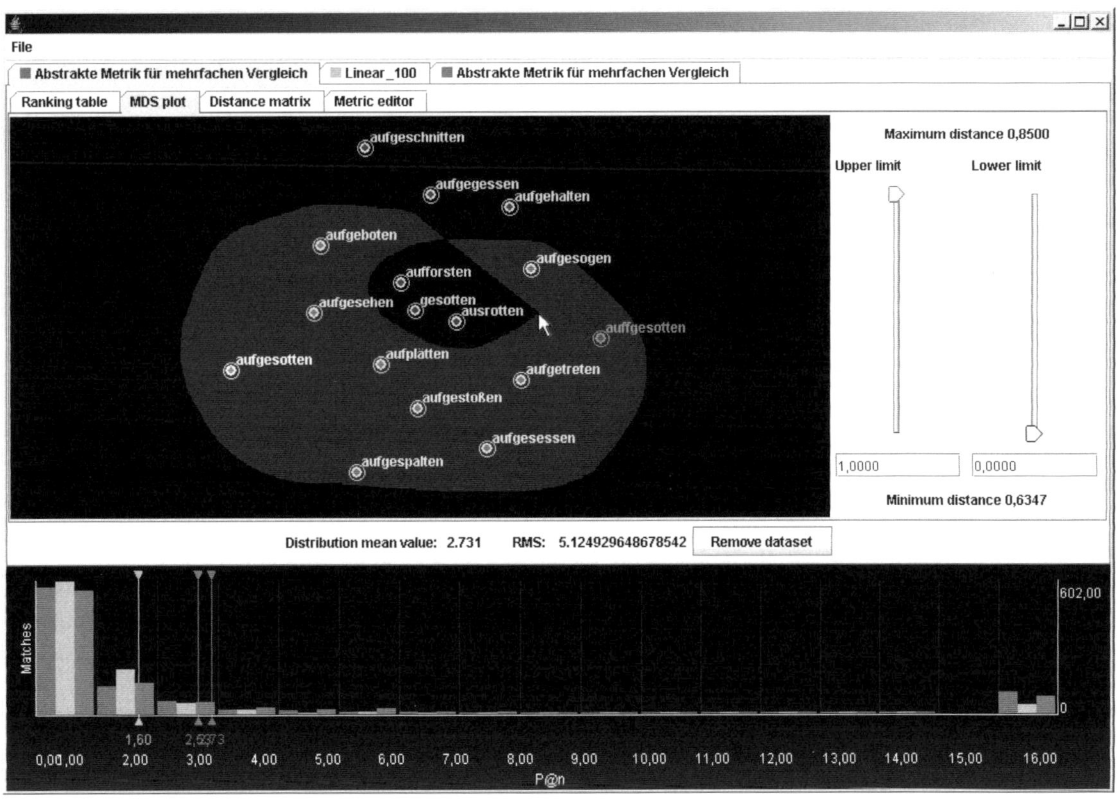

Figure 3. The user interface of the Metric Evaluation Tool showing the evaluation of six metrics trained on different historical training sets, polygon selection in the MDS view and cut-off sliders.

Kruskal's "raw stress" value is then determined by summarizing the error over the elements of the upper triangular matrix. The sum can be restricted to this reduced element set due to the symmetric nature of the matrix.

$$\sigma_r(X) = \sum_{(i<j)} \left[f(\delta_{ij}) - d_{ij}(X) \right]^2$$

In our Metric Evaluation Tool (MET) we used the SMACOF algorithm (see below) to calculate a stress-minimizing configuration. Finding such a configuration is a numerical optimization problem. Because a direct solution of such a problem is often not feasible, numerous iterative algorithms have been developed to calculate an approximate solution close enough to the direct solution, where one actually exists. The SMACOF algorithm (scaling by majorizing a complicated function) is such an approach (De Leeuw, 1977). We start by arranging the items in a checkerboard grid configuration. The algorithm then calculates the raw stress, modifies the current configuration so that it yields a lesser stress value by applying a Guttman Transformation (Guttman, 1968) and then compares the new configuration's stress with the old one. This step is repeated until the change in stress drops below a set threshold or a maximum number of iteration steps is exceeded.

The resulting configuration is usually not an optimal one. Optimal in this case would be a distortionless representation with vanishing stress value. Such a configuration is rarely, if ever, achieved in MDS. There are three main reasons for this:

- Some calculated spelling distances can conflict such that there is no spatial configuration that represents the distances without distortion. For example, a spelling may be determined to be close to several other spellings, which, however, are widely spread out. This is due to the fact that spelling distances do not always fulfill the triangle inequality.
- Although geometric distances, being mathematical metrics, require the spelling distances to be symmetric, the spelling distances calculated will not necessarily be so. For instance, the distance between spellings A and B could be different from that between spellings B and A.
- Even if an optimal configuration were to exist, the iterative optimization process might not actually find it. The algorithm might terminate due to iteration limits or because of being "trapped" in a local minimum.

This restriction on the MDS result, however, is not severe enough to derogate its usage as a visualization tool. Its task is not to reconstruct the calculated distance perfectly but to uncover characteristics of the spelling distances and spelling sets used. These characteristics, such as clusters and outliers, usually outweigh the distortions. Applied to a set of spellings and their distance measure, MDS generates a spatial configuration fit for a plot view. The spellings' positions in relation to one another represent their similarity. Clusters of closely related spellings and outliers are easy to recognize and can be used as starting points for detailed analyses of subsets.

An advantage of this type of visualization is that it considers the calculated distances among all spellings instead of only two. An initial comparison of the difference or similarity of multiple spellings is possible at a single glance and without switching between different views. Additional visual hints can improve the overview even further. Certain spellings, such as the standard spelling or the variant, can be made easily recognizable through color or shape indications. The selection of subsets is aided by zoom and filtering features applied to the plot view. Densely packed clusters can be made less cluttered by changing the plot's zoom factor or by blending irrelevant items into the background. Selecting the spellings by either clicking or encircling allows the subsets to be determined easily. The reduced item set can then be used for a detail view, for example the display of operations and distances like the tabular view. In the MET, the components used to calculate a distance for a given subset can be viewed. In this way, it is easy to understand, for example, why a certain spelling is not as "close" to another spelling as expected.

This visualization approach is applicable to a wide variety of spelling distances as long as they provide a quantitative measurement of two spellings. There are no assumptions made about the distance value except that small values represent a high degree of similarity.

	kundt>kind	kundt>kund	kundt>kunde	kundt>kunz
Distance sum	1.572	0.572	0.903	1.326
del(t) : 0.572	0.572	0.572	0.572	0.572
ins(e) : 0.331			0.331	
repl(d, z) : 0.754				0.754
repl(u, i) : 1.0	1.0			

Figure 4. Table view of replacement costs mirroring deletion, insertion and replacement costs. These costs can be manually adjusted to trigger an MDS view update.

3.3 Tabular views

After refining the selections from several thousand down to a few items, a detailed display of relevant information about the spellings and their calculated distances is needed. At this stage the actual values are more important than a visually comprehensible display of relations.

Two different views in the MET use a tabular arrangement of values. One represents the distance matrix between a set of spellings, similar to the one used to calculate the MDS solution. However, in this case, the distances are not combined to a mean value for both directions. At this point the difference between the two directions can be of interest and should be visible. Standard spelling and spelling variant are displayed in different colors so they can be found more easily.

The second tabular view displays the distances between the standard spelling and the ranked variants. To obtain a better understanding, the results are split up into their components using a Levenshtein-based distance mirroring the replacement costs that occurred when transforming one spelling into the other. These components are displayed in the rows according to their classification, while the different spelling variants appear in the columns (cf. Figure 4). By reordering the columns, the user can move the spellings next to each other in order to compare them more closely.

Another benefit of representing the values in this way is that detailed modifications to the spelling distance can be made interactively. Here, the replacement costs can be changed inside the table itself, allowing an instant evaluation on what effect such a change will have on the distance measure.

4 Interaction

There are several ways to interact with the application. Selection of data triggers an update of the view(s) on the next level of detail: by selecting columns of the histogram, the ranking table is activated; selecting spellings in the ranking table triggers the MDS view where spellings can be selected to be shown in the distance matrix and metric editor. While selections in the tabular views and the histogram can easily be performed with a rectangular selection box, the MDS needed a more elaborate way of selecting data. A polygonal form can be drawn with the mouse that also allows inverted selection (cf. Figure 3). Using two sliders or numerical input, the upper and lower cut-off for selection can be defined. For example, all spellings with a distance higher than 2.5 to the search term can be excluded (cf. right side of Figure 3). Zooming can be performed using the mouse wheel. In the metric editor, showing the highest degree of detail, the costs for the operations of deletion, insertion and replacement can be adjusted. These changes are instantly represented in the MDS view, therefore allowing for the manual calibration of the distance measures (cf. Figure 4).

5 Exemplary application of the interface

To give an example of our MET, we will apply it to a situation we have encountered more than once in the last two years of our research: a set of historical German text documents *T* from between 1500 and 1600 which contains nonstandard spellings. As shown in (Kempken, 2006), the number of spelling variants in old documents is monotonically nondecreasing with advancing age. *T* might also contain errors originating from bad OCR or obsolete characters. Nonetheless, we want to be able to perform retrieval on the document. To simulate a successful full-text search, we manually collected all 1,165 spelling variants *V* in *T* and aligned them with their equivalent standard spellings *S*. We will call those word pairs *evidences*. *S* is now merged into a contemporary dictionary—the OpenOffice German dictionary, which contains approximately 80,000 words. For a reliable evaluation we need a high quality dictionary without typos or historical spellings. The OO-dictionary is the best such wordlist available to us. Our algorithm is able to process dictionaries of up to ~5 million words. Bigger dictionaries can be kept in a database instead of the computer's main memory.

We used the MET applied with six different distance measures to determine the one that works best in finding all the standard spellings *S* "hidden" in the dictionary related to the spelling variants *V*. A normal search task in a historical database would be to find a spelling variant by querying a standard spelling. Because a coherent wordlist of historical spellings was not available, to ensure a more reliable result, we performed the task the other way around. This conforms to the way automatic annotators like VARD work (see above).

Such experiments can be used not only to find the best metric but also to answer general questions:

- Will an SM specifically trained on data from the same time period as *T* work best or will the extension of the time period lower or raise the retrieval quality?
- Is there a level where a "saturation" of training data is reached and the measures' quality cannot be enhanced any further?
- Does the amount of necessary training data vary with the time/location of *T*?

For our first experiment the six measures M_1, $M_2 \dots M_6$ were trained by the same number of evidences from 14th- to 19th-century German texts. Prior to the training, the evidences had been diachronically clustered (1300-1500, 1300-1700, 1300-1900, 1500-1700, 1500-1900, 1700-1900) into sets, each containing 1,500 word pairs. In general, performance is measured in precision (proportion of retrieved and relevant documents to all documents retrieved) and recall (proportion of retrieved and relevant documents to all relevant documents). Since we ensured that for every historical spelling there is a standard spelling, retrieved and relevant documents are equal and so are precision and recall. We therefore use precision at *n* (*P@n*). This measure is often used in cases where instead of boolean retrieval a ranking of documents is returned, for example in web-retrieval. Precision at 10 is the precision that relevant documents are retrieved within the 10 documents with the highest ranking. In standard settings the MET is using $n \leq 15$.

The task of our prototype now was

- to determine the metric most suitable for the retrieval task, and
- to figure out deficiencies in the metrics to further enhance their quality.

	DMV	SD
1300–1500	*1.37*	*3.174*
1300–1700	*1.384*	*3.222*
1300–1900	*1.261*	*2.983*
1500–1700	*1.375*	*3.1825*
1500–1900	*1.29*	*3.052*
1700–1900	*1.43*	*3.342*

Table 1. Distribution mean value and standard deviation of the evaluated measures

Looking at *P@1* the measures 1300-1500 (58.6%), 1300-1700 (58.7%), 1500-1700 (59.1%) and 1700-1900 (59.4%) seem to be more or less equally efficient. However, by looking at Table 1 we can see that this assumption is not totally correct. The measure trained on evidences from 1700 to 1900 holds a slightly higher distribution mean value and standard deviation than the other two. Interestingly the 1500-1700 measure is not the most efficient one. 1300-1900 and 1500-1900 show better results in *P@1*, DMV and SD. Even though the inclusion of 1300-1500 evidences seems to be of minor significance, the 1300-1900 measure is still slightly better (60.5% *P@1*). Those results are – of course – not significant because of the small dictionary we used. We hope to acquire a bigger freely available dictionary for more expressive results.

The ranking table is now able to show the actual words that led to the result, therefore supporting the expert in further interpretations. The MDS plot and distance matrix let the user explore the words at each rank interactively. Especially interesting are, of course, those words that could not be found within the top 15 ranks. The 1500-1900 and 1700-1900 measures have some difficulties with elder spellings (e.g. *sammatin* [=velvety]). It is also evident that many of the 3.9% of words > *P@10* share certain characteristics:

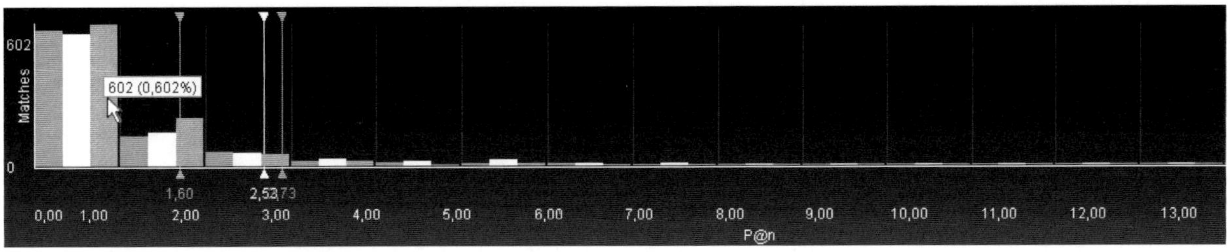

Figure 5. Histogram and DMV comparison of Jaro metric, standard bigram measure and SM 1300-1900.

- a lot of words are short in length (e.g. *vmb, nit, het, eer*). Even a single letter replacement changes a high percentage of the word's recognizability
- some words consist of very frequent graphemes, therefore increasing the space of potential matches in standard spelling (e.g. *hendlen – enden, handeln, hehlen* ...)
- some evidences feature high variability (e.g. *ewig – eehefig*)

Those cases complicate successful retrieval.

Comparing the replacement costs in the metric editor (cf. Figure 4) indicates where the SM needs improvement. In our example we noticed that the costs for the replacement of <s> with the German ess-tset <ß> were a little too high, and therefore spellings were not optimally retrieved. A slight manual correction, a control in the MDS view and a recalculation of the histogram showed improved quality of the SM.

Further experiments suggested a "training saturation" (see above) of about 4,000 variants. We trained M_1 on 1,500 evidences from 1300-1900, M_2 on 4,000, M_3 on 6,000 and M_4 on 12,000. While M_1 still shows a small drop in retrieval quality, the differences between M_2 to M_4 are almost unnoticeable. We also performed a cross-language evaluation between historical English and German as we already did manually in (Archer et al, 2006). Our prior results could be confirmed using the MET.

For the comparison of truly different distance measures, as we did in (Kempken, 2006), we used the same data as above with our SM 1300-1900, Jaro metric (Jaro, 1995) and a standard bigram measure (cf. Figure 5). The histogram values of p@<4 for the SM (86.6%) are already 9.2% better than Jaro (77.4%) and 9.9% better than the bigram measure (76.7%). DMV and SD also show how much better the SM performed (cf. Table 2).

	DMV	SD
SM 1300-1900	*1.604*	*3.73*
Jaro	*2.731*	*5.124*
Bigrams	*2.533*	*4.754*

Table 2. DMV and SD comparison of SM, Jaro-Winkler and bigram measure.

6 Conclusion and outlook

While table views will probably not become obsolete any time soon, there are multiple ways to ease and enhance the understanding of abstract data. It has already been documented that users often prefer visual data representations when dealing with complex problems (Kempken, 2007).

In this paper we presented the prototype of our Metric Evaluation Tool and showed that this software is helpful in the evaluation of distance measures. The combination of overview, details and interactivity eases the complex task of determining quality problem-specific distance measures.

Because the MET is a prototype, there is room for improvement. The graphical MDS display could be extended in various ways to further improve the configuration found. Displaying the numerical distance values between spellings as a tooltip or graphical overlay, group highlighting and interactive insertion or removal of additional spelling variants are just a few examples. The bar charts of the histogram view could easily be extended using pixel-matrix displays as proposed by (Hao et al, 2007) to conveniently represent additional information like the distribution of distance ranges.

The MET is only one of the visualization tools we are working on at the moment. No single application will be able to satisfy all the many and various needs that arise in the field of language research. It is our goal to build applications that access and reflect spelling variation in a more natural and intuitive manner. To narrow the field of potentially suitable distance measures, we are also working on automatic text classification. The Word-

Explorer, for instance, is an additional approach to presenting details. Similar to the MDS view in appearance, it is used to further examine words' possible spelling variants, the graphematic space of solution (Neef, 2005). Based on the renowned Prefuse-package for Java (prefuse.org), it provides methods that support easy access and usability, including fisheye, zoom and context menus.

7 Acknowledgements

We would like to thank the Deutsche Forschungsgemeinschaft for supporting this research and our anonymous reviewers whose detailed and helpful reports have helped us to improve this paper.

References

Archer D, Ernst-Gerlach A, Pilz T, Rayson P (2006). The Identification of Spelling Variants in English and German Historical Texts: Manual or Automatic?. Proceedings Digital Humanities 2006, July 5-9 2006, Paris, France

Card S K, Mackinlay J D, Shneiderman B (1999). Readings in Information Visualization; Using Vision to think. Morgan Kaufman, Los Altos, California

De Leeuw J (1977). Applications of convex analysis to multidimensional scaling

Guttman L (1968). A general nonmetric technique for finding the smallest coordinate space for a configuration of points, Psychometrika

Hao M C, Dayal U, Keim D, Schreck T (2007). A visual analysis of multi-attribute data using pixel matrix displays. Proceedings Visualization and Data Analysis (EI 108), Jan 29-30 2007, San Jose, California

Jaro M A (1995) Probabilistic linkage of large public health data file. In: Statistics in Medicine 14, pp. 491-498

Kempken S, Luther W, Pilz T (2006). Comparison of distance measures for historical spelling variants. Proceedings IFIP AI 2006, Sep 8-12 2006, Santiago, Chile

Kempken S, Pilz T, Luther W (2007). Visualization of rule productivity in deriving nonstandard spellings. Proceedings Visualization and Data Analysis (EI 108), Jan 29-30 2007, San Jose, California

Knuth D (1973). The Art Of Computer Programming. vol 3: Sorting and Searching, Addison-Wesley, pp. 391-392

Kruskal J B (1964). Multidimensional scaling by goodness-of-fit to a nonmetric hypothesis, Psychometrika, 29:1-27

Neef M (2005). Die Graphematik des Deutschen. Niemeyer, Tübingen, Germany

Rayson P, Archer D, Smith N (2005). VARD versus Word: A comparison of the UCREL variant detector and modern spell checkers on English historical corpora. Proceedings of Corpus Linguistics 2005, July 14-17 2005, Birmingham, UK.

Ristad E; Yianilos P (1997). Learning string edit distance. Proceedings of the Fourteenth International Conference, July 8-11 1997, San Francisco, California

Shneiderman B (1996). The eyes have it: A task by data type taxonomy for information visualization. Proceedings Symposium of Visual Languages, Sep 3-6 1996, Boulder, Colorado

Data nonlinearity in exploratory multivariate analysis of language corpora

Hermann Moisl
School of English Literature, Language, and Linguistics
University of Newcastle
Newcastle upon Tyne NE1 7RU
United Kingdom

hermann.moisl@ncl.ac.uk

Abstract

Data nonlinearity has historically not been and currently is not an issue in work on exploratory multivariate analysis of language corpora. However, the presence of nonlinearity in data has a fundamental bearing on the conduct of exploratory analysis. The first part of the discussion explains why this is so in principle, and the second exemplifies the explanation via exploratory analysis of the *Newcastle Electronic Corpus of Tyneside English* (NECTE), an historical speech corpus. The conclusion is that data should be screened for nonlinearity prior to analysis and, if a substantial degree of it is found, a nonlinear analytical method should be used.

1. Introduction

Exploratory multivariate analysis methods are used across a wide range of research disciplines to identify interesting structure in multidimensional data whose characteristics are not well known, and, if structure is found, to generate hypotheses about the domain which the data describes (Andrienko and Andrienko, 2005). Corpus-based linguistics has long been among these disciplines, and, as computational power has increased and ever-larger natural language corpora have become available, the application of exploratory analysis in empirical linguistic research has grown. When one surveys the relevant linguistics literature, it becomes clear that data nonlinearity has historically not been and is not currently an issue. An exhaustive review cannot be undertaken here, but a snapshot of recent literature is symptomatic: neither the relevant papers in the *Literary and Linguistic Computing* journal's special issue on 'Progress in Dialectometry' (2006) nor Manning and Schütze's discussion of clustering in their subject-standard *Foundations of Statistical Natural Language Processing* (2000) refer to it, except perhaps in passing. However, the presence of nonlinearity in data has a fundamental bearing on the conduct of exploratory analysis. The first part of the discussion explains why this is so in principle, and the second exemplifies the explanation via exploratory analysis of the *Newcastle Electronic Corpus of Tyneside English* (NECTE), an historical speech corpus. The conclusion is that data should be screened for nonlinearity prior to analysis and, if a substantial degree of it is found, a nonlinear analytical method should be used.

2. Nonlinearity and exploratory analysis

In physical systems, nonlinearity is the breakdown of proportionality between cause and effect, and it manifests itself in a variety of complex and often unexpected --including chaotic-- behaviours. Since nonlinearity pervades the physical world (see for example Bertuglia, 2005), data that describes it is likely to contain nonlinearity as well. If the data is in vector space representation, such nonlinearity manifests itself as curvature in the data manifold, which can range from simple curves and surfaces to highly convoluted fractals.

Many of the commonly used exploratory multivariate methods, henceforth called 'linear methods', are insensitive to nonlinearity, and as such can generate results that misrepresent the structure of a nonlinear data manifold. This insensitivity stems from the way in which the linear methods measure distance between pairs of vectors in the manifold --as the shortest straight-line

Proceedings of Ninth Meeting of the ACL Special Interest Group in Computational Morphology and Phonology, pages 93–100, Prague, June 2007.

distance between them. This is not, however, the only possible measure. This distance between two cities can be measured linearly as in figure 1a or nonlinearly along the curve of the earth's surface, as in figure 1b:

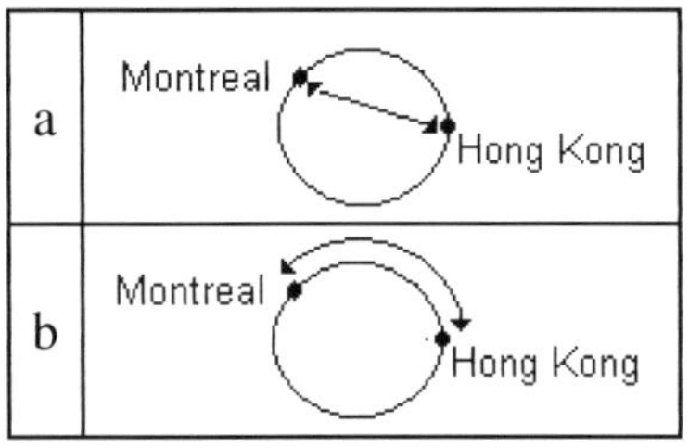

Figure 1: Linear and nonlinear distance measure

Linear distance in this case seriously misrepresents the true distance. The same applies to nonlinear data manifolds. Figure 2 shows an extreme example frequently used in discussions of nonlinear dimensionality reduction (i.e. Tenenbaum et al., 2000), in which linear distance and distance along the surface of the manifold differ markedly.

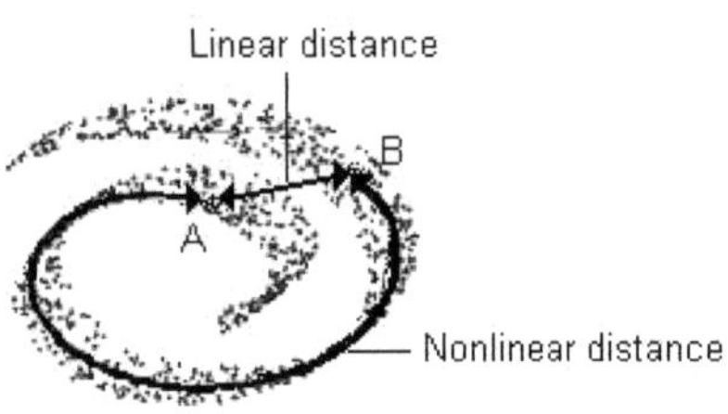

Figure 2: Linear and nonlinear distance in a nonlinear manifold

Linear exploratory methods base their representation of data structure on linear distance between vectors in the data space. If the manifold diverges significantly from linearity, linear distance measures can give distorted results.

The classic response to the discovery of nonlinearity in data is to remove it using well established methods like log-transformation (i.e. Clarke and Cooke, 1998:571-4), and then to analyze the linearized data using a linear method. This risks throwing the proverbial baby out with the bathwater. Nonlinearity is not always just a nuisance to be eliminated, but may reflect a fundamental aspect of the thing being studied; in fact, the study of nonlinearity in natural systems is now well established across a range of disciplines (Scott, 2004). If nonlinearity is found in natural language corpus data, the default should be to retain it on the grounds that it might reflect a scientifically interesting aspect of corpus structure. If it is retained, however, linear analytical methods become inapplicable in principle, and nonlinear ones which measure distance along the curvature of the manifold must be used.

3. Exploratory analysis of the NECTE data

3.1 The NECTE data

The *Newcastle Electronic Corpus of Tyneside English* (NECTE) is a corpus of dialect speech from Tyneside in North-East England (Allen et al., 2005). It includes phonetic transcriptions of 63 interviews together with social data about the speakers, and as such offers an opportunity to study the sociophonetics of Tyneside speech of the late 1960s. Moisl et al. (2006) and Moisl and Maguire (2007) have begun that study using exploratory analysis of the transcriptions with the aim of generating hypotheses about phonetic variation among speakers in the Tyneside dialect area. These studies were based on comparison of profiles associated with each of the informants. A profile for any speaker S is the number of times S uses each of the phonetic segments in the NECTE transcription scheme in his or her interview. More specifically, the profile P associated with S is a vector having as many elements as there are segments such that each vector element P_j represents the *j*'th segment, where *j* is in the range 1..number of segments in the NECTE phonetic transcription scheme, and the value stored at P_j is an integer representing the number of times S uses the *j*'th segment. There are 156 segments, and so a speaker profile is a length-156 vector. There are 63 TLS speakers, and their profiles are represented in a matrix M having 63 rows, one for each profile.

3.2 Identifying nonlinearity

Where the data dimensionality is 3 or less, nonlinearity can be identified by creating a scatterplot of the manifold and looking for curvature. Visual interpretation is subjective, however. It can be unreliable when the shape of the manifold is not as clear cut as, say, in figure 2, and needs to be supplemented with some quantitative measure of nonlinearity; for high-dimensional data direct graphical representation is impossible (Andrienko and Andrienko, 2005, ch. 4), and quantitative measurement is the only alternative. The most straightforward measures are based the residuals in linear and nonlinear regression: the sum of squares of residuals, or SS_R, gives the total divergence of the data variables from the line of best fit, and the standard error their average dispersion around the line in a way analogous to univariate standard deviation.

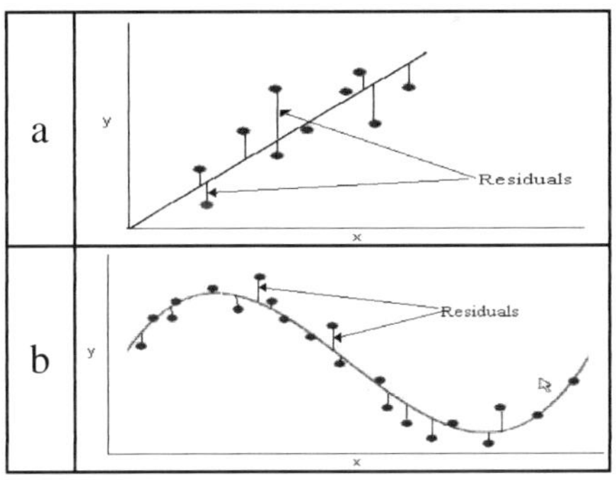

Figure 3: Lines of best fit in linear and nonlinear regression

For a given pair of variables, if the SS_R and standard error from a nonlinear regression are less than those from a linear one, then a curve fits the data better than a straight line and the relationship of the two variables is nonlinear.

In applications where the dimensionality of the data can be in the hundreds or even thousands, pairwise regression-based testing of nonlinearity can quickly become onerous since, for any given dimensionality n,

$$p_n = \frac{n(n-1)}{2}$$

For $n = 100$, there would be 4950 different variable pairs to consider. The situation can be salvaged in cases where some variables are more important than others relative to the research question by examining only a tractable subset of important variables. Several criteria for variable importance are available, such as variance, term frequency / inverse document frequency (Robertson, 2004) and Poisson distribution (Church and Gale, 1995a, 1995b); the use of variance for this purpose is exemplified below.

With a dimensionality of 156, 12090 variable pairs would have to be tested for nonlinearity, which is not impossible but certainly onerous. The number of pairs to be considered was therefore reduced to a manageable level using the relative variances of the 156 variables as a selection criterion. The justification for using variance for this purpose is as follows. Classification of objects in any domain of study depends on there being variation in their characteristics. When the objects to be classified are described by variables, then a variable is only useful for the purpose if there is significant variation in the values that it takes; those with little or no variation can be disregarded. The variances of the column vectors of M were calculated, sorted in descending order of magnitude, and plotted in figure 4.

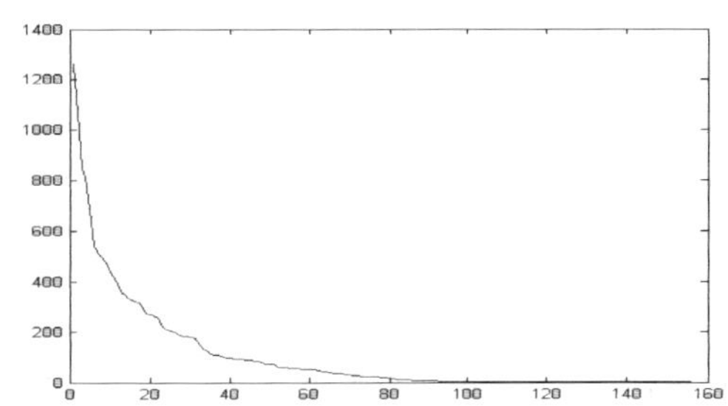

Figure 4: Variances of column vectors of N

The highest-variance dozen variables were selected and linear, quadratic, and cubic regression were applied to all 66 distinct pairings of them, in each case calculating SS_R and standard error. Three examples are given: figure 5a is representative of the linearly-related pairs, figure 5b of moderately nonlinear pairs, and figure 5c of strongly nonlinear ones. The frequencies of these are 12 linear, 25 moderately nonlinear, and 29 strongly nonlinear.

	Regression plots	Quantifications
a	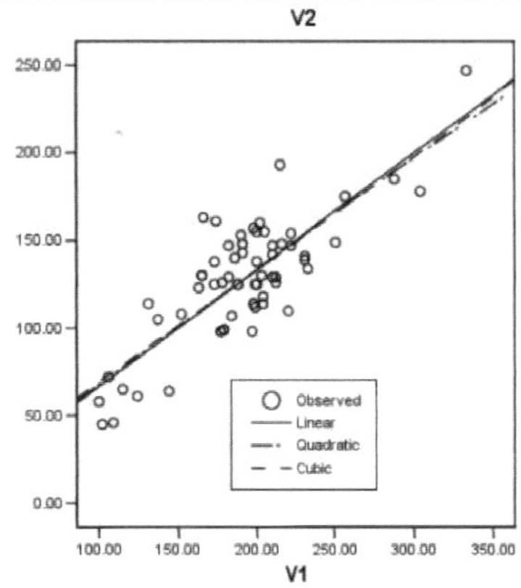	see table a below
b	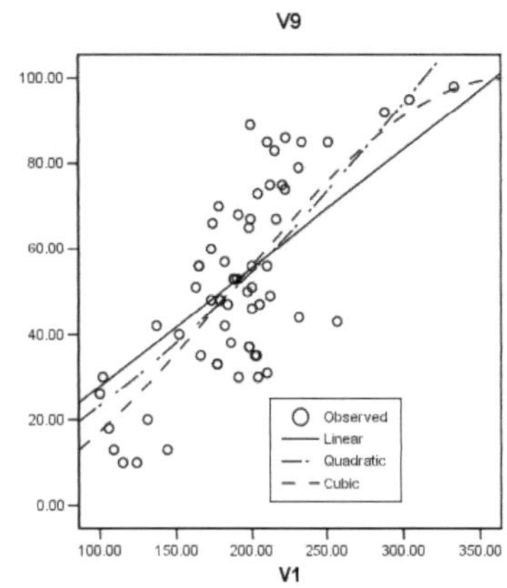	see table b below
c	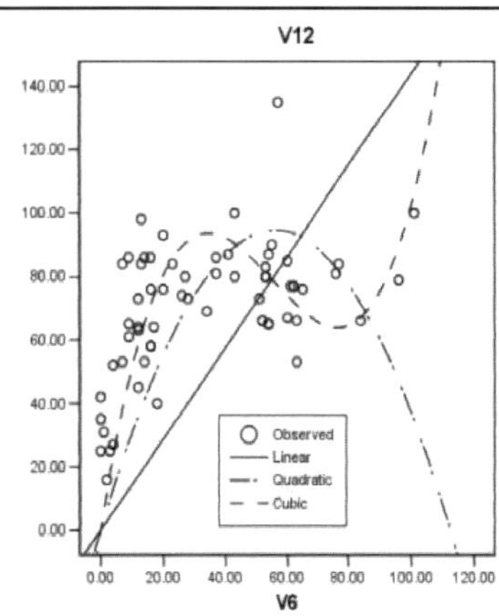	see table c below

a

Linear	
SS_R	26682.00
Standard Error	20.74
Quadratic	
SS_R	26622.40
Standard Error	20.89
Cubic	
SS_R	26598.20
Standard error	21.05

b

Linear	
SS_R	53703.43
Standard Error	29.67
Quadratic	
SS_R	53496.58
Standard Error	29.86
Cubic	
SS_R	38880.40
Standard error	25.67

c

Linear	
SS_R	95071.21
Standard error	39.16
Quadratic	
SS_R	49281.20
Standard error	28.42
Cubic	
SS_R	22206.88
Standard error	19.24

Figure 5: Sample regressions of variable pairs from data matrix M

The essentially linear relationship of v1 and v2 is clear both visually and in the uniformity of SS_R and standard error measures, where the nonlinear regressions yield no meaningful improvement over the linear. For v1 and v9 cubic regression shows some improvement over linear and quadratic both visually and quantitatively. For v6 and v12 the quadratic regression line is visually a much better fit to the data than the linear one, and the cubic one is even better; correspondingly, the quadratic quantifications show a substantial improvement over the linear ones, and the cubic ones even more so. The relationships between the highest-variance variables in M can, therefore, be said to range from linear to strongly nonlinear.

3.3 Linear and nonlinear analysis of the NECTE data

Moisl et al. (2006) analyzed the NECTE data with what is probably the most widely used of the linear exploratory methods: hierarchical cluster analysis (Everitt et al., 2001). This is actually a class of methods each of which defines clusters differently, but all of which represent cluster structure as nested constituency trees. Infamously --and unsurprisingly, given that each uses a different definition of what constitutes a cluster-- the variant methods can and often do assign different tree structures to the same data, and it is not usually clear which is to be preferred (Everitt et al., 2001, ch. 4). In the NECTE case, however, a range of variants (single link, complete link, average link, Ward's Method) converged on a stable structure of four main clusters exemplified by the Ward tree shown in figure 6.

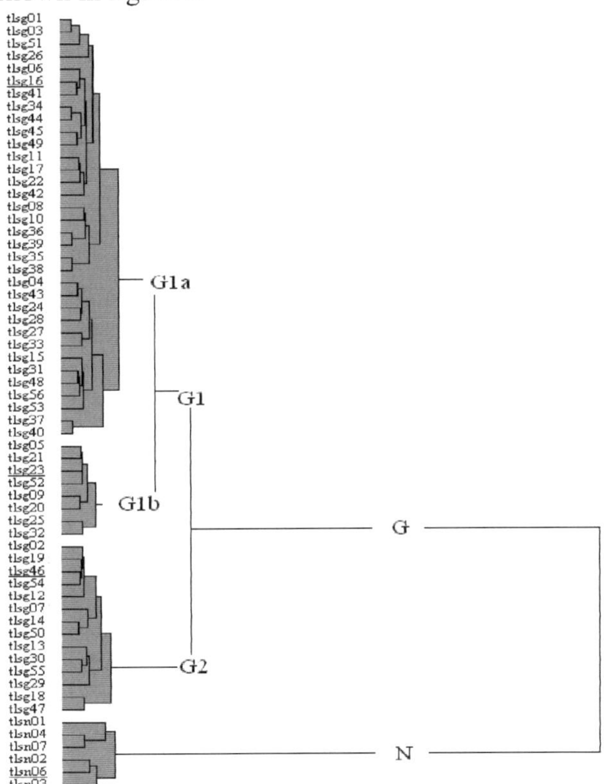

Figure 6: Ward's Method cluster tree for data matrix M

When interpreted in terms of the social data that NECTE provides for the speakers, a clear correlation between phonetic usage and social factors emerged. The main distinction is between middle class, well educated speakers from Newcastle on the north side of the river Tyne, labelled N, and working class, less well educated speakers from Gateshead on the south side of the Tyne, labelled G. The Gateshead speakers are categorized into G2 (exclusively male), and G1 (mainly through not exclusively female); G1 is subcategorized into G1a (working class males and females) and G1b (males and females with relatively higher socioeconomic status). Moisl and Maguire (2007) subsequently used the centroids of these clusters to identify the phonetic features most characteristic of each. Three sets of vowels were found to be of particular importance. Although all of these had been commented on before, their relative (and cumulative) sociolinguistic importance had hitherto escaped attention. They are:

- various types of [ə].
- [ɔː] and [ɑː], which correspond to RP [əʊ], and are found in words of the GOAT lexical set as defined by Wells (1982:146-7).
- [aɪ], [ɑː], and [eɪ], which correspond to RP [aɪ], and are found in words belonging to the PRICE lexical set as defined by Wells (1982:149-50).

For nonlinear analysis the self-organizing map, or SOM, was selected from among the various available nonlinear exploratory methods because it has been successfully used in a very wide range of applications (Kaski et al., 1998; Oja et al., 2001). The standard SOM (Kohonen, 2001) projects the topology of a data manifold in a space of arbitrary dimensionality n onto a two-dimensional lattice, where the structure of the manifold can be visually inspected. It does this by partitioning the vectors on the manifold surface into a Voronoi tesselation (Aurenhammer and Klein, 2000), thereby assigning all the data vectors within a defined topological neighborhood to the same cell of the tesselation, as shown in figure 7.

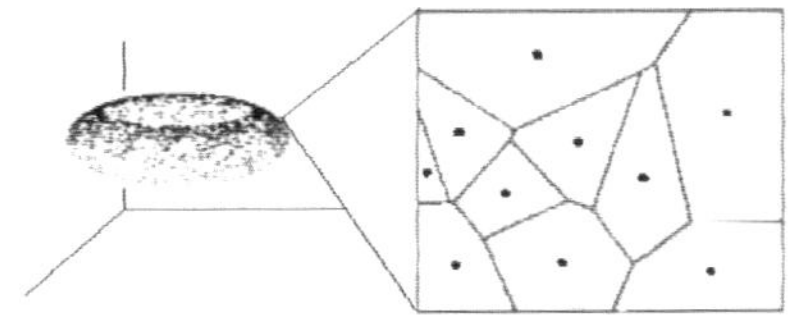

Figure 7: Voronoi tesselation of a manifold surface

For example, the doughnut shape on the left of figure 7 is a manifold in 3-dimensional space, and the square on the right represents the way in which a SOM partitions its surface: each dot represents a quantized vector and the lines enclosing a dot represent the boundaries of the area of the tesselation cell containing the *k* vectors within the specified topological neighborhood. All the vectors in a given cell are mapped to the same lattice unit, and the vectors in adjoining cells are mapped to adjacent lattice units. The result of this topology preservation is that all vectors close to one another in the input space in the sense that they are in the same or adjoining topological neighbourhoods will be close on the SOM output lattice (for further discussion see Ritter et al., (1992), ch. 4). The topology preservation is, moreover, nonlinear because the tesselation is based not on a global distance measure between vectors on the manifold but on local neighborhood distance, and as such the tesselation follows the manifold surface: if the surface is nonlinear, so is the topology-preserving representation of it.

The NECTE data was analyzed using a range of SOM parameters for output lattice size and shape and various initializations such as starting neighborhood, learning rate, and rate of neighborhood decrease. The results converged on a stable analysis of which the following map is representative.

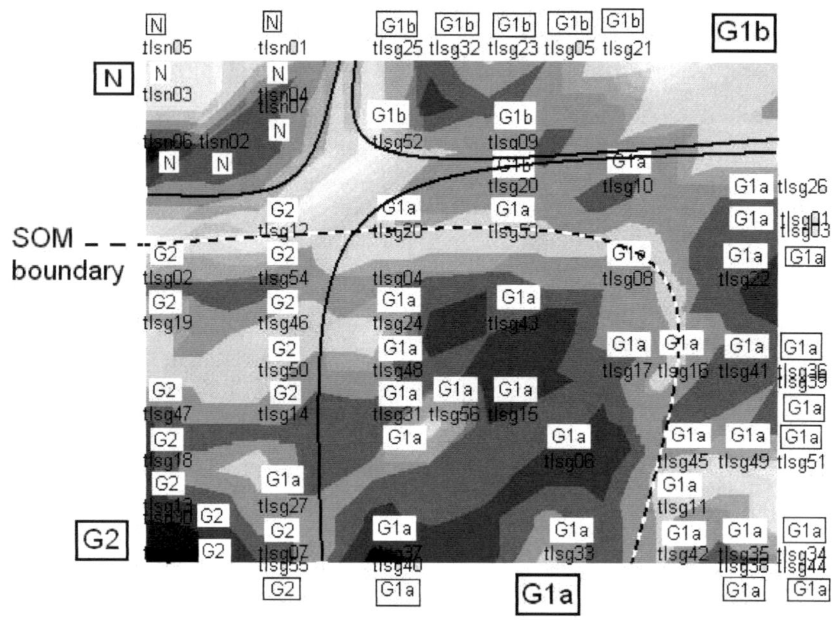

Figure 8: SOM analysis of the NECTE data

The speaker labels were positioned automatically on the lattice by the SOM's input-to-lattice mapping function, and the shading was generated using the U-matrix method (Ultsch, 1993). This shading must be understood in order to interpret the above SOM correctly, so a brief explanation is given here. It has already been noted that the SOM preserves the topology of the *n*-dimensional input manifold in the sense that vectors which are close in the input space are also close in the two-dimensional output space. The converse is not true, however: just because vectors are close in the output space does not necessarily mean that they are close on the input manifold. This apparently-paradoxical situation arises because the SOM mapping function does not use a global distance measure but only local neighborhood distance, and it consequently cannot and does not represent proportionality of distance between vector pairs in the input space. Instead, is squeezes its representation of the input topology onto the lattice in such a way that closely adjacent lattice cells may represent vectors which are far apart on the input manifold. Because, therefore, spatial distance is a delphic guide to interpretation of the SOM, some way must be found of demarcating the shape of the manifold representation given by the lattice. The U-matrix is a way of doing this. How it works can only be explained in terms of the details of SOM architecture, which cannot be given here on account of space constraints. It is, however, important to understand that lighter regions of the map represent manifold boundaries and darker ones the manifold surface; metaphorically, the darker areas are islands representing the shape of the manifold, and the lighter areas the sea separating them. The remaining annotations in figure 8, finally, were added by hand to facilitate discussion in the next subsection, and are explained there.

3.4 Discussion

Associated with each speaker on the SOM is a label which shows that speaker's place in the hierarchical cluster tree --tlsg08 on the SOM is in cluster G1a in the tree, for example. In addition, solid-line curves have been added to the SOM which show the approximate areas of the map that correspond to the main hierarchical clusters and, for each region, the relevant hierarchical cluster label has been shown surrounded by a square --the upper left corner of the SOM, for example, is bounded by a solid curve and labelled N to show that the speaker vectors found there correspond to those in the N hierarchical cluster. Using these annotations, it might appear that the hierarchical and SOM analyses are similar: the hierarchical analysis shows four main clusters, and the SOM has four disjoint regions corresponding to those clusters. This perception of correspondence is, however, based on spatial placement of the speaker vectors on the SOM, and, as we have seen, relative spatial distance on a SOM can be misleading. If one looks instead at the U-matrix shading that demarcates the manifold boundaries, the Newcastle group is as clearly distinguished from the Gateshead speakers by the SOM as by the hierarchical analysis, but the Gateshead speakers are grouped in a way that differs subtly from the hierarchical analysis. The hierarchical analysis says that there are three distinct Gateshead groups: G1a consists of working class men and women, G1b of lower middle class men and women, and G2 of working class men. The SOM, on the other hand, says that the Gateshead speakers fall into only two main groups the boundary between which is shown in figure 8 as a dotted-line curve. The one above and to the right of the dotted line (and excluding the Newcastle group) consists of lower middle class men and women and working class women. The other, below and to the left of the dotted line, comprises working class men together with two women (tlsg37 and tlsg40) who are classified with men both here and in the hierarchical analysis.

The linear and nonlinear methods, therefore, offer results that differ substantively. From a methodological point of view, the SOM result must be preferred because the data contains nonlinearity, and a nonlinear method can be expected to give a more accurate analysis of nonlinear data than a linear one. A sociolinguist might find the SOM analysis preferable on grounds of simplicity: there is no obvious distinction in the social data between the working class men that the hierarchical analysis assigns to separate clusters. The present paper is, however, a methodological one, and no further comment is ventured on this.

5. Conclusion

The discussion began with the observation that existing work on exploratory analysis of linguistic corpora does not take the possibility of data nonlinearity into account, and claimed that the presence of nonlinearity in data has a fundamental bearing on the conduct of exploratory analysis. The first part of the discussion explained why this is so in principle, and the second exemplified the explanation via exploratory analysis of the *Newcastle Electronic Corpus of Tyneside English* using both linear and nonlinear methods. That the two types of method gave substantively different results supports the case in principle that data should be screened for nonlinearity prior to exploratory analysis and that, if substantial degree of it is found, a nonlinear analytical method should be used.

References

Will Allen, Joan Beal, Karen Corrigan, Warren Maguire, and Hermann Moisl. 2007. A Linguistic Time Capsule: the Newcastle Electronic Corpus of Tyneside English. In: Joan Beal, Karen Corrigan, and Hermann Moisl (eds.). 2007. *Using Unconventional Digital Language Corpora: Diachronic Corpora.* Palgrave Macmillan, Basingstoke, 16-48.

Natalie Andrienko and Gennady Andrienko. 2005. *Exploratory Analysis of Spatial and Temporal Data: a Systematic Approach.* Springer-Verlag, Berlin.

Franz Aurenhammer and R. Klein. 2000. Voronoi Diagrams. In: J.-R. Sack and J. Urrutia (eds.) *Handbook of Computational Geometry*. North-Holland, Amsterdam, 201-290.

Cristoforo Bertuglia and Franco Vaio. 2005. *Nonlinearity, Chaos, and Complexity: The Dynamics of Natural and Social Systems*. Oxford University Press, Oxford.

Kenneth Church and William Gale. 1995a. Poisson mixtures. *Natural Language Engineering*, 1: 163-190.

Kenneth Church and William Gale. 1995b. Inverse Document Frequency (IDF): A Measure of Deviation from Poisson. *Proceedings of the Third Workshop on Very Large Corpora*. Association for Computational Linguistics. Reed Elsevier, 121-130.

G. Clarke and D. Cooke. 1998. *A Basic Course in Statistics*. 4th ed. Arnold, London.

Brian Everitt, Sabine Landau, and Morven Leese. 2001. *Cluster Analysis*. 4th ed. Arnold, London.

Samuel Kaski, J. Kangas, and Teuvo Kohonen. 1998. Bibliography of Self-Organizing Map (SOM) Papers: 1981-1997. *Neural Computing Surveys*, 1:102-350.

Teuvo Kohonen. 2001. *Self-Organizing Maps*. 3rd ed. Springer-Verlag, Berlin.

Christopher Manning and Hinrich Schütze. 2000. *Foundations of Statistical Natural Language Processing*. MIT Press, Cambridge, Mass.

Hermann Moisl, Warren Maguire, and Will Allen. 2006. Phonetic variation in Tyneside: exploratory multivariate analysis of the Newcastle Electronic Corpus of Tyneside English. In: Frans Hinskens (ed.). *Language Variation-European Perspectives*. John Benjamins Publishing, Amsterdam, 127-141.

Hermann Moisl and Warren Maguire. 2007. Identifying the Main Determinants of Phonetic Variation in the Newcastle Electronic Corpus of Tyneside English. *Journal of Quantitative Linguistics* 2007, 14: to appear.

M. Oja, Samuel Kaski, and Teuvo Kohonen. 2001. Bibliography of self-organizing map (SOM) papers: 1998-2001. *Neural Computing Surveys*, 3:1-156.

Helge Ritter, T. Martinetz, and K. Schulten. 1992. *Neural computation and self -organizing maps*. Addison-Wesley, Wokingham, UK.

Stephen Robertson. 2004. Understanding inverse document frequency: on theoretical arguments for IDF. *Journal of Documentation*, 60:503-520.

Alwyn Scott. 2004. *Encyclopedia of Nonlinear Science*. Fitzroy Dearborn Publishers. .

Josh Tenenbaum, V. de Silva, and John Langford. 2000. A global framework for nonlinear dimensionality reduction. *Science*, 290:2319--2323.

Alfred Ultsch. 1993. Self-organizing neural networks for visualization and classification. In: O.Opitz, B. Lausen, and R. Klar, (eds.), *Information and classification :concepts, methods, and applications*. Springer-Verlag, Berlin, 307-313.

John Wells. 1982. *Accents of English*. Cambridge: Cambridge University Press, Cambridge, UK.

Emergence of Community Structures in Vowel Inventories: An Analysis based on Complex Networks

Animesh Mukherjee, Monojit Choudhury, Anupam Basu, Niloy Ganguly
Department of Computer Science and Engineering,
Indian Institute of Technology, Kharagpur
{animeshm,monojit,anupam,niloy}@cse.iitkgp.ernet.in

Abstract

In this work, we attempt to capture patterns of co-occurrence across vowel systems and at the same time figure out the nature of the force leading to the emergence of such patterns. For this purpose we define a weighted network where the vowels are the nodes and an edge between two nodes (read vowels) signify their co-occurrence likelihood over the vowel inventories. Through this network we identify communities of vowels, which essentially reflect their patterns of co-occurrence across languages. We observe that in the assortative vowel communities the constituent nodes (read vowels) are largely uncorrelated in terms of their features indicating that they are formed based on the principle of maximal perceptual contrast. However, in the rest of the communities, strong correlations are reflected among the constituent vowels with respect to their features indicating that it is the principle of feature economy that binds them together.

1 Introduction

Linguistic research has documented a wide range of regularities across the sound systems of the world's languages (Liljencrants and Lindblom, 1972; Lindblom, 1986; de Boer, 2000; Choudhury et al., 2006; Mukherjee et al., 2006a; Mukherjee et al., 2006b). Functional phonologists argue that such regularities are the consequences of certain general principles like *maximal perceptual contrast* (Liljencrants and Lindblom, 1972), which is desirable between the phonemes of a language for proper perception of each individual phoneme in a noisy environment, *ease of articulation* (Lindblom and Maddieson, 1988; de Boer, 2000), which requires that the sound systems of all languages are formed of certain universal (and highly frequent) sounds, and *ease of learnability* (de Boer, 2000), which is required so that a speaker can learn the sounds of a language with minimum effort. In the study of vowel systems the optimizing principle, which has a long tradition (Jakobson, 1941; Wang, 1968) in linguistics, is maximal perceptual contrast. A number of numerical studies based on this principle have been reported in literature (Liljencrants and Lindblom, 1972; Lindblom, 1986; Schwartz et al., 1997). Of late, there have been some attempts to explain the vowel systems through multi agent simulations (de Boer, 2000) and genetic algorithms (Ke et al., 2003); all of these experiments also use the principle of perceptual contrast for optimization purposes.

An exception to the above trend is a school of linguists (Boersma, 1998; Clements, 2004) who argue that perceptual contrast-based theories fail to account for certain fundamental aspects such as the patterns of co-occurrence of vowels based on similar acoustic/articulatory *features*[1] observed across

[1] In linguistics, features are the elements, which distinguish one phoneme from another. The features that describe the vowles can be broadly categorized into three different classes namely the *height*, the *backness* and the *roundedness*. Height refers to the vertical position of the tongue relative to either the roof of the mouth or the aperture of the jaw. Backness refers to the horizontal tongue position during the articulation of a vowel relative to the back of the mouth. Roundedness refers to whether the lips are rounded or not during the articulation of a

Proceedings of Ninth Meeting of the ACL Special Interest Group in Computational Morphology and Phonology, pages 101–108,
Prague, June 2007.

the vowel inventories. Instead, they posit that the observed patterns, especially found in larger size inventories (Boersma, 1998), can be explained only through the principle of *feature economy* (de Groot, 1931; Martinet, 1955). According to this principle, languages tend to maximize the combinatorial possibilities of a few distinctive features to generate a large number of sounds.

The aforementioned ideas can be possibly linked together through the example illustrated by Figure 1. As shown in the figure, the initial plane P constitutes of a set of three very frequently occurring vowels /i/, /a/ and /u/, which usually make up the smaller inventories and do not have any single feature in common. Thus, smaller inventories are quite likely to have vowels that exhibit a large extent of contrast in their constituent features. However, in bigger inventories, members from the higher planes (P' and P'') are also present and they in turn exhibit feature economy. For instance, in the plane P' comprising of the set of vowels /ĩ/, /ã/, /ũ/, we find a nasal modification applied equally on all the three members of the set. This is actually indicative of an economic behavior that the larger inventories show while choosing a new feature in order to reduce the learnability effort of the speakers. The third plane P'' reinforces this idea by showing that the larger the size of the inventories the greater is the urge for this economy in the choice of new features. Another interesting facet of the figure are the relations that exist across the planes (indicated by the broken lines). All these relations are representative of a common linguistic concept of *robustness* (Clements, 2004) in which one less frequently occurring vowel (say /ĩ/) implies the presence of the other (and not vice versa) frequently occurring vowel (say /i/) in a language inventory. These cross-planar relations are also indicative of feature economy since all the features present in the frequent vowel (e.g., /i/) are also shared by the less frequent one (e.g., /ĩ/). In summary, while the basis of organization of the vowel inventories is perceptual contrast as indicated by the plane P in Figure 1, economic modifications of the perceptually distinct vowels takes place with the increase in the inventory size (as indicated by the planes P' and P'' in Figure 1).

In this work we attempt to corroborate the above conjecture by automatically capturing the patterns of co-occurrence that are prevalent *in* and *across* the planes illustrated in Figure 1. In order to do so, we define the "**Vo**wel-Vowel **Net**work" or **VoNet**, which is a weighted network where the vowels are the nodes and an edge between two nodes (read vowels) signify their co-occurrence likelihood over the vowel inventories. We conduct community structure analysis of different versions of VoNet in order to capture the patterns of co-occurrence in and across the planes P, P' and P'' shown in Figure 1. The plane P consists of the communities, which are formed of those vowels that have a very high frequency of occurrence (usually *assortative* (Newman, 2003) in nature). We observe that the constituent nodes (read vowels) of these assortative vowel communities are largely uncorrelated in terms of their features. On the other hand, the communities obtained from VoNet, in which the links between the assortative nodes are absent, corresponds to the co-occurrence patterns of the planes P' and P''. In these communities, strong correlations are reflected among the constituent vowels with respect to their features. Moreover, the co-occurrences across the planes can be captured by the community analysis of VoNet where only the connections between the assortative and the non-assortative nodes, with the non-assortative node co-occurring very frequently with the assortative one, are retained while the rest of the connections are filtered out. We find that these communities again exhibit a high correlation among the constituent vowels.

This article is organized as follows: Section 2 describes the experimental setup in order to explore the co-occurrence principles of the vowel inventories. In this section we formally define VoNet, outline its construction procedure, and present a community-finding algorithm in order to capture the co-occurrence patterns across the vowel systems. In section 3 we report the experiments performed to obtain the community structures, which are representative of the co-occurrence patterns in and across the planes discussed above. Finally, we conclude in section 4 by summarizing our contributions, pointing out some of the implications of the current work

vowel. There are however still more possible features of vowel quality, such as the velum position (e.g., nasality), type of vocal fold vibration (i.e., phonation), and tongue root position (i.e., secondary place of articulation).

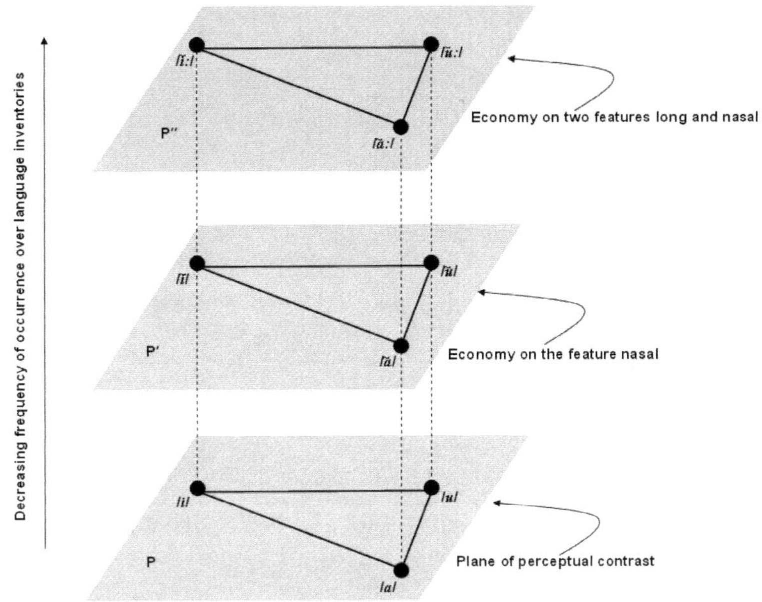

Figure 1: The organizational principles of the vowels (in decreasing frequency of occurrence) indicated through different hypothetical planes.

and indicating the possible future directions.

2 Experimental Setup

In this section we systematically develop the experimental setup in order to investigate the co-occurrence principles of the vowel inventories. For this purpose, we formally define VoNet, outline its construction procedure, describe a community-finding algorithm to decompose VoNet to obtain the community structures that essentially reflects the co-occurrence patterns of the vowel inventories.

2.1 Definition and Construction of VoNet

Definition of VoNet: We define VoNet as a network of vowels, represented as G = $\langle$ V_V, E $\rangle$ where V_V is the set of nodes labeled by the vowels and E is the set of edges occurring in VoNet. There is an edge $e \in$ E between two nodes, if and only if there exists one or more language(s) where the nodes (read vowels) co-occur. The weight of the edge e (also *edge-weight*) is the number of languages in which the vowels connected by e co-occur. The weight of a node u (also *node-weight*) is the number of languages in which the vowel represented by u occurs. In other words, if a vowel v_i represented by the node u occurs in the inventory of n languages then the node-weight of u is assigned the value n. Also if the vowel v_j is represented by the node v and there are w languages in which vowels v_i and v_j occur together then the weight of the edge connecting u and v is assigned the value v. Figure 2 illustrates this structure by reproducing some of the nodes and edges of VoNet.

Construction of VoNet: Many typological studies (Lindblom and Maddieson, 1988; Ladefoged and Maddieson, 1996; Hinskens and Weijer, 2003; Choudhury et al., 2006; Mukherjee et al., 2006a; Mukherjee et al., 2006b) of segmental inventories have been carried out in past on the UCLA Phonological Segment Inventory Database (UPSID) (Maddieson, 1984). Currently UPSID records the sound inventories of 451 languages covering all the major language families of the world. The selection of the languages for the inclusion on UPSID is governed by a quota principle seeking maximum genetic diversity among extant languages in order to reduce bias towards any particular family. In this work we have therefore used UPSID comprising of these 451 languages and 180 vowels found across them, for

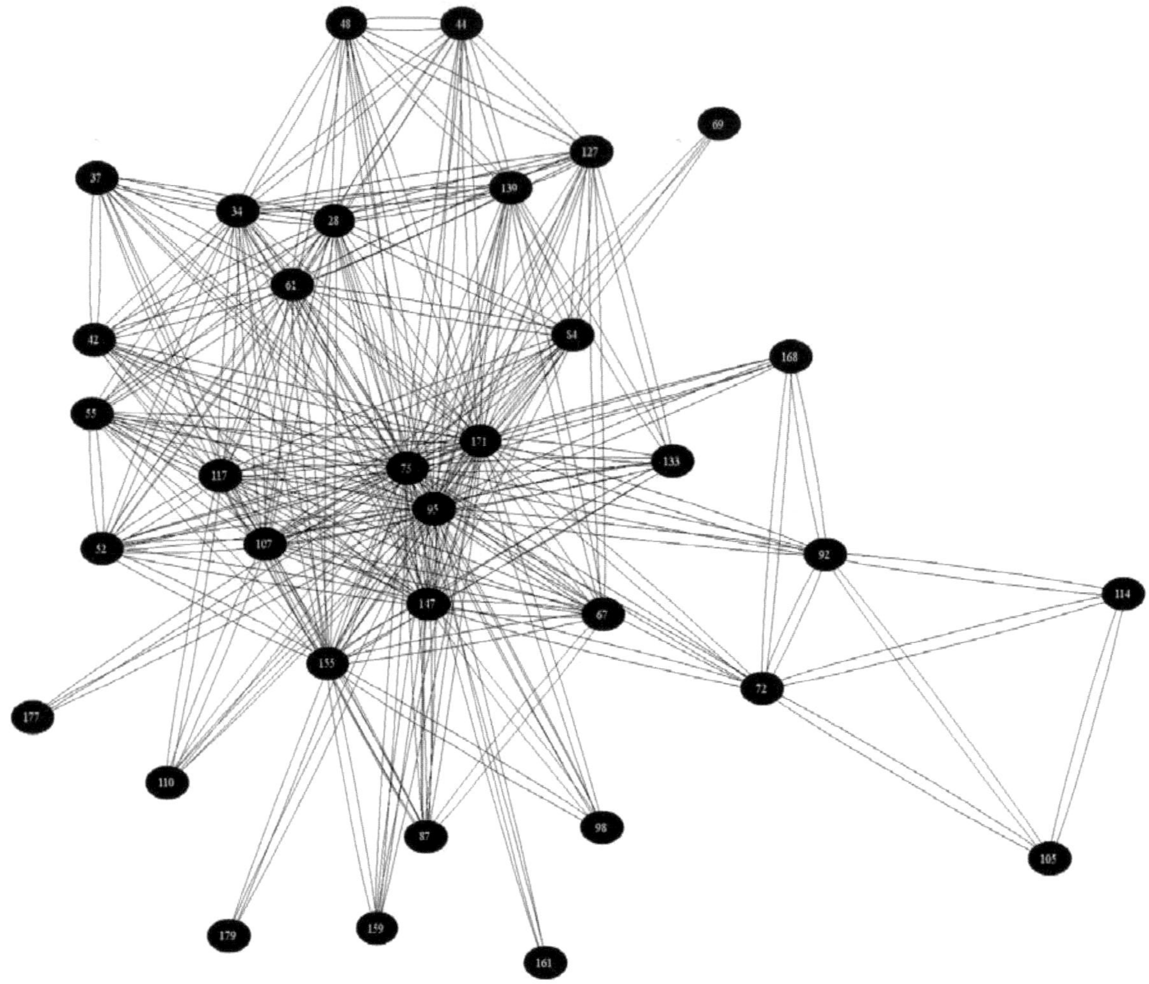

Figure 3: A partial illustration of VoNet. All edges in this figure have an edge-weight greater than or equal to 15. The number on each node corresponds to a particular vowel. For instance, node number 72 corresponds to /ĩ/.

constructing VoNet. Consequently, the set V_V comprises 180 elements (nodes) and the set E comprises 3135 elements (edges). Figure 3 presents a partial illustration of VoNet as constructed from UPSID.

2.2 Finding Community Structures

We attempt to identify the communities appearing in VoNet by the extended Radicchi et al. (Radicchi et al., 2003) algorithm for weighted networks presented in (Mukherjee et al., 2006a). The basic idea is that if the weights on the edges forming a triangle (loops of length three) are comparable then the group of vowels represented by this triangle highly occur together rendering a pattern of co-occurrence while if these weights are not comparable then there is no such pattern. In order to capture this property we define a strength metric S (in the lines of (Mukherjee et al., 2006a)) for each of the edges of VoNet as follows. Let the weight of the edge (u,v), where u, $v \in V_V$, be denoted by w_{uv}. We define S as,

$$S = \frac{w_{uv}}{\sqrt{\sum_{i \in V_C - \{u,v\}} (w_{ui} - w_{vi})^2}} \qquad (1)$$

if $\sqrt{\sum_{i \in V_C - \{u,v\}} (w_{ui} - w_{vi})^2} > 0$ else $S = \infty$. The denominator in this expression essentially tries to capture whether or not the weights on the edges forming triangles are comparable (the higher the value of S the more comparable the weights are). The network can be then decomposed into clusters

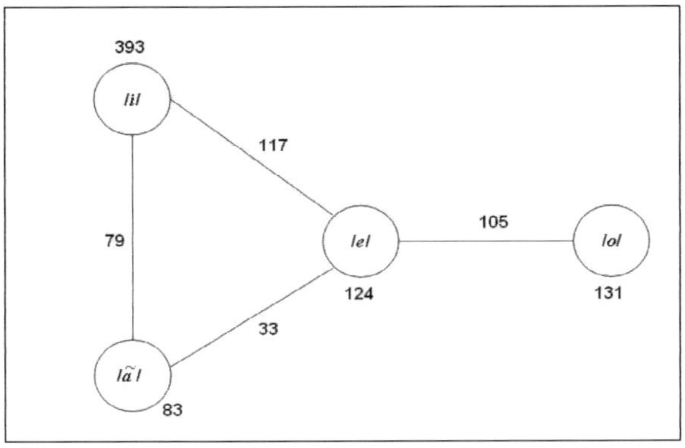

Figure 2: A partial illustration of the nodes and edges in VoNet. The labels of the nodes denote the vowels represented in IPA (International Phonetic Alphabet). The numerical values against the edges and nodes represent their corresponding weights. For example /i/ occurs in 393 languages; /e/ occurs in 124 languages while they co-occur in 117 languages.

or communities by removing edges that have S less than a specified threshold (say η).

At this point it is worthwhile to clarify the significance of a vowel community. A community of vowels actually refers to a set of vowels which occur together in the language inventories very frequently. In other words, there is a higher than expected probability of finding a vowel v in an inventory which already hosts the other members of the community to which v belongs. For instance, if /i/, /a/ and /u/ form a vowel community and if /i/ and /a/ are present in any inventory then there is a very high chance that the third member /u/ is also present in the inventory.

3 Experiments and Results

In this section we describe the experiments performed and the results obtained from the analysis of VoNet. In order to find the co-occurrence patterns in and across the planes of Figure 1 we define three versions of VoNet namely VoNet$_{assort}$, VoNet$_{rest}$ and VoNet$_{rest'}$. The construction procedure for each of these versions are presented below.

Construction of VoNet$_{assort}$: VoNet$_{assort}$ comprises the assortative[2] nodes having node-weights above 120 (i.e, vowels occurring in more than 120 languages in UPSID), along with only the edges inter-connecting these nodes. The rest of the nodes (having node-weight less than 120) and edges are removed from the network. We make a choice of this node-weight for classifying the assortative nodes from the non-assortative ones by observing the distribution of the occurrence frequency of the vowels illustrated in Figure 4. The curve shows the frequency of a vowel (y-axis) versus the rank of the vowel according to this frequency (x-axis) in log-log scale. The high frequency zone (marked by a circle in the figure) can be easily distinguished from the low-frequency one since there is distinct gap featuring between the two in the curve.

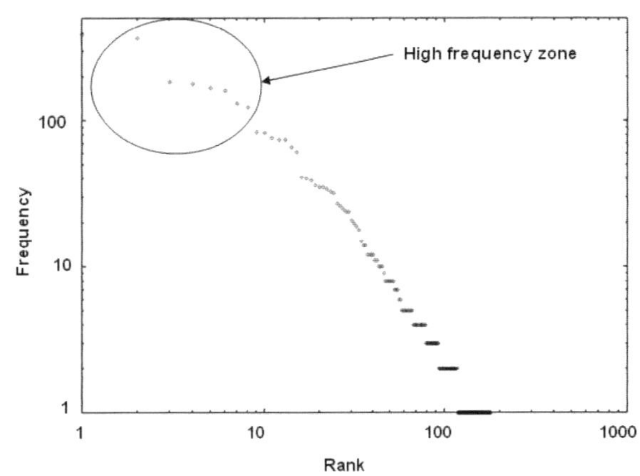

Figure 4: The frequency (y-axis) versus rank (x-axis) curve in log-log scale illustrating the distribution of the occurrence of the vowels over the language inventories of UPSID.

Figure 5 illustrates how VoNet$_{assort}$ is constructed from VoNet. Presently, the number of nodes in VoNet$_{assort}$ is 9 and the number of edges is 36.

Construction of VoNet$_{rest}$: VoNet$_{rest}$ comprises all the nodes as that of VoNet. It also has all the edges of VoNet except for those edges that inter-connect the assortative nodes. Figure 6 shows how VoNet$_{rest}$ can be constructed from VoNet. The number of nodes and edges in VoNet$_{rest}$ are 180

[2]The term "assortative node" here refers to the nodes having a very high node-weight, i.e., consonants having a very high frequency of occurrence.

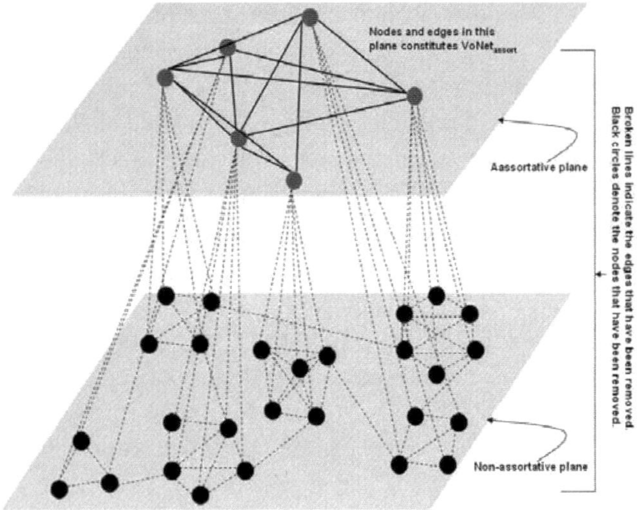

Figure 5: The construction procedure of VoNet$_{assort}$ from VoNet.

and 1293[3] respectively.

Construction of VoNet$_{rest'}$: VoNet$_{rest'}$ again comprises all the nodes as that of VoNet. It consists of only the edges that connect an assortative node with a non-assortative one if the non-assortative node co-occurs more than ninety five percent of times with the assortative nodes. The basic idea behind such a construction is to capture the co-occurrence patterns based on robustness (Clements, 2004) (discussed earlier in the introductory section) that actually defines the cross-planar relationships in Figure 1. Figure 7 shows how VoNet$_{rest'}$ can be constructed from VoNet. The number of nodes in VoNet$_{rest'}$ is 180 while the number of edges is 114[4].

We separately apply the community-finding algorithm (discussed earlier) on each of VoNet$_{assort}$, VoNet$_{rest}$ and VoNet$_{rest'}$ in order to obtain the respective vowel communities. We can obtain different sets of communities by varying the threshold η. A few assortative vowel communities (obtained from VoNet$_{assort}$) are noted in Table 1. Some of the communities obtained from VoNet$_{rest}$ are presented in Table 2. We also note some of the communities obtained from VoNet$_{rest'}$ in Table 3.

Tables 1 , 2 and 3 indicate that the communities in VoNet$_{assort}$ are formed based on the principle of perceptual contrast whereas the formation of the communities in VoNet$_{rest}$ as well as VoNet$_{rest'}$ is largely governed by feature economy. Hence, the smaller vowel inventories which are composed of mainly the members of VoNet$_{assort}$ are organized based on the principle of maximal perceptual contrast whereas the larger vowel inventories, which also contain members from VoNet$_{rest}$ and VoNet$_{rest'}$ apart from VoNet$_{assort}$, show a considerable extent of feature economy. Note that the groups presented in the tables are quite representative and the technique described above indeed captures many other such groups; however, due to paucity of space we are unable to present all of them here.

4 Conclusion

In this paper we explored the co-occurrence principles of the vowels, across the inventories of the world's languages. In order to do so we started with a concise review of the available literature on vowel inventories. We proposed an automatic procedure to extract the co-occurrence patterns of the vowels across languages.

Some of our important findings from this work are,

- The smaller vowel inventories (corresponding to the communities of VoNet$_{assort}$) tend to be organized based on the principle of maximal perceptual contrast;
- On the other hand, the larger vowel inventories (mainly comprising of the communities of VoNet$_{rest}$) reflect a considerable extent of feature economy;
- Co-occurrences based on robustness are prevalent across vowel inventories (captured through the communities of VoNet$_{rest'}$) and their emergence is again a consequence of feature economy.

Until now, we have concentrated mainly on the methodology that can be used to automatically cap-

[3] We have neglected nodes with node-weight less than 3 since these nodes correspond to vowels that occur in less than 3 languages in UPSID and the communities they form are therefore statistically insignificant.

[4] The network does not get disconnected due to this construction since, there is always a small fraction of edges that run between assortative and low node-weight non-assortative nodes of otherwise disjoint groups.

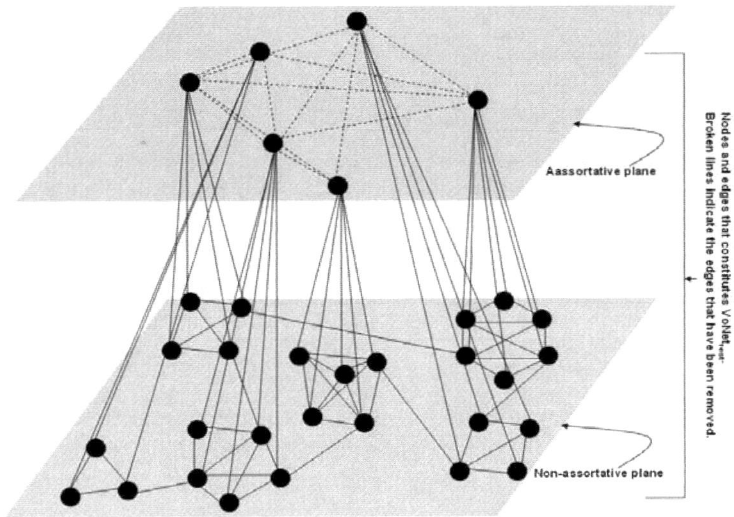

Figure 6: The construction procedure of VoNet$_{rest}$ from VoNet.

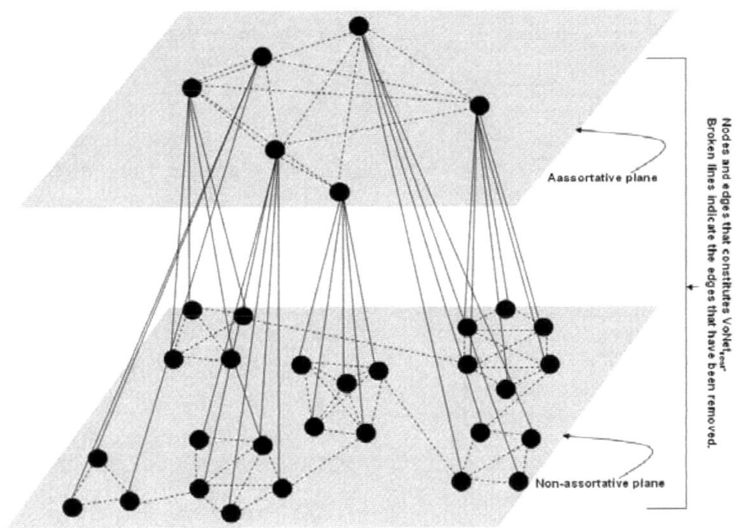

Figure 7: The construction procedure of VoNet$_{rest'}$ from VoNet.

Community	Features in Contrast
/i/, /a/, /u/	(low/high), (front/central/back), (unrounded/rounded)
/e/, /o/	(higher-mid/mid), (front/back), (unrounded/rounded)

Table 1: Assortative vowel communities. The contrastive features separated by slashes (/) are shown within parentheses. Comma-separated entries represent the features that are in use from the three respective classes namely the height, the backness, and the roundedness.

ture the co-occurrence patterns across the vowel systems. However, it would be also interesting to investigate the extent to which these patterns are governed by the forces of maximal perceptual contrast and feature economy. Such an investigation calls for quantitative definitions of the above forces and

Community	Features in Common
/ĩ/, /ã/, /ũ/	nasalized
/ĩ:/, /˜a:/, /ũ:/	long, nasalized
/i:/, /u:/, /a:/, /o:/, /e:/	long

Table 2: Some of the vowel communities obtained from VoNet_{rest}.

Community	Features in Common
/i/, /ĩ/	high, front, unrounded
/a/, /ã/	low, central, unrounded
/u/, /ũ/	high, back, rounded

Table 3: Some of the vowel communities obtained from $\text{VoNet}_{rest'}$. Comma-separated entries represent the features that are in use from the three respective classes namely the height, the backness, and the roundedness.

a thorough evaluation of the vowel communities in terms of these definitions. We look forward to accomplish the same as a part of our future work.

References

B. de Boer. 2000. Self-organisation in vowel systems, *Journal of Phonetics*, **28**(4), 441–465.

P. Boersma. 1998. *Functional phonology*, Doctoral thesis, University of Amsterdam, The Hague: Holland Academic Graphics.

M. Choudhury, A. Mukherjee, A. Basu and N. Ganguly. 2006. Analysis and synthesis of the distribution of consonants over languages: A complex network approach, *Proceedings of COLING–ACL*, 128–135, Sydney, Australia.

N. Clements. 2004. Features and sound inventories, *Symposium on Phonological Theory: Representations and Architecture*, CUNY.

A. W. de Groot. 1931. Phonologie und Phonetik als funktionswissenschaften, *Travaux du Cercle Linguistique de*, **4**, 116–147.

F. Hinskens and J. Weijer. 2003. Patterns of segmental modification in consonant inventories: A cross-linguistic study, *Linguistics*, **41**, 6.

R. Jakobson. 2003. *Kindersprache, aphasie und allgemeine lautgesetze*, Uppsala, reprinted in *Selected Writings I. Mouton*, (The Hague, 1962), 328-401.

J. Ke, M. Ogura and W.S.-Y. Wang. 2003. Optimization models of sound systems using genetic algorithms, *Computational Linguistics*, **29**(1), 1–18.

P. Ladefoged and I. Maddieson. 1996. *Sounds of the worlds languages*, Oxford: Blackwell.

J. Liljencrants and B. Lindblom. 1972. Numerical simulation of vowel quality systems: the role of perceptual contrast, *Language*, **48**, 839–862.

B. Lindblom. 1986. Phonetic universals in vowel systems, *Experimental Phonology*, 13–44.

B. Lindblom and I. Maddieson. 1988. Phonetic universals in consonant systems, *Language, Speech, and Mind*, Routledge, London, 62–78.

I. Maddieson. *Patterns of sounds*, 1984. Cambridge University Press, Cambridge.

A. Martinet. 1955. *Èconomie des changements phonétiques*, Berne: A. Francke.

A. Mukherjee, M. Choudhury, A. Basu and N. Ganguly. 2006. Modeling the co-occurrence principles of the consonant inventories: A complex network approach, *arXiv:physics/0606132 (preprint)*.

A. Mukherjee, M. Choudhury, A. Basu and N. Ganguly. 2006. Self-organization of the Sound Inventories: Analysis and Synthesis of the Occurrence and Co-occurrence Networks of Consonants. *arXiv:physics/0610120 (preprint)*.

M. E. J. Newman. 2003. The structure and function of complex networks, *SIAM Review*, **45**, 167–256.

F. Radicchi, C. Castellano, F. Cecconi, V. Loreto and D. Parisi. 2003. Defining and identifying communities in networks, *PNAS*, **101**(9), 2658–2663.

J-L. Schwartz, L-J. Boë, N. Vallée and C. Abry. 1997. The dispersion-focalization theory of vowel systems, *Journal of Phonetics*, *25*, 255–286.

W. S.-Y. Wang. 1968. The basis of speech. Project on linguistic analysis reports, University of California, Berkeley, (reprinted in *The Learning of Language* in 1971).

Cognate identification and alignment using practical orthographies

Michael Cysouw
Max Planck Institute for Evolutionary Anthropology, Leipzig
cysouw@eva.mpg.de

Hagen Jung
Max Planck Institute for Evolutionary Anthropology, Leipzig
jung@eva.mpg.de

Abstract

We use an iterative process of multi-gram alignment between associated words in different languages in an attempt to identify cognates. To maximise the amount of data, we use practical orthographies instead of consistently coded phonetic transcriptions. First results indicate that using practical orthographies can be useful, the more so when dealing with large amounts of data.

1 Introduction

The comparison of lexemes across languages is a powerful method to investigate the historical relations between languages. A central prerequisite for any interpretation of historical relatedness is to establish lexical cognates, i.e. lexemes in different languages that are of shared descend (in contrast to similarity by chance). If a pair of lexemes in two different languages stem from the same origin, this can be due to the fact that both languages derive from a common ancestor language, but it can also be caused by influence from one language on another (or influence on both language from a third language). To decide whether cognates are indicative of a common ancestor language ("vertical transmission") or due to language influence ("horizontal transmission") is a difficult problem with no shortcuts. We do not think that one kind of cognacy is more interesting that another. Both loans (be it from a substrate or a superstrate) and lexemes derived from a shared ancestor are indicative of the history of a language, and both should be acknowledged in the unravelling of linguistic (pre)history.

In this paper, we approach the identification of cognate lexemes on the basis of large parallel lexica between languages. This approach is an explicit attempt to reverse the "Swadesh-style" wordlist method. In the Swadesh-style approach, first meanings are selected that are assumed to be less prone to borrowing, then cognates are identified in those lists, and these cognates are then interpreted as indicative of shared descend. In contrast, we propose to first identify (possible) cognates among all available information, then divide these cognates into strata, and then interpret these strata in historical terms. (Because of limitations of space, we will only deal with the first step, the identification of cognates, in this paper.) This is of course exactly the route of the traditional historical-comparative approach to language comparison. However, we think that much can be gained by applying computational approaches to this approach.

A major problem arises when dealing with large quantities of lexical material from many different languages. In most cases it will be difficult (or very costly and time consuming in the least) to use coherent and consistent phonetic transcriptions of all available information. Even if we would have dictionaries with phonetic transcriptions for all languages that we are interested in, this would not necessarily help, as the details of phonetic transcription are normally not consistent across different authors. In this paper, we will therefore attempt to deal with unprocessed material in practical orthographies. This will of course pose problems for history-ridden orthographies like in English or French. However, we beleve that for most of the world's languages the practical

Proceedings of Ninth Meeting of the ACL Special Interest Group in Computational Morphology and Phonology, pages 109–116,
Prague, June 2007.

orthographies are not as inconsistent as those (because they are much younger) and might very well be useful for linguistic purposes.

In this paper, we will first discuss the data used in this investigation. Then we will describe the algorithm that we used to infer alignments between word pairs. Finally, we will discuss a few of the results using this algorithm on large wordlists in practical orthography.

2 Resources

In this study we used parallel wordlists that we extracted from the Intercontinental Dictionary Series (IDS) database, currently under development at the Max Planck Institute for Evolutionary Anthropology in Leipzig (see http://www.eva.mpg.de/lingua/files/ids.html for more information). The IDS wordlists contain more than thousand entries of basic words from each language, and many entries contain alternative wordforms. At this time, there are only a few basic transcription languages (English, French and Portuguese) and some Caucasian languages available. We choose some of them for the purpose of the present study and preprocessed the data. To compare languages, we chose only word pairs that were available and non-compound in both languages. For all words that occurred several times in the whole collection of a language, we accepted only one randomly choosen wordform and left out all others. We also deleted content in brackets or in between other special characters. If, after these preparation, a wordform is still longer than twelve UTF-8 characters, we disregard these for reasons of computational efficiency. After this, we are still left with a large number of about 900 word pairs for each pair of languages.

3 Alignment

An alignment of two words w_a and w_b is a bijective and maintained ordered one-to-one correspondence from all subsequences s_a of the word w_a with $w_a = concat(s_{a_1}, s_{a_2}, \ldots, s_{a_k})$ to all subsequences s_b of the word w_b with $w_b = concat(s_{b_1}, s_{b_2}, \ldots, s_{b_k})$. It is possible that one of the associated subsequences is the empty word ϵ. In general one may construct a distance measure from such a linked sequence of two given words by assigning a cost for each single link of the alignment. There are many such alignment/cost functions described in the literature, and they are often used to calculate a distance measure between two sequences of characters (Inkpen et al., 2005). A measurement regularly used for linguistic sequences is the Levenshtein distance, or a modifications of it. Other distance measures detect, for example, the longest common subsequences or the longest increasing subsequences.

It is our special interest to use multi-character mappings for calculating a distance between two words. Therefore, we adapt and extend the Levenshtein measurement. First, we allow for mapping of any arbitrary string length (not just strings of one character as in Levenshtein) and, second, we assign a continuous cost between 0 and 1 for every mapping.

Our algorithm consist basically of two steps. In the first step, all possible subsequence pairs between associated words are considered, and a cost function is extracted for every multi-gram pair from their co-occurrences in the whole wordlist. In a second step, this cost function is used to infer an alignment between whole words. On the basis of this alignment a new cost function is established for all multi-gram pairs. This second step can be iterated until the cost function stabilizes.

3.1 Cost of an multi-gram pair

For every pair of subsequences s_{a_i} and s_{b_j} we count the number of co-occurrences. The subsequences s_{a_i} and s_{b_j} co-occur when they are found in two associated words w_a and w_b from a language wordlist of two languages L_a and L_b. We then use a simple Dice coefficient as a cost function between all possible subsequences. For computational reasons, it is necessary to limit the size of the multi-grams considered. We decided to limit the multi-gram size to a number of maximally four UTF-8 characters. Still, in the first step of our algorithm, there is a very large set of such subsequence pairs because all possible combinations are considered. When an alignment is inferred in the iterative process, only the aligned subsequences are counted as co-occurrences, so the number of possible combinations is considerably lower. Further, to prevent low frequent co-occurrences to have a disproportional impact, we added an attestation threshold of 2% of the wordlist size for two subsequences to be accepted for the alignment process.

3.2 Alignment of words

An alignment of two words is a complete ordered linking of subsequences. We annotate it in the following way (vertical dashes delimit the subsequences; note that subsequences may be empty):

$(\ | w | ool)$(щерс | ть |)

There is a huge amount of possible combinations of aligned subsequences. On the basis of the cost function, a distance is established for every word pair alignment. The summation of all multi-gram mapping costs represents the distance of the alignment. Because we are dealing with multi-grams of variable length, alternative alignments of the same word pair will consist of a different number of subsequences. So, simple summation would lead to distances out of the range from 0 to 1. To counteract this, we normalized the word distance. We weighted each subsequence relative to the number of characters in the subsequence. For example, the mapping of w and ть in the example above would be multiplied by $\frac{3}{10}$, because w and ть have together 3 characters and the complete words have in total 10 characters.

To make use of efficient divide and conquer solving strategies and to get meaningful linguistic statements with the base of the calculated best alignments, we decided to look for a special subset of best alignments. As (Kondrak, 2002) pointed out, there are some situations in which the consideration of local alignment gets the required results. If only a part of a word aligning sequence is of high similarity then sometimes a linguistic justification of the whole word similarity is given. Those alignments contain the lowest cost multi-gram pairs, but are not necessarily of best similarity in total.

To illustrate the difference between local and global alignment, consider an example that shows different results, depending whether the total sum of multi-gram similarities is taken or the best local one. Look at the two words 'abc' and '$\alpha\beta\gamma$' and a part of its multi-gram cost function in Table 1. The summation of the costs would prefer alignment A_2, as can be seen in Table 2. But we prefer A_1, because it contains the subsequence pair $(ab \mid \alpha\beta)$ with the lowest cost.

multi-gram 1	multi-gram 2	cost
ab	$\alpha\beta$	0.1
bc	$\beta\gamma$	0.3
a	α	0.4
c	γ	0.8
⋮	⋮	⋮

Table 1: Costs for constructed subsequence pairs (ordered by cost)

Index	Alignment	Distance
A_2	$(a \mid bc)(\alpha \mid \beta\gamma)$	$0.4 + 0.3 = 0.7$
A_1	$(ab \mid c)(\alpha\beta \mid \gamma)$	$0.1 + 0.8 = 0.9$
⋮	⋮	⋮

Table 2: Alignments with distance

With these assumptions, we composed a fast and easy method to find the best alignment. We prefer alignments where some links are very good, but the rest might not be. We assume that words are more related to each other, if there are such highly rated pairs. This approach can also be found in other string based comparing methods like, for example, the Longest Common Increasing Subsequence method, which calculates the longest equal multi-gram and neglects the rest of the word. We first order all possible multi-gram mappings by their costs and pick the subsequence pair with the lowest cost. Starting from this mapping seed, we look for mappings for the rest of the word pair, both before and after the initial mapped subsequence. For both these suffixes and prefixes, we again search for the subsequence with the lowest cost. This process is re-applied until the whole words are mapped. If there is more than one optimal linking subsequence pair, then all possible alignments are considered. In this way, we do not restrict, in contrast to Kondrak, which position for the multi-gram mapping will be preferred for the local alignment. The algorithm runs in $O(n^6)$. It takes $O(n^4)$ time for all combinations of different multi-gram pairs within $O(n)$ steps in $O(n)$ iterations.

4 Experimental Evaluation

As mentioned above, we applied our model to some test data from the IDS database. For later analyses, we also constructed some random wordlists. With these we are able to say something about how significant our results are. To make these random wordlists we remap each word w_a from L_a to an arbitrarily chosen word w_b from collection L_b. This new mapped word was adjusted to the size of the originally associated word from L_b. The adjustment works by stretching or shrinking the new word to the required length by doubling the word several times and cutting of the overlaying head or tail afterwards. In this way, we controlled for word length and multi-gram frequencies. This randomization process was performed five times from L_a to L_b, and five the times from L_b to L_a, and the results were averaged over all these ten cases.

For the calculation process, we stored all lists in SQL tables. We first built a preprocessed working table with the lexemes from the languages to be compared, and afterwards we constructed the resulting tables that hold all the results:

- compare table: the word pairs, their alignments and alignment goodness;
- subsequence table: the subsequence pairs found and their co-occurrence coefficients;
- random compare table: pseudo random word pairs like the compare table;
- random subsequence table: the subsequence pairs found from random compare table.

Table 3 consists of the best alignments for word pairs of English and French after 30 iterations, and Table 4 shows the best alignments for the comparison of English and Hunzib (a Caucasian language). First note that our algorithm works independently of the orthography used. We do not assume that the same UTF-8 characters in the two languages are identical. The fact that ⟨c⟩ is mapped between English *clan* and French *clan* is a result of the statistical distribution of these characters in the two languages. This orthography-independence means that we can apply our algorithm without modifications to cyrillic scripts as shown with the English-Hunzib comparison. Second, we payed close attention to the fact that the word similarity values are comparable among different language comparisons. This means that it is highly significant that the highest word similarities between English and French are much higher than those between English and Hunzib (actually, the alignments between English and Hunzib are nonsensical, but more about that later). Further, our algorithm finds vowel-consonant multi-grams in some cases (e.g. see Table 5). As far as we can see, there are not linguistically meaningful and should be considered an artifact of our current approach. We hope to fine-tune the algorithm in the future to prevent this behavior.

Our method finds alignments, but also the subsequences in the alignments are of interest. The best mapped multi-grams between English and French are illustrated in Table 5. Strangely, the highest ranked ones are a few vowel+consonant bigrams, that occur not very often. Since the Dice coefficient depends on the size of the investigated collection, we assumed a minimum frequency of co-occurrences in each calculation step of 2% of the collection size (which is 20 cases in the English-French comparison). The high-ranked bigrams are all just above this threshold. Therefore, we might argue that all the bigrams from the top of the list are a side-effect of the collection size itself.

Following these bigrams are many one-to-one matches of all alphabetic characters except ⟨j,k,q,w,x,y,z⟩. These mappings are found without assuming any similarity based on the UTF-8 encoding of the characters. What we actually find here is a mapping for the orthography of the stratum of the French loan words in English. As can be seen in the histogram in Figure 1, the mapping between multi-grams falls off dramatically after these links.

<table>
<tr><th>English</th><th>French</th><th>Alignment</th><th>similarity</th></tr>
<tr><td>tribe,clan</td><td>tribu,clan</td><td>(| c | | l | | an |) (| c | | l | | an |)</td><td>0.955872</td></tr>
<tr><td>long</td><td>long</td><td>(| l | | on | | g |) (| l | | on | | g |)</td><td>0.925542</td></tr>
<tr><td>lion</td><td>lion</td><td>(| l | | i | | on |) (| l | | i | | on |)</td><td>0.916239</td></tr>
<tr><td>canoe</td><td>canoe,pirogue</td><td>(| c | | an | | o | | e |) (| c | | an | | o | | e |)</td><td>0.911236</td></tr>
<tr><td>famine</td><td>famine,disette</td><td>(| f | | a | | m | | in | | e |) (| f | | a | | m | | in | | e |)</td><td>0.910465</td></tr>
<tr><td>innocent</td><td>innocent</td><td>(| in | | n | | o | | c | | e | | n | | t |) (| in | | n | | o | | c | | e | | n | | t |)</td><td>0.908913</td></tr>
<tr><td>prison,jail</td><td>prison</td><td>(| p | | r | | i | | s | | on |) (| p | | r | | i | | s | | on |)</td><td>0.9089</td></tr>
<tr><td>poncho</td><td>poncho</td><td>(| p | | on | | c | | h | | o |) (| p | | on | | c | | h | | o |)</td><td>0.907496</td></tr>
<tr><td>sure,certain</td><td>sûr,certain</td><td>(| c | | e | | r | | t | | a | | in |) (| c | | e | | r | | t | | a | | in |)</td><td>0.905022</td></tr>
<tr><td>tapioca,manioc</td><td>manioc</td><td>(| m | | an | | i | | o | | c |) (| m | | an | | i | | o | | c |)</td><td>0.904811</td></tr>
<tr><td>⋮</td><td>⋮</td><td>⋮</td><td>⋮</td></tr>
</table>

Table 3: English-French best rated alignments after 30 iterations

<table>
<tr><th>English</th><th>Hunzib</th><th>Alignment</th><th>similarity</th></tr>
<tr><td>jewel</td><td>жавгьар,йакъут</td><td>(| j | | e | | w | | e | | l |) (| ж | | а | в | гь | | а | | р |)</td><td>0.507094</td></tr>
<tr><td>see</td><td>нацIа</td><td>(| s | | e | | e |) (| н | | а | цI | а |)</td><td>0.489442</td></tr>
<tr><td>grease,fat</td><td>маъа</td><td>(g | r | | e | a | s | | e |) (| м | | а | | ъ | | а |)</td><td>0.464667</td></tr>
<tr><td>heaven</td><td>гIалжан</td><td>(| h | | e | | a | | v | | e | | n |) (г | I | | а | | л | | ж | | а | | н |)</td><td>0.445626</td></tr>
<tr><td>ocean</td><td>акеан</td><td>(| o | | c | | e | a | n |) (а | к | | е | | а | | н |)</td><td>0.419629</td></tr>
<tr><td>pocket</td><td>киса,жиби</td><td>(p | o | | c | | k | | e | t) (| к | | и | | с | | а |)</td><td>0.410143</td></tr>
<tr><td>sweep</td><td>лъалIа</td><td>(| s | w | e | | e | p) (л | ъ | | а | лI | а |)</td><td>0.395264</td></tr>
<tr><td>measure</td><td>маса</td><td>(| m | | e | a | s | ur | e |) (| м | | а | | с | | а |)</td><td>0.393806</td></tr>
<tr><td>flower</td><td>гьакI</td><td>(flo | w | | e | | r |) (| гь | | а | | к | I)</td><td>0.391867</td></tr>
<tr><td>rebuke,scold</td><td>акьа</td><td>(r | e | | b | | u | k | e |) (| а | | к | | ь | | а |)</td><td>0.387163</td></tr>
<tr><td>⋮</td><td>⋮</td><td>⋮</td><td>...</td></tr>
</table>

Table 4: English-Hunzib best rated alignments after 30 iterations

E	F	freq	dice
ar	ar	21	1
in	in	26	1
on	on	22	1
an	an	22	1
m	m	80	0.92786
n	n	188	0.92161
c	c	120	0.91815
p	p	78	0.91798
r	r	277	0.91665
f	f	35	0.90647
l	l	132	0.90534
v	v	26	0.90346
t	t	165	0.8719
b	b	44	0.86301
s	s	126	0.85915
d	d	66	0.82913
o	o	192	0.82325
e	e	417	0.81479
a	a	229	0.81367
g	g	34	0.79683
h	h	53	0.7856
i	i	183	0.75961
u	u	94	0.69546
⋮	⋮	⋮	⋮

Table 5: Best English (E) and French (F) multi-gram mappings after 30 iterations.

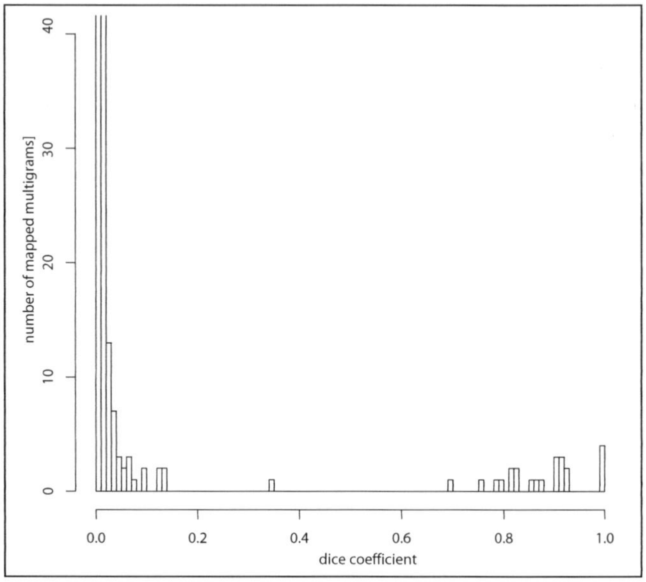

Figure 1: Histogram of dice-coefficients for English-French multi-gram mappings.

The character-independence of our method is illustrated by the character mapping between English and Russian in Table 6. Shown in the table are only the highest ranked orthographic mappings. Again we see an almost complete alphabetic linkage, probably caused by the French loanwords shared by both English and Russian.

With this approach, we are also able to find some vestiges of sound changes, as illustrated by the character mapping between Spanish and Portuguese in Table 7. Shown here are only the highest ranked *non-identical* multi-grams. The dice coefficients of the pairs ⟨h⟩ – ⟨ll⟩, ⟨f⟩ – ⟨h⟩ show the results of sound changes that were dramatically enough to be represented in the orthography. The pairs ⟨ç⟩ – ⟨z⟩ and ⟨n⟩ – ⟨ñ⟩ show difference in orthographic convention (though the best pair should have been ⟨nh⟩ – ⟨ñ⟩).

E	R	freq	dice
r	р	184	0.88874745
n	н	115	0.8461936
l	л	104	0.79646295
s	с	114	0.7927922
t	т	165	0.7701921
m	м	47	0.7699933
o	о	184	0.7510106
k	ть	21	0.74458015
p	п	50	0.7388723
i	и	102	0.7034591
a	а	221	0.6866478
u	у	40	0.6449104
c	к	77	0.6251676
e	е	219	0.59066784
b	б	32	0.525643
w	в	46	0.46787763
d	д	42	0.381996
⋮	⋮	⋮	⋮

Table 6: Best English (E) and Russian (R) multi-gram mappings after 30 iterations.

P	S	freq	dice
⋮	⋮	⋮	⋮
ç	z	20	0.6316202
h	ll	20	0.4552776
f	h	34	0.43381172
n	ñ	24	0.37720457
ã	n	33	0.31106696
h	h	23	0.23646937
v	b	32	0.2165933
t	h	29	0.2127131
z	c	24	0.15424858
o	e	305	0.12838262
⋮	⋮	⋮	⋮

Table 7: Spanish (S) and Portuguese (P) multi-gram mappings after 30 iterations. Only the highest ranking non-identical mappings are shown

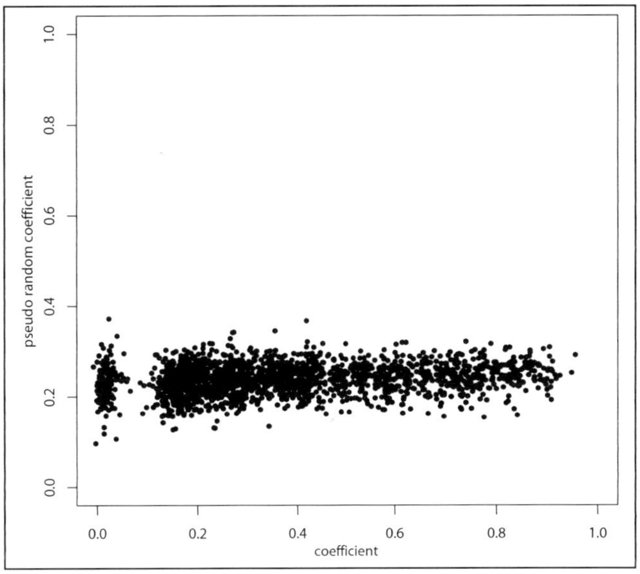

Figure 2: English-French similarities for word alignments plotted against the similarities with random language entries.

A promising indicator for cognate identification is the comparison of word alignment similarities with the similarities between randomly associated word pairs. We generated pseudo random word pairs as described above. Therefore we caluclate for each word from one language one coeffiecent value for the linkage with the assocciated word and a second avarage value for the linkage with some random words. In Figure 2 we plot these two values for all words of English and all words of French (after 30 iterations) against each other. Each dot represents a word. The x-axis shows the similarity coefficient between the real words and the y-axis shows the similarity coefficient from the comparison with the pseudo random words. As can be seen, many of the actual similarities are more to the right of the $y = x$ line indicating more than chance frequency similarity.

In contrast, in comparing English with Hunzib in Figure 3 there is only a slight tendency of stretching of the scatterplot. So one could conclude that English and Hunzib have probably no cognates at all, although there are some strongly related word pairs. However, some slight stretching will always be seen, because of the usage of an algorithm with iterations. Such a process will always strengthen some random tendencies.

The iterative process is illustrated in Figure 4. Shown here are the alignment similarities for all word pairs between French and Portuguese. After the first round of alignment, there is only a slight stretch in the scatterplot. Already after the second iteration, the plot is stretched strongly. In the further iterations the situation changes only slightly. Apparently, two rounds of alignment and reassignment of the cost function suffice for convergence.

5 Conclusion

The big advantage of using original orthographies in the study of linguistic relationships is that much more information is readily available. Because of the wealth of available data, we can use computational approaches for the comparison of wordlists. In principle, the kind of approach that we have sketched out in this paper can just as well be used for the comparison of complete dictionaries. The comparison of real wordlists with randomly shuffled wordlists indicated that even on purely statistical grounds it might be possible to separate meaningful alignments from random alignments.

The most promising result of our investigation is

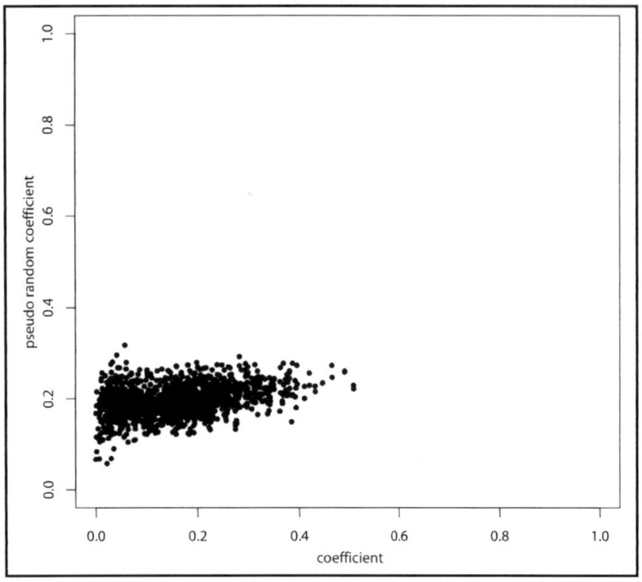

Figure 3: English-Hunzib similarities for word alignments plotted against the similarities with random language entries.

that we were able to find cognates even without any knowledge about the orthographic conventions used in the languages that were compared. In the comparison English-French and English-Russian there appear to be many French loanwords among the well-aligned wordpairs. If this impresion holds, we are in fact only able to infer the stratum of French influence in European languages. An interesting next step would then be to redo the analyses after removing this stratum from the data and look for deeper strata in the lexicon. As shown by the Spanish-Portuguese comparison, sound changes can be picked up by our approach as long as the changes have left a trace in the orthography.

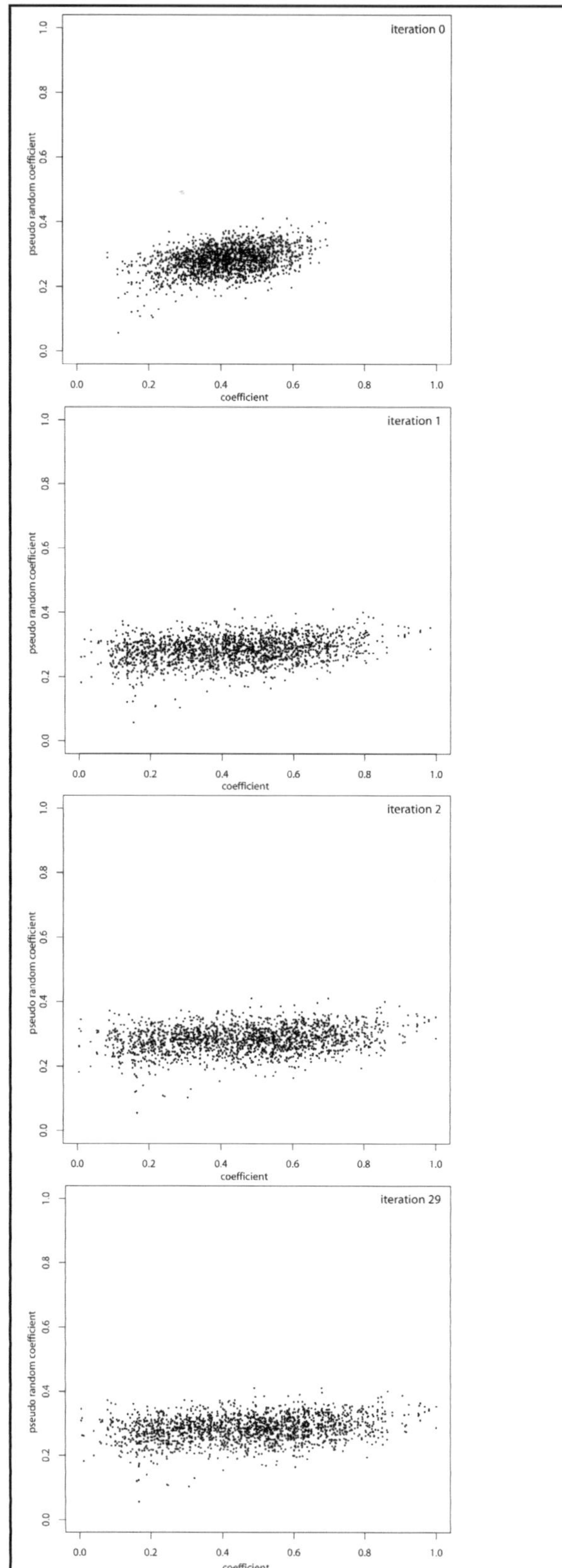

Figure 4: Plots of four iterations after 1, 2, 3 and 30 rounds of the French-Portuguese comparison. The coefficients are plotted against coefficients that were build with randomized language entries.

References

Diana Inkpen, Oana Frunza, and Grzegorz Kondrak. 2005. Automatic identification of cognates and false friends in french and english. In *RANLP-2005, Bulgaria*, pages 251–257, September.

Grzegorz Kondrak. 2002. *Algorithms for language reconstruction*. Ph.D. thesis, University of Toronto.

ParaMor: Minimally Supervised Induction of Paradigm Structure and Morphological Analysis

Christian Monson, Jaime Carbonell, Alon Lavie, Lori Levin
Language Technologies Institute
Carnegie Mellon University
5000 Forbes Ave.
Pittsburgh, PA, USA 15213
{cmonson, alavie+, jgc+, lsl+}@cs.cmu.edu

Abstract

Paradigms provide an inherent organizational structure to natural language morphology. ParaMor, our minimally supervised morphology induction algorithm, retrusses the word forms of raw text corpora back onto their paradigmatic skeletons; performing on par with state-of-the-art minimally supervised morphology induction algorithms at morphological analysis of English and German. ParaMor consists of two phases. Our algorithm first constructs sets of affixes closely mimicking the paradigms of a language. And with these structures in hand, ParaMor then annotates word forms with morpheme boundaries. To set ParaMor's few free parameters we analyze a training corpus of Spanish. Without adjusting parameters, we induce the morphological structure of English and German. Adopting the evaluation methodology of Morpho Challenge 2007 (Kurimo et al., 2007), we compare ParaMor's morphological analyses with Morfessor (Creutz, 2006), a modern minimally supervised morphology induction system. ParaMor consistently achieves competitive F_1 measures.

1 Introduction

Words in natural language (NL) have internal structure. Morphological processes derive new lexemes from old ones or inflect the surface form of lexemes to mark morphosyntactic features such as tense, number, person, etc. This paper address minimally supervised induction of productive natural language morphology from text. Minimally supervised induction of morphology interests us both for practical and theoretical reasons. In linguistic theory, the morpheme is often defined as the smallest unit of language which conveys meaning. And yet, without annotating for meaning, recent work on minimally supervised morphology induction from written corpora has met with some success (Creutz, 2006). We are curious how far this program can be pushed. From a practical perspective, minimally supervised morphology induction would help create morphological analysis systems for languages outside the traditional scope of NLP. However, to develop our method we induce the morphological structure of three well-understood languages, English, German, and Spanish.

1.1 Inherent Structure in NL Morphology

The approach we have taken to induce morphological structure has explicit roots in linguistic theory. Cross-linguistically, natural language organizes inflectional morphology into *paradigms* and *inflection classes*. A paradigm is a set of mutually exclusive operations that can be performed on a word form. Each mutually exclusive morphological operation in a paradigm marks a lexeme for some set or *cell* of morphosyntactic features. An inflection class, meanwhile, specifies the procedural details that a particular set of adherent lexemes follow to realize the surface form filling each paradigm cell. Each lexeme in a language adheres to a single inflection class for each paradigm the lexeme realizes. The lexemes belonging to an inflection class may have no relationship binding them together beyond an arbitrary morphological stipulation that they adhere to the same inflection class. But for this paper, an inflection class may

Proceedings of Ninth Meeting of the ACL Special Interest Group in Computational Morphology and Phonology, pages 117–125,
Prague, June 2007.

Paradigm Cells	Inflection Class	
	'eat'	**'silent-e'**
Unmarked	eat	dance, erase, …
Present, 3rd	eats	dances, erases, …
Past Tense	ate	danced, erased, …
Progressive	eating	dancing, erasing, …
Passive	eaten	danced, erased, …

Table 1: The English verbal paradigm, left column, and two inflection classes of the verbal paradigm. The verb *eat* fills the cells of its inflection class with the five surface forms shown in the second column. Verbs belonging to the 'silent-e' inflection class inflect following the pattern of the third column.

also refer to a set of lexemes that inflect similarly for phonological or orthographic reasons. Working with text we intentionally blur phonology and orthography.

A simple example will help illustrate paradigms, inflection classes, and the mutual exclusivity of cells. As shown in Table 1, all English verbs belong to a single common paradigm of five cells: One cell marks a verb for the morphosyntactic feature values *present tense 3rd person*, as in *eats*; another cell marks *past tense*, as in *ate*; a third cell holds a surface form typically used to mark *progressive aspect*, *eating*; a fourth produces a *passive participle*, *eaten*; and finally there is the unmarked cell, in this example *eat*.

Aside from inflection classes each containing only a few irregular lexemes, such as that containing *eat*, there are no English verbal inflection classes that arbitrarily differentiate lexemes on purely morphological grounds. There are, however, several inflection classes that realize surface forms only for verbs with particular phonology or orthography. The 'silent-e' inflection class is one such. To adhere to the 'silent-e' inflection class a lexeme must fill the unmarked paradigm cell with a form that ends in an unspoken character *e*, as in *dance*. The other paradigm cells in the 'silent-e' inflection class are filled by applying orthographic rules such as:

Progressive Aspect Cell – replace the final *e* of the unmarked form with the string *ing*, *dance* → *dancing*

Past Cell – substitute *ed*, *dance* → *danced*

Paradigm cells are mutually exclusive. In the English verbal paradigm, although English speakers can express progressive past actions with a grammatical construction, viz. *was eating*, there is no surface form of the lexeme *eat* that simultaneously fills both the *progressive* and the *past* cells of the verbal paradigm, **ateing*.

1.2 ParaMor

Paradigms and inflection classes, the inherent structure of natural language morphology, form the basis of ParaMor, our minimally supervised morphological induction algorithm. In ParaMor's first phase, we find sets of mutually exclusive strings which closely mirror the inflection classes of a language—although ParaMor does not differentiate between syncretic word forms of the same lexeme filling different paradigm cells, such as *ed*-suffixed forms which can fill either the *past* or the *passive* cells of English verbs. In ParaMor's second phase we employ the structured knowledge contained within the discovered inflection classes to segment word forms into morpheme-like pieces.

Languages employ a variety of morphological processes to arrive at grammatical word forms—processes including suffix-, prefix-, and infixation, reduplication, and template filling. Furthermore, the application of word forming processes often triggers phonological (or orthographic) change, such a as the dropped final *e* of the 'silent-e' inflection class, see Table 1. Despite the wide range of morphological processes and their complicating concomitant phonology, a large caste of inflection classes, and hence paradigms, can be represented as mutually exclusive substring substitutions. In the 'silent-e' inflection class, for example, the word-final strings *e.ed.es.ing* can be substituted for one another to produce the surface forms that fill the paradigm cells of lexemes belonging to this inflection class. In this paper we focus on identifying word final suffix morphology. While we focus on suffixes, the methods we employ can be straightforwardly generalized to prefixes and ongoing work seeks to model sequences of concatenative morphemes.

Inducing the morphology of a language from a naturally occurring text corpus is challenging. In languages with a rich morphological structure, surface forms filling particular cells of an inflection class may be relatively rare. In the Spanish newswire text over which we developed ParaMor there are 50,000 unique types. Among these types, instances of first and second person verb forms are few. The suffix *imos* which fills the *first person plural indicative present* cell for the *ir* verbal inflection class of Spanish occurs on only 77 unique lexemes. And yet we aim to identify candidate inflection classes which closely model the true inflection classes of a language, covering as many inflectional paradigm cells as possible.

Fortunately, we can leverage the paradigm structure of natural language morphology itself to retain many inflections which, because of data sparseness, might be missed if considered in isolation. ParaMor begins with a recall-centric search for partial candidate inflection classes. Many of the candidates which result from this initial search are incorrect. But intermingled with the false positives are candidates which collectively model significant fractions of true inflection classes. Hence, ParaMor's next step is to cluster the initial partial candidate inflection classes into larger groups. This clustering effectively uses the larger correct initial candidates as nuclei to which smaller correct candidates accrete. With as many initial true candidates as possible safely corralled with other candidates covering the same inflection class, ParaMor completes the paradigm discovery phase by discarding the large number of erroneous initially selected candidate inflection classes. Finally, with a strong grasp on the paradigm structure, ParaMor straightforwardly segments the words of a corpus into morphemes.

1.3 Related Work

In this section we highlight previously proposed minimally supervised approaches to the induction of morphology that, like ParaMor, draw on the unique structure of natural language morphology. One facet of NL morphological structure commonly leveraged by morphology induction algorithms is that morphemes are recurrent building blocks of words. Brent et al. (1995), Goldsmith (2001), and Creutz (2006) emphasize the building block nature of morphemes when they each use recurring word segments to efficiently encode a corpus. These approaches then hypothesize that those recurring segments which most efficiently encode a corpus are likely morphemes. Another technique that exploits morphemes as repeating sub-word segments encodes the lexemes of a corpus as a character tree, i.e. trie, (Harris, 1955; Hafer and Weis, 1974), or as a finite state automaton (FSA) over characters (Johnson, H. and Martin, 2003; Altun and M. Johnson, 2001). A trie or FSA conflates multiple instances of a morpheme into a single sequence of states. Because the choice of possible succeeding characters is highly constrained within a morpheme, branch points in the trie or FSA are likely morpheme boundaries. Often trie similarities are used as a first step followed by further processing to identify morphemes (Schone and Jurafsky, 2001).

The paradigm structure of NL morphology has also been previously leveraged. Goldsmith (2001) uses morphemes to efficiently encode a corpus, but he first groups morphemes into paradigm like structures he calls signatures. To date, the work that draws the most on paradigm structure is Snover (2002). Snover incorporates paradigm structure into a generative statistical model of morphology. Additionally, to discover paradigm like sets of suffixes, Snover designs and searches networks of partial paradigms. These networks are the direct inspiration for ParaMor's morphology scheme networks described in section 2.1.

2 ParaMor: Inflection Class Identification

2.1 Search

A Search Space: The first stage of ParaMor is a search procedure designed to identify partial inflection classes containing as many true productive suffixes of a language as possible. To search for these partial inflection classes we must first define a space to search over. In a naturally occurring corpus not all possible surface forms occur. In a corpus, each stem adhering to an inflection class will likely be observed in combination with only a subset of the suffixes in that inflection class. Each box in Figure 1 depicts a small portion of the empirical co-occurrence of suffixes and stems from a Spanish newswire corpus of 50,000 types. Each box in this figure contains a list of suffixes at the top in **bold**, together with the total number, and a few examples (in *italics*), of stems that occurred in separate word forms with each suffix in that box. For example, the box containing the suffixes **e**, **erá**, **ieron**, and **ió** contains the stems *deb* and *padec* because the word forms *debe*, *padece*, *deberá*, *padecerá*, etc. all occurred in the corpus. We call each possible pair of suffix and stem sets a *scheme*, and say that the **e.erá.ieron.ió** scheme covers the words *debe*, *padece,* etc. Note that a scheme contains both stems that occurred with exactly the set of suffixes in that scheme, as well as

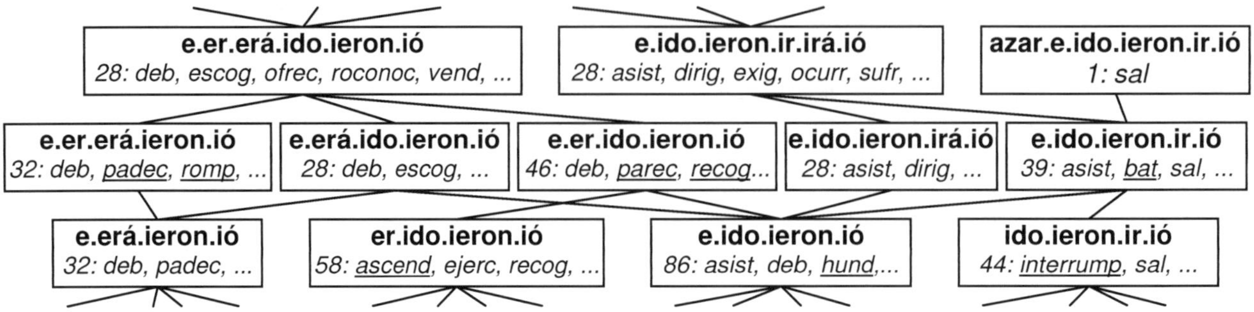

Figure 1: A small portion of a morphology scheme network—our search space of partial empirical inflection classes. This network was built from a Spanish Newswire corpus of 50,000 types, 1.26 million tokens. Each box contains a scheme. The suffixes of each scheme appear in **bold** at the top of each box. The total number of adherent stems for each scheme, together with a few exemplar stems, is in *italics*. Stems are underlined if they do not appear in any parent shown in this figure.

stems that occurred with suffixes beyond just those in the scheme. For example, in addition to the four suffixes **e**, **erá**, **ieron**, and **ió,** the stem *deb* occurred with the suffixes **er** and **ido**, as evident from the top left scheme **e.er.erá.ido.ieron.ió** which contains the stem *deb*. Intuitively, a scheme is a subset of the suffixes filling the paradigm cells of a true inflection class together with the stems that empirically occurred with that set of suffixes.

The schemes in Figure 1 cover portions of the *er* and the *ir* Spanish verbal inflection classes. The top left scheme of the figure contains suffixes in the *er* inflection class, while the top center scheme contains suffixes in the *ir* inflection class. The six suffixes in the top left scheme and the six suffixes in the top center scheme are just a few of the suffixes in the full *er* and *ir* inflection classes. As is fairly common for inflection classes across languages, the sets of suffixes in the Spanish *er* and *ir* inflection classes overlap. That is, verbs that belong to the *er* inflection class can take as a suffix certain strings of characters that verbs belonging to the *ir* inflection class can also take. The suffixes that are unique to the *er* verb inflection class in the top left scheme are **er** and **erá**; while the unique suffixes for the *ir* class in the top center scheme are **ir** and **irá**. In the third row of the figure, the scheme **e.ido.ieron.ió** contains only suffixes found in both the *er* and *ir* schemes.

While the example schemes in Figure 1 are correct and do occur in a real Spanish newswire corpus, the schemes are atypically perfect. There is only one suffix appearing in Figure 1 that is not a true suffix of Spanish—**azar** in the upper right scheme. In unsupervised morphology induction we do not know a priori the correct suffixes of a language. Hence, we form schemes by proposing candidate morpheme boundaries at every character boundary in every word, including the character boundary after the final character in each word form, to allow for empty suffixes.

Schemes of suffixes and their exhaustively co-occurring stems define a natural search space over partial inflection classes because schemes readily organize by the suffixes and stems they contain. We define a parent-child relationship between a parent scheme, P and a child scheme C, when P contains all the suffixes that C contains and when P contains exactly one more suffix than C. In Figure 1, parent child relations are represented by solid lines connecting boxed schemes. The scheme **e.er.erá.ido.ieron.ió**, for example, is the parent of three depicted children in Figure 1, one of which is **e.er.erá.ieron.ió**.

Our search strategy exploits a fundamental aspect of the relationship between parent and child schemes. Consider the number of stems in a parent scheme P as compared to the number of stems in any one of its children C. Since P contains all the suffixes which C contains, and because P only contains stems that occurred with every suffix in P, P can at most contain exactly the stems C contains and typically will contain fewer. In the Spanish corpus from which the scheme network of Figure 1 was built, 32 stems occur in forms with each of the five suffixes **e**, **er**, **erá**, **ieron**, and **ió** attached. But only 28 of these 32 stems occur in yet another form involving **ido**—the stem *deb* did but the stems *padec* and *romp* did not, for example.

A Search Strategy: To search for schemes which cover portions of the true inflection classes of a language, ParaMor's search starts at the bottom of the network. The lowest level in the scheme network consists of schemes which contain exactly one suffix together with all the stems that occurred in the corpus with that suffix attached. ParaMor considers each one-suffix scheme in turn beginning with that scheme containing the most stems, working toward schemes containing fewer. From each bottom scheme, ParaMor follows a single greedy upward path from child to parent. As long as an upward path takes at least one step, making it to a scheme containing two or more alternating suffixes, our search strategy accepts the terminal scheme of the path as likely modeling a portion of a true inflection class.

Each greedily chosen upward step is based on two criteria. The first criterion considers the number of adherent stems in the current scheme as compared to its parents' adherent sizes. A variety of statistics could judge the stem-strength of parent schemes: ranging from simple ratios through (dis)similarity measures, such as the dice coefficient or mutual information, to full fledged statistical tests. After experimenting with a range of such statistics we found, somewhat surprisingly, that measuring the ratio of parent stem size to child stem size correctly identifies parent schemes which contain only true suffixes just as consistently as more sophisticated tests. While a full report of our experiments is beyond the scope of this paper, the short explanation of this behavior is data sparseness. Many upward search steps start from schemes containing few stems. And when little data is available no statistic is particularly reliable.

Parent-child stem ratios have two additional computational advantages over other measures. First, they are quick to compute and second, the parent with the largest stem ratio is always that parent with the most stems. So, being greedy, each search step simply moves to that parent, P, with the most stems, as long as the parent-child stem ratio to P is large. The threshold above which a stem ratio is considered large enough to warrant an upward step is a free parameter. As the goal of this initial search stage is to identify schemes containing as wide a variety of productive suffixes as possible, we want to set the parent-child stem ratio threshold as low as possible. But a ratio threshold that is too small will allow search paths to schemes containing unproductive and spurious suffixes. In practice, for Spanish, we have found that setting the parent-child stem ratio cutoff much below 0.25 results in schemes that begin to include only marginally productive derivational suffixes. For this paper we leave the parent-child stem ratio cutoff parameter at 0.25.

Alone, stem strength assessments of parent schemes, such as parent-child stem ratios, falter as a search path nears the top of the morphology scheme network. Monotonically decreasing adherent stem size causes statistics that assess parents' stem-strength to become less and less reliable. Hence, the second criterion governing each search step helps to halt upward search paths before judging parents' worth becomes impossible. While there are certainly many possible stopping criteria, ParaMor's policy stops each upward search path when there is no parent scheme with more stems than it has suffixes. We devised this halting condition for two reasons. First, requiring each path scheme to contain more stems than suffixes attains high suffix recall. High recall results from setting a low bar for upward movement at the bottom of the network. Search paths which begin from schemes whose single suffix is rare in the text corpus can often take one or two upward search steps and reach a scheme containing the necessary three or four stems. Second, this halting criterion requires the top scheme of search paths that climb high in the network to contain a comparatively large number of stems. Reigning in high-reaching search paths before the stem count falls too far, captures path-terminal schemes which cover a large number of word types. In the second stage of ParaMor's inflection class identification phase these larger terminal schemes effectively vacuum up the useful smaller paths that result from the more rare suffixes. Figure 2 contains examples of schemes selected by ParaMor's initial search.

To evaluate ParaMor at paradigm identification, we hand compiled an answer key of the inflection classes of Spanish. This answer key contains nine productive inflection classes. Three contain the suffixes of the *ar*, *er*, and *ir* verbal inflection classes. There are two orthographically differentiated inflection classes for nouns in the answer key: one for nouns that form the plural by adding *s*, and one for nouns that take *es*. Adjectives in Spanish inflect for gender and number. Arguably, gender and number each constitute separate paradigms, each with two cells. But here we conflated these into a single inflection class with four cells. Finally, there are three inflection classes in our answer key covering Spanish clitics. Spanish verbal clitics behave orthographically as agglutinative sequences of suffixes.

1) **Ø.s** 5501 stems
2) **a.as.o.os** 892 stems
...
5) **a.aba.aban.ada.adas.ado.ados.an.ando.ar.aron.arse.ará.arán.ó** 25 stems
...
12) **a.aba.ada.adas.ado.ados.an.ando.ar.aron.ará.arán.e.en.ó** 21 stems
...
209) **e.er.ida.idas.ido.idos.imiento.ió** 9 stems
...
1590) **Ø.ipo** 4 stems
1591) **ido.idos.ir.iré** 6 stems
1592) **Ø.e.iu** 4 stems
1593) **iza.izado.izan.izar.izaron.izarán.izó** 8 stems
...

Figure 2: The suffixes of some schemes selected by the initial search over a Spanish corpus of 50,000 types. While some selected schemes contain large numbers of correct suffixes, such as the 1st, 2nd, 5th, 12th, 209th, and 1591st selected schemes; many others are incorrect collections of word final strings.

In a corpus of Spanish newswire text of 50,000 types and 1.26 million tokens, the initial search identifies schemes containing 92% of all ideal inflectional suffixes of Spanish, or 98% of the ideal suffixes that occurred at least twice in the corpus. There are selected schemes which contain portions of each of the nine inflection classes in the answer key. The high recall of the initial search comes, of course, at the expense of precision. While there are nine inflection-classes and 87 unique suffixes in the hand-built answer key for Spanish, 8339 schemes are selected containing 9889 unique candidate suffixes.

2.2 Clustering Partial Inflection Classes

While the third step of inflection class identification, discussed in Section 2.3, directly improves the initial search's low precision by filtering out bogus schemes, the second step, described here, conflates selected schemes which model portions of the same inflection class. Consider the fifth and twelfth schemes selected by ParaMor from our Spanish corpus, as shown in Figure 2. Both of these schemes contain a large number of suffixes from the Spanish *ar* verbal inflection class. And while each contains many overlapping suffixes, each possesses correct suffixes which the other does not. Meanwhile, the 1591st selected scheme contains four suffixes of the *ir* verbal inflection class, including the only instance of *iré* that occurs in any selected scheme. Containing only six stems, the 1591st scheme could accidentally be filtered out during the third phase of inflection class identification. Hence, the rationale for clustering initial selected schemes is two fold. First, by consolidating schemes which cover portions of the same inflection class we produce sets of suffixes which more closely model the paradigm structure of natural language morphology. And, second, corralling correct schemes safeguards against losing unique suffixes.

The clustering of schemes presents two unique challenges. First, we must avoid over-clustering schemes which model distinct inflection classes. As noted in Section 2.1, it is common, cross-linguistically, for the suffixes of inflection classes to overlap. Looking at Figure 2, we must be careful not to merge the 209th selected scheme, which models a portion of the *er* verbal inflection class, with the 1591st selected scheme, which models the *ir* class—despite these schemes sharing two suffixes, *ido* and *idos*. As the second challenge, the many small schemes which the search strategy produces act as distractive noise during clustering. While small schemes containing correct suffixes do exist, e.g. the 1591st scheme, the vast majority of schemes containing few stems and suffixes are incorrect collections of word final strings that happen to occur in corpus word forms attached to a small number of shared initial strings. ParaMor's clustering algorithm should, for example, avoid placing **Ø.s** and **Ø.ipo**, respectively the 1st and 1590th selected schemes, in the same cluster. Although **Ø.ipo** shares the null suffix with the valid nominal scheme **Ø.s**, the string 'ipo' is not a morphological suffix of Spanish.

To form clusters of related schemes while addressing both the challenge of observing a language's paradigm structure as well as the challenge of merging in the face of many small incorrectly selected schemes, ParaMor adapts greedy hierarchical agglomerative clustering. We modify vanilla bottom-up clustering by placing restrictions on which clusters are allowed to merge. The first restriction helps ensure that schemes modeling distinct but overlapping inflection classes remain separated. The restriction: do not place into the same cluster suffixes which share no stem in the corpus. This restriction retains separate clusters for separate inflection classes because a lexeme's stem occurring with suffixes unique to that lexeme's inflection class will not occur with suffixes unique to some other inflection class.

Alone, requiring all pairs of suffixes in a cluster to occur in the corpus with some common stem will not prevent small bogus schemes, such as **Ø.ipo** from attaching to correct schemes, such as **Ø.s**—the **ipo.s** scheme contains two 'stems,' the word form initial strings 'ma' and 't'. And so a second restriction is required. This second restriction employs a heuristic specifically adapted to ParaMor's initial search strategy. As discussed in Section 2.1, in addition to many schemes which contain only few suffixes, ParaMor's initial network search also identifies multiple overlapping schemes containing significant subsets of the suffixes in an inflection class. The 5th, 12th, and 209th selected schemes of Figure 2 are three such larger schemes. ParaMor restricts cluster merges heuristically by requiring at least one large scheme for each small scheme the cluster contains, where we measure the size of a scheme as the number of unique word forms it covers. The threshold size above which schemes are considered large is the second of ParaMor's two free parameters. The scheme size threshold is reused during ParaMor's filtering stage. We discuss the unsupervised procedure we use to set the size threshold when we present the details of cluster filtering in Section 2.3.

We have found that with these two cluster restrictions in place, the particular metric we use to measure the similarity of scheme-clusters does not significantly affect clustering. For the experiments we report here, we measure the similarity of scheme-clusters as the cosine between the sets of all possible stem-suffix pairs the clusters contain. A stem-suffix pair occurs in a cluster if some scheme belonging to that cluster contains both that stem and that suffix. With these adaptations, we allow agglomerative clustering to proceed until there are no more clusters that can legally be merged.

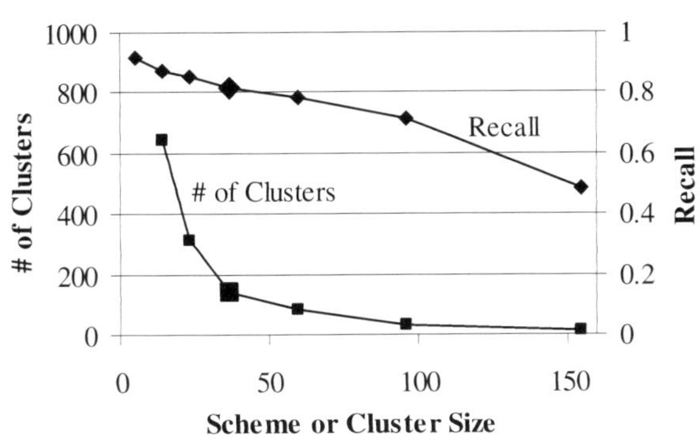

Figure 3: The # of clusters and their recall of unique Spanish suffixes as the scheme-cluster size cutoff is varied. The value of each function at the threshold we use in all experiments reported in this paper is that of the larger symbol.

2.3 Filtering of Inflection Classes

With most valid schemes having found a safe haven in a cluster with other schemes modeling the same inflection class, we turn our attention to improving scheme-cluster precision. ParaMor applies a series of filters, culling out unwanted scheme-clusters. The first filter is closely related to the cluster restriction on scheme size discussed in Section 2.2. ParaMor discards all unclustered schemes falling below the size threshold used during clustering. Figure 3 graphs the number of Spanish clusters which survive this size-based filtering step as the threshold size is varied. Figure 3 also contains a plot of the recall of unique Spanish suffixes as a function of this threshold. As the size threshold is increased the number of remaining clusters quickly drops. But suffix recall only slowly falls during the steep decline in cluster count, indicating ParaMor discards mostly bogus schemes containing illicit suffixes. Because recall is relatively stable, the exact size threshold we use should have only a minor effect on ParaMor's final morphological analyses. In fact, we have not fully explored the ramifications various threshold values have on the final morphological word segmentations, but have simply picked a reasonable setting, 37 covered word types. At this threshold, the number of scheme-clusters is reduced by more than 98%, while the number of unique candidate suffixes in any cluster is reduced by more than 85%. Note that the initial number of selected schemes, 8339, falls outside the scale of Figure 3.

Of the scheme-clusters which remain after size based filtering is complete, by far the largest category of incorrect clusters contains schemes which, like the 1593rd selected scheme, shown in Figure 2, incorrectly hypothesize morpheme boundaries one or more characters to the left of the true boundary. To filter out these incorrectly segmented clusters we use a technique inspired by Harris (1955). For each initial string common to all suffixes in the cluster, for each scheme in the cluster, we examine the network scheme containing the suffixes formed by stripping the initial string from the scheme's suffixes. We then measure the entropy of leftward trie characters of the stripped scheme. If the entropy is large, then the character stripped scheme is likely at a morpheme boundary and the original scheme is likely modeling an incorrect morpheme boundary. This algorithm would throw out the 1593rd selected scheme because the stems in the scheme **a.ado.an.ar.aron.arán.ó** end in a wide variety of characters, yielding high trie entropy, and signaling a likely morpheme boundary. Because we apply morpheme boundary filtering after we have clustered, the redundancy of the many schemes in the cluster makes this filter quite robust, letting us set the cutoff parameter as low as we like avoiding another free parameter.

2.4 Segmentation and Evaluation

Word segmentation is our final step of morphological analysis. ParaMor's current segmentation algorithm is perhaps the most simple paradigm inspired segmentation algorithm possible. Essentially, ParaMor strips off suffixes which likely participate in a paradigm. To segment any word, w, ParaMor identifies all scheme-clusters that contain a non-empty suffix that matches a word final string of w. For each such matching suffix, $f \in C$, where C is the cluster containing f, we strip f from w obtaining a stem t. If there is some second suffix $f' \in C$ such that $t.f'$ is a word form found in either of the training or the test corpora, then ParaMor proposes a segmentation of w between t and f. ParaMor, here, identifies f and f' as mutually exclusive suffixes from the same paradigm. If ParaMor finds no complex analysis, then we propose w itself as the sole analysis of the word. Note that for each word form, ParaMor may propose multiple separate segmentation analyses each containing a single proposed stem and suffix.

To evaluate ParaMor's morphological segmentations we follow the methodology of Morpho Challenge 2007 (Kurimo et al., 2007), a minimally supervised morphology induction competition. Word segmentations are evaluated in Morpho Challenge 2007 by comparing against hand annotated morphological analyses. The correctness of proposed morphological analyses is computed in Morpho Challenge 2007 by comparing pairs of word forms which share portions of their analyses. Recall is measured by first sampling pairs of words from the answer analyses which share a stem or morphosyntactic feature and then noting if that pair of word forms shares a morpheme in any of their proposed analyses. Precision is measured analogously, sampling morpheme-sharing pairs of words from the proposed analyses and noting if that pair of words shares a feature in any correct analysis of those words.

We evaluate ParaMor on two languages not examined during the development of ParaMor's induction algorithms: English and German. And we evaluate with each of these two languages at two tasks:

1. Analyzing inflectional morphology alone
2. Jointly analyzing inflectional and derivational morphology.

We constructed Morpho Challenge 2007 style answer keys for each language and each task using the Celex database (Burnage, 1990). The English and German corpora we test over are the corpora available through Morpho Challenge 2007. The English corpus contains nearly 385,000 types, while the German corpus contains more than 1.26 million types. ParaMor induced paradigmatic scheme-clusters over these larger corpora by reading just the top 50,000 most frequent types. But with the scheme-clusters in hand, ParaMor segmented all the types in each corpus.

We compare ParaMor to Morfessor v0.9.2 (Creutz, 2006), a state-of-the-art minimally supervised morphology induction algorithm. Morfessor has a single free parameter. To make for stiff competition, we report results for Morfessor at that parameter setting which maximized F_1 on each separate test scenario. We did not vary the two free parameters of ParaMor, but hold each of ParaMor's parameters at a setting which produced reasonable *Spanish* suffix sets, see sections 2.1-2.2. Table 2 contains the evaluation results. To estimate the variance of our experimental results we measured Morpho Challenge 2007 style precision, recall, and F_1 on multiple non-overlapping pairs of 1000 feature-sharing words.

Neither ParaMor nor Morfessor arise in Table 2 as clearly superior. Each algorithm outperforms the other at F_1 in some scenario. Examining precision and recall is more illuminating. ParaMor attains particularly high recall of inflectional affixes for both English and German. We conjecture that ParaMor's strong performance at identifying inflectional morphemes comes from closely modeling the natural paradigm structure of language. Conversely, Morfessor places its focus on precision and does not rely on any property exclusive to inflectional (or derivational) morphology. Hence,

	Inflectional Morphology Only								Inflectional & Derivational Morphology							
	English				German				English				German			
	P	R	F_1	σ	P	R	F_1	σ	P	R	F_1	σ	P	R	F_1	σ
Morfessor	53.3	47.0	**49.9**	1.3	38.7	44.2	41.2	0.8	**73.6**	34.0	46.5	1.1	**66.9**	37.1	**47.7**	0.7
ParaMor	33.0	**81.4**	47.0	0.9	42.8	**68.6**	**52.7**	0.8	48.9	53.6	**51.1**	0.8	60.0	33.5	43.0	0.7

Table 2: ParaMor segmentations compared to Morfessor's (Creutz, 2006) evaluated for **P**recision, **R**ecall, $\mathbf{F_1}$, and standard deviation of F_1, **σ**, in four scenarios. Segmentations over English and German are each evaluated against correct morphological analyses consisting, on the left, of inflectional morphology only, and on the right, of both inflectional and derivational morphology.

Morfessor attains high precision with reasonable recall when graded against an answer key containing both inflectional and derivational morphology.

We are excited by ParaMor's strong performance and are eager to extend our algorithm. We believe the precision of ParaMor's simple segmentation algorithm can be improved by narrowing down the proposed analyses for each word to the most likely. Perhaps ParaMor and Morfessor's vastly different strategies for morphology induction could be combined into a hybrid strategy more successful than either alone. And ambitiously, we hope to extend ParaMor to analyze languages with agglutinative sequences of affixes by generalizing the definition of a scheme.

Acknowledgements

The research reported in this paper was funded in part by NSF grant number IIS-0121631.

References

Altun, Yasemin, and Mark Johnson. "Inducing SFA with є-Transitions Using Minimum Description Length." *Finite State Methods in Natural Language Processing Workshop at ESSLLI* Helsinki: 2001.

Brent, Michael R., Sreerama K. Murthy, and Andrew Lundberg. "Discovering Morphemic Suffixes: A Case Study in MDL Induction." *The Fifth International Workshop on Artificial Intelligence and Statistics* Fort Lauderdale, Florida, 1995.

Burnage, Gavin. *Celex—A Guide for Users.* Springer, Centre for Lexical information, Nijmegen, the Netherlands, 1990.

Creutz, Mathias. "Induction of the Morphology of Natural Language: Unsupervised Morpheme Segmentation with Application to Automatic Speech Recognition." Ph.D. Thesis in Computer and Information Science, Report D13. Helsinki: University of Technology, Espoo, Finland, 2006.

Goldsmith, John. "Unsupervised Learning of the Morphology of a Natural Language." *Computational Linguistics* 27.2 (2001): 153-198.

Hafer, Margaret A., and Stephen F. Weiss. "Word Segmentation by Letter Successor Varieties." *Information Storage and Retrieval* 10.11/12 (1974): 371-385.

Harris, Zellig. "From Phoneme to Morpheme." *Language* 31.2 (1955): 190-222. Reprinted in Harris 1970.

Harris, Zellig. *Papers in Structural and Transformational Linguists.* Ed. D. Reidel, Dordrecht 1970.

Johnson, Howard, and Joel Martin. "Unsupervised Learning of Morphology for English and Inuktitut." *Human Language Technology Conference / North American Chapter of the Association for Computational Linguistics (HLT-NAACL).* Edmonton, Canada: 2003.

Kurimo, Mikko, Mathias Creutz, and Matti Varjokallio. "Unsupervised Morpheme Analysis – Morpho Challenge 2007." March 26, 2007. <http://www.cis.hut.fi/morphochallenge2007/>

Schone, Patrick, and Daniel Jurafsky. "Knowledge-Free Induction of Inflectional Morphologies." *North American Chapter of the Association for Computational Linguistics (NAACL).* Pittsburgh, Pennsylvania: 2001. 183-191.

Snover, Matthew G. "An Unsupervised Knowledge Free Algorithm for the Learning of Morphology in Natural Languages." Sever Institute of Technology, Computer Science Saint Louis, Missouri: Washington University, M.S. Thesis, 2002.

Dynamic Correspondences: An Object-Oriented Approach to Tracking Sound Reconstructions

Tyler Peterson
University of British Columbia
E270-1866 Main Mall
Vancouver, BC, Canada V6T-1Z1
tylerrp@interchange.ubc.ca

Gessiane Picanço
Universidade Federal do Pará
Belém – Pará – Brasil
CEP 66075-110
picanco.g@hotmail.com

Abstract

This paper reports the results of a research project that experiments with cross-tabulation in aiding phonemic reconstruction. Data from the Tupí stock was used, and three tests were conducted in order to determine the efficacy of this application: the confirmation and challenging of a previously established reconstruction in the family; testing a new reconstruction generated by our model; and testing the upper limit of simultaneous, multiple correspondences across several languages. Our conclusion is that the use of cross tabulations (implemented within a database as *pivot tables*) offers an innovative and effective tool in comparative study and sound reconstruction.

1 Introduction

In the past decade databases have transitioned from a useful resource as a searchable repository of linguistic tokens of some type, to an actual tool capable of not only organising vast amounts of data, but executing complex statistical functions and queries on the data it stores. These advances in database technology complement those made in computational linguistics, and both have recently begun to converge on the domain of comparative and historical linguistic research.

This paper contributes to this line of research through describing the database project *Base de Dados para Estudos Comparativos – Tupí* (BDEC-T) (Database for Comparative Studies – Tupí), which is part of a larger research program investigating the phonemic reconstruction of the Tupí languages. The database component of the BDEC-T is designed to capitalise on the functionality of cross-tabulation tables, commonly known as *pivot tables*, a recent innovation in the implementation SQL queries in many database and spreadsheet applications. Pivot tables can be described as an 'object-oriented' representation of SQL statements in the sense that columns of data are treated as objects, which allow the user to create multidimensional views of the data by 'dragging and dropping' columns into various sorting arrangements. We have found that this dynamic, multidimensional manipulation of the data can greatly aid the researcher in identifying relationships and correspondences that are otherwise difficult to summarize by other query types.

In this paper we report on the results of an experiment that tests the applicability of pivot tables to language data, in particular, the comparative and historical reconstruction of the proto-phonemes in a language family. In doing this, three tests were conducted:

1. The confirmation and challenging of a 'manual' and/or previously established reconstruction of a proto-language, Proto-Tupí;

2. The testing of a new reconstruction generated by our model, and checking it against a manual reconstruction;

3. The testing the upper limit of simultaneous, multiple correspondences across several languages.

Proceedings of Ninth Meeting of the ACL Special Interest Group in Computational Morphology and Phonology, pages 126–133,
Prague, June 2007.

It is argued that this type of object-oriented implementation of SQL statements using pivot tables, offers two unique features: the first is the ability to check several one-to-one and one-to-many correspondences simultaneously across several languages; and secondly, the ability to dynamically survey the language-internal distribution of segments and their features.

The former feature represents a notable advantage over other 'manual' methods, as the reconstructed forms may be entered in the database as proto-languages, which can be continually revised and tested against all other languages. The latter feature offers the ability to check the language-internal distribution of the (proto-)segments which will aid in preventing possible cases of skewed occurrences, as is shown below. Basic statistical analyses, such as numbers of occurrences, can also be reported, graphed and plotted by the pivot tables, thus providing further details of individual languages and proto-languages, and, ultimately, a more quantitatively reliable analysis.

The net outcome of this is the presentation of a practical methodology that is easily and quickly implementable, and that makes use of a function that many people already have with their database or spreadsheet.

1.1 The Data

The Tupí stock of language families is concentrated in the Amazon river basin of Brazil (and areas of neighbouring countries) and comprises 10 families of languages: Arikém, Awetí, Juruna, Mawé, Mondé, Mundurukú, Puruborá, Ramarama, Tuparí, and Tupí-Guaraní (Rodrigues 1958; revised in Rodrigues 1985), totaling approximately 64 languages. Tupí-Guaraní is the largest family with more than 40 languages, while the other families range from one language (e.g. Awetí, Puruborá) to six languages (e.g. Mondé). From these, the Tupí-Guaraní family is the only family that has been mostly analized from a historical point of view (e.g. Lemle 1971, Jensen 1989, Schleicher 1998, Mello 2000, etc.); there is also a proposal for Proto-Tuparí (Tuparí family), by Moore and Galúcio (1993), and Proto-Mundurukú (Mundurukú family), by Picanço (2005). A preliminary reconstruction at level of the Tupí stock was proposed by Rodrigues (1995), in which he reconstructs a list of 67 items for Proto-Tupí (see further details below). The BDEC-T also includes these reconstructed languages, as they allow us to compare the results obtained from the database with the results of previous, manual historical-comparative studies.

2 The Application: Design and Method

The BDEC-T was initially developed as repository database for language data from various Tupí languages described above, with the purpose of allowing the user to generate lists of word and phoneme correspondences through standard boolean search queries or SQL statements. These lists aided the researcher in exploring different correspondences in the course of a proto-phoneme or word reconstruction. The BDEC-T is implemented within MS Access 2003, which provides the user an interface for entering language data that is then externally linked to tab-delimited text files in order to preserve its declarative format.[1] This also allowed flexibility in accessing the data for whatever purpose in the platform or program of the researcher's choosing.

At present, the BDEC-T for the Tupí stock contains a glossary of 813 words and up to 3,785 entries distributed across 15 Tupían languages. Approximately 18% of this 813-word list appear to have cognates in the majority of languages entered so far, and which can be used as reference for a reliable set of robust cognates across the entire Tupí stock.[2] This number is continually increasing as more languages are entered in the database, and at least 50% of the glossary is filled up for all languages. The average number of entries for each language varies considerably as it depends largely on available sources; yet, in general, the average is of approximately 250 words per language (i.e. about 30%).

[1]The choice of using a proprietary database such as MS Access is mostly a practical one: after considering various factors such as programming, maintenance, distribution and other practical issues, we decided that a database of this type should be useable by researchers with little or no programming experience, as it is fairly easy to learn and modify (see also Bredenkamp, Sadler and Spencer (1998: 149) for similar arguments). It should also be noted that all the procedures outlined here are implementable in open source database and spreadsheet programs such as OpenOffice Calc and Base (vers. 2.3).

[2]There is a separate function in the BDEC-T for assessing and tracking cognates and how they map to semantic sets (see Peterson 2007a for details).

2.1 Data entry and Segmentation

Each of the 65 languages and 4 proto-languages in BDEC-T is associated with its own data entry form. Each data entry form is divided into three main parts:

1. The *word entry fields* where the word for that language is entered (along with two other optional features);
2. The *comparison viewer* that contains fields which simultaneously display that same word in the all the other languages in the database;
3. The *segmentation section* which contains an arrangement fields for recording segment data.

The structure of the stored data is straightforward: the data entered in these forms is stored in a master table where all of the languages are represented as columns. Glosses are the rows, where each gloss is assigned a unique, autogenerated number in the master record when it is entered into the database. This serves as the primary key for all the translations of that gloss across all of the languages.

The third component of the language data entry form, the segmentation section (Fig. 1), contains a linear arrangement of ten columns, S1 to S10, and three rows, each cell of which corresponds to a field. The first row of the ten columns are fields where the user can enter in the segmentation of that particular word, which contains the segments themselves. The second and third rows correspond to optional features (F) that are associated with that segment. In this particular version F1 is unused, while F2 encodes syllable structure (i.e. 'O' onset, 'N' nucleus).[3]

For example, Figure 1 is a screenshot of a portion of the segmentation section in the language data entry form for Mundurukú. The word being entered is 'moon', and the word in Mundurukú is *káʃi*. Segment slots S3 to S6 are used to segment the word.

As a convention, a word will typically be segmented starting with the S3 slot, and not with S1. The reason for this is to allow for at least two segment fields (S1 and S2) to accommodate cognates in

[3]There is no restriction on the kind of information that can be stored in the two Feature fields. However, in order for them to be useful, they would need to contain a limited set of comparable features across all the languages.

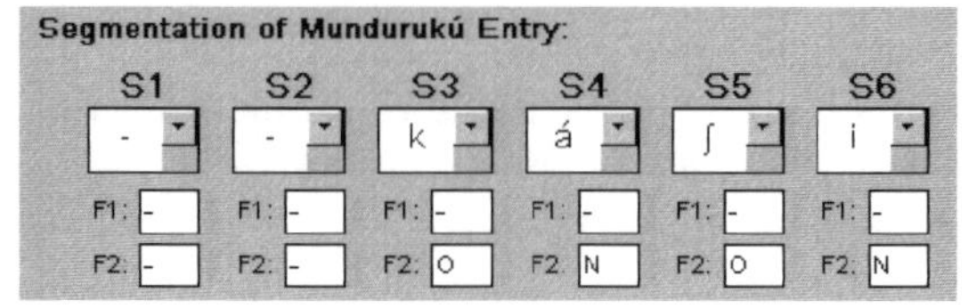

Figure 1: Screenshot of a portion of the Segmentation section in the Mundurukú Data entry form.

Segmentation slot	S1	S2	S3	S4	S5
Avá-Canoeiro			ɨ	t	ɨ
Guajá		w	ɨ	t	ɨ
Araweté	i	w	i	t	ɨ

Table 1: Segmentation of *'wind'*

other languages that have segments that occur before S3, but are entered into the database at a later time. This is done in order to maintain a consistency between correspondences, regardless of what slot they are in the data base. In other words, we need to be prepared to handle cases that are shown in Tables 1 and 2 above. If the Avá Canoeiro word for 'wind' is entered first in Table 1, it is prudent to have segment slots available for languages that are entered later that may have additional segments occurring before. Guajá and Araweté were entered into the database after Avá Canoeiro, and both have additional segments. Keeping S1 and S2 available as a general rule can accommodate these cases.

Our purpose in designing the segmentation component of the form this way was to give the researcher complete control over how words are segmented. This also allows the researcher to cross-check their segmentations in real time with those in the other languages already in the database, which can be done in the comparison viewer (not shown due to space limitations). This is essential for more complicated cases, such as those in Table 2, where there are not only word edge mismatches, but also gaps and (grammaticalized) morphological boundaries that need to be properly corresponded. The significance of this will be demonstrated below.[4]

[4]Cases where gaps result in languages already entered would require the user to go back to the other languages entered and re-segment them to include the corresponding gap. This would be the case if *iap* was entered without the gap in S3 before the other languages in Table 2. This is facilitated within the database: multiple language forms can be open simultaneously,

Segmentation slot	S1	S2	S3	S4	S5
Avá-Canoeiro		ɨ		a	p
Guajá		u	ʔ	ɨ	
Mbyá	h –	u	ʔ	ɨ	
Kamayurá	h	ɨ	ʔ	ɨ	p

Table 2: Segmentation of *'arrow'*

The data entered in the segmentation section of a language's data entry form is stored in language-specific tables, which has columns for each of the ten segments, and columns recording the two optional features associated with that segment. All of the segment data in the language-specific tables are coordinated by the primary key generated and kept in the master table. The next subsection describes how this segmental data can be used in two specific ways: 1) to track correspondences between languages for a particular cognate or segment slot; and 2), for monitoring the language-internal distribution of segments. We propose that this is achieved through using cross-tabulations of the segment data recorded in each column, and outline a practical implementation of this is using pivot tables.

2.2 Cross-tabulation: 'Pivot tables'

Access 2003 includes a graphical implementation of SQL statements in the form of cross tabulations, or *pivot tables*, which provide the user an interface with which they can manipulate multiple columns of data to create dynamic, multi-dimensional organizations of the data. There are three basic reasons for organizing data into a pivot table, all of which are relevant to the task at hand: first, to summarize data contained in lengthy lists into a compact format; secondly, to find relationships within that data that are otherwise hard to see because of the amount of detail; and thirdly, to organize the data into a format that is easy to chart. Pivot tables are dynamic because columns of data are treated as objects that can be moved, or literally 'swapped' in, out our around in relation to other columns. They are multi-dimensional because column data can be organized along either axis, yielding different 'snapshots' of the data. It is this kind of functionality that will be capitalised on in examining correspondences between columns of segment data (S1-10) across any number of languages in the database.

A cross tabulation displays the joint distribution of two or more variables. They are usually presented as a contingency table which describes the distribution of two or more variables simultaneously. Thus, cross tabulation allows us to examine frequencies of observations that belong to specific categories on more than one variable. By examining these frequencies, we can identify relations between cross-tabulated variables. Typically, only variables with a relatively small number of different meaningful values are cross tabulated. We suggest that phonemes fit this criteria, as there is a finite and relatively low number of total unique phonemes that can ever be potentially cross tabulated.

For example, Figure 2 (below) is a screen shot of a pivot table generated in the BDEC-T that shows the distribution of word and morpheme-initial voiceless stops in Mundurukú in relation to those in the same position for three other languages: Karitiana, Gavião and Karo. This was achieved in the following way: as described above, we assume that the word-initial segment for most words is S3. The S3 column for Mundurukú is then taken to the 'drop field' (shaded grey), where all of the values in the S3 of Mundurukú become dependent variables. The S3 columns for Karitiana, Gavião and Karo become independent variables, which allow us to monitor the distribution of voiceless stops in these languages in relation to the S3 segments in Mundurukú. In essence, Mundurukú S3 becomes a sort function on any other S3 columns to the right of it.[5]

Where this method becomes effective is when we 'swap' out Mundurukú S3 and replace it with Gavião S3, which is done by pulling the column header and placing it into the grey 'drop field'. This is shown in Figure 3 below. What Figure 3 immediately demonstrates is the asymmetric correspondence between Mundurukú and Gavião for S3: broadly speaking, the correspondences between Mundurukú and Karitiana, Gavião and Karo are more general, whereas the same correspondences for

or switched between by the master switchboard.

[5] Given space considerations, the data in these Tables are just samples - the voiceless stop series was picked from a separate list which acts as a filter on the segments in the Mundurukú S3. Cells where there is a gap '-' do not represent a gap or lack of correspondence, but rather the word for that language possibly hasn't been segmented yet (gaps are represented by '∅')

M	K	G	K	Mund	Karitia	Gavião	Karo	#	Gloss
k	ŋ	g	n	kíp	ɨita ŋep	git	nãp?	15	piolho
	ø	g	–	káʃi	oti	gát ti	-	44	lua
	?	–	–	kə̃j	eɲ / ?ej	-	ɨ-ganã	69	terra-1
	–	k	–	kədá	-	gakoráá	-	71	procurar
	g/ŋ	g	n	ikopí	ŋop / gop	gap	nãp	12	caba
	ŋ	g	–	ikopí	ŋɨp / gɨp	góôɤ-aá	-	13	cupim
p	–	b	m	pə̨jbə́	moroɲa	baj	mãjgãra	27	cobra
	–	–	p	pə̨	-	bâbe / ci-pabı	pə̃	37	braço
	–	b	p	pík	peɲetet	ő̃ő̃-baa	pək	60	queimar
	p	–	–	pə	pɨ	–	i-pábe	36	mão
	p	b	p	poʃi	pɨti	ő̃-batĩi	pi?ti-rem	6	pesado
t	s	z/s	c	tap	sop	zêp / sép	a?-cap	17	pêlo
	–	c	–	təp	-	cap	na?jop cɨ?	20	folha-2
	s	z	c	tajʃi	sooɲ	ő̃-zaj / ci-zaj	a?-cej	32	esposa
	s	c	c	ti	se	ci	-ci/ɨ	24	líquido
	s	z/s	j	top	ɨ-sɨp	ő̃-zop / ci-sop	ijõ̃m	25	pai-1
	ɲ	j	j	tə̃j	ɲõɲ	ẽẽ-jẽẽj	jə̃j	33	dente
	–	s	c	tap	–	sép	a?cap	18	pena
	s	z/s	c	patét	sat	zêt / ci-set	cet	11	nome

Figure 2: Screenshot of a pivot table for voiceless stops in Mundurukú (shaded) corresponding with Karitiana, Gavião and Karo in BDEC-T.

G	M	K	K	Mund	Karitiana	Gavião	Karo	#	Gloss
k	k	–	–	kadá	-	gakoráá	-	71	procurar
	ʃ	k	k	ʃét	kat	két	i-ket	9	dormir
p	–	p	-	ŋə̨bá	pa?ep / papɨ	pepó-tẽẽ	-	38	asa
t	tʃ	-	t	tʃó / dʒó	-	ma-tóó	top	47	ver

Figure 3: Screenshot of a pivot table for voiceless stops in Gavião (shaded) corresponding with Mundurukú, Karitiana and Karo in BDEC-T.

Gavião are more restricted.

There is no restriction on the number of independent or dependent variables, and this can be used to investigate the language-internal distribution of segments. Figure 4 shows how the segment data in S3 and S4 from the same language can be used in a pivot table, allowing the user to track the distribution of certain word or morpheme-initial segments and the segments that follow them. This arrangement gives us a snapshot of consonant-vowel patterns in Karo, where S3 has been additionally filtered to show the distribution of vowels that follow the palatals [c] and [j].

One important advantage to this arrangement of data and the use of pivot tables is the potential for tracking multiple correspondences across several languages simultaneously. So far, this is only limited by processor speed and viewing space. We have tested up to five segment correspondences (i.e. S3-8) across three languages, or one correspondence (i.e.

3	4	Karo	Número	Gloss
c	a	a?-cap	17	pêlo
		a-capóp	59	cauda-1
	á	cán	49	fogo/lenha
	e	cet	11	nome
	ə	a?cəp	18	pena
	ej	a?-cej	32	esposa
	ĩ	a?-cĩn	53	flor
	ɨ	cɨ?	19	folha-1
	I/ɨ	-ci/ɨ	24	líquido
	Total			
j	a	jate	55	queixada-1
		ja?o	62	calango-1
		jajo	28	tatu-1
	ã	jãj	33	dente
	o	jokãn	22	tucano
	õ	ijõm	25	pai-1

Figure 4: Screenshot of a pivot table for language-internal distribution of [c] and [j] morpheme and syllable-initially in Karo.

S3) for as many as ten languages simultaneously. Given that most words in the Tupí language family have on average three to five segments, the former of these amounts to the ability of corresponding the segments of entire words simultaneously. Considering that any segment column can be swapped in and out dynamically, this adds a substantial amount of power in tracking single correspondences simultaneously across a variety of languages, proto-languages, and potentially even entire families.

Various statistics can be applied to these pivot tables, where the results can be graphed and exported. The analyst may now take these results and proceed with the appropriate detailed investigation, an example of which is presented in the following sections.

3 Proto-Tupí and Mundurukú

To demonstrate the efficacy of this approach, we show now the results obtained with the BDEC-T and the use of pivot tables, and compare them with the results of a previously established set of sound correspondences and reconstructed proto-phonemes. For this, we chose Proto-Tupí, for which Rodrigues (1995) reconstructed 67 lexical proto-forms and established a consonant inventory composed of four complex series of stops, divided into plain, labialized (still uncertain), palatalized, and glottalized (ejectives), shown Table 3.

Rodrigues based his analysis on various synchronic reflexes found in several Tupían languages,

Plain	p	t, ʦ	ʧ	k
Labialized	(p^{w})	w		(k^{w})
Palatalized		t^{j}		k^{j}
Glottalized	p^{ʔ}, (p^{ʔw})	t^{ʔ}, ʦ^{ʔ}	ʧ^{ʔ}	k^{ʔ}, (k^{ʔw})

Table 3: Proto-Tupí stop series (Rodrigues 1995)

Rodrigues		**BDEC-T**		**Rodrigues**		**BDEC-T**	
P-T	Mund.	P-T	Mund.	P-T	Mund.	P-T	Mund.
*p	p	*p	p	*ʧ	ʃ	*ʧ	ʃ
			∅		ʧ		ʧ
			ps		ʤ		ʤ
			p/b				
*p^{ʔ}	b	*p^{ʔ}	b	*ʧ^{ʔ}	t	*ʧ^{ʔ}	t
			p		d		d
*t	n	*t	n	*ʦ	ʤ	*ʦ	ʤ
			s				ʧ, ʤ
			ʧ		ʃ		ʃ
			t/n				
*t^{ʔ}	d	*t^{ʔ}	d	*ʔ	ʔ	*ʔ	ʔ
			ʤ		∅	*VʔV	V̰
			t/d				
*k	k	*k	k	*k^{ʔ}	ʔ	*k^{ʔ}	ʔ
			ʃ				

Table 4: The correspondence sets as proposed by Rodrigues (1995) compared with those generated by the BDEC-T.

including Mundurukú. Here we compare the correspondence sets postulated by Rodrigues and compare them to those generated by the BDEC-T. The results of the pivot table analysis are shown in Table 4. Note that the BDEC-T predicts a larger set of correspondences than those posited by Rodrigues. However, there are a few cases where both lists agree; for example, for Proto-Tupí *ʧ which corresponds to ʃ, ʧ and ʤ in both cases.

Another important result obtained with the BDEC-T is the possibility of relating other types of segmental information. For example, Mundurukú exhibits a feature that makes it distinct from any other Tupían language: it is the only Tupían language known to make a phonological contrast between modal and creaky (laryngealised) vowels (Picanço 2005). Mundurukú phonation types are crucial for any reconstruction at the stock level – especially in the case of the ejectives proposed by Rodrigues – but this was completely ignored in his proposal. As shown in Table 5 (on the following page), some Proto-Tupí sequences *(C)VʔV yielded (C)V̰ sequences (where the tilde underneath a vowel marks creaky voice on the vowel).

	S1	S2	S3	S4	S5	S6
Proto-Tupí: **upiʔa*	∅	u	p	i	**ʔ**	**a**
Mundurukú: *topsa̰*	t	o	ps	∅	∅	**a̰**
Mekéns: *upia*	∅	u	p	i	∅	**a**

Table 5: *(C)VʔV corresponding with (C)V̰

A comparison that considers only a segment-to-segment correspondence will mistakenly posit the correspondence set *ʔ/∅ for both Mundurukú and Sakirabiá (Mekéns, Tuparí family), when the correspondence is in fact *ʔ/∅ for Sakirabiá but *(C)VʔV/(C)V̰ for Mundurukú. This is true for Rodrigues' analysis, which mistakenly established that "in Mundurukú [the glottal stop] has dropped" (1995: 6). The BDEC-T, on the other hand, allows us to compare features to segments, and to examine various correspondences of segments in a sequence. This is a particular advantage as there will be no missing information. With this, this unique property of Mundurukú, specifically creaky voice, can be explained historically in a principled way.

3.1 Language-internal distribution

A major feature offered by the BDEC-T is the possibility of examining the distribution of segments within the same language, which allow us to better capture the proper environment for correspondences between languages. As Picanço (2005) notes, phonotactic restrictions may, in many cases, be gaps left behind by historical changes. Table 6 provides an example of the distribution of the pairs plain-glottalized stops. At least in the case of *p versus *p^{ʔ}, the only occurrences of the latter is preceding the high central vowel *ɨ; in this environment, both consonants appear to contrast as *p also occurs before *ɨ. In the case of the coronal pairs *t/*t^{ʔ} and *ʧ/*ʧ^{ʔ}, there is no occurrence of the first pair before *ɨ, whereas *ʧ/*ʧ^{ʔ} occur mostly in this environment. As for *ʦ versus *ʦ^{ʔ}, these also appear to be in complementary distribution. By using

p	e	pˀ	ɨ	t	ã	tˀ	a
	ɨ				a		i
	i				ĩ		u
	o				ũ		
					u		
ʧ	ɨ	ʧˀ	ɨ	ʦ	u	ʦˀ	a
			a		ɨ		

Table 6: Language-internal distribution of segments

pivot tables, the analyst is able to easily monitor and track distributional gaps or contrasts and so provide a more systematic diachronic analysis.

Another case which illustrates the applicability of pivot tables in arranging segment data concerns the vowels. Rodrigues' comparison produced vowel correspondences between Proto-Tupí and Mundurukú. Again we compare his findings with those detected by the database: Table 7 compares the oral vowel correspondences as in Rodrigues (1995) with those obtained by the pivot tables in the BDEC-T, supplemented by the total of words with the respective correspondence.

In Rodrigues' analysis, the correspondences between proto-Tupí oral vowels and their reflexes in Mundurukú are straightforward: it is a one-to-one correspondence. BDEC-T, however, challenges this analysis as there appear to be other correspondences that have not been observed, with the exception of the correspondence set *e/e, where both methods achieved the same results. Rodrigues' intuitions are, nonetheless, relatively close to what the database produced: the largest number of correspondences match the ones posited by Rodrigues, indicating that a 'manual' analysis, although valid, still has the potential to miss details that the database captures.

In sum, we employed the function of cross tabulations in the form of pivot tables to arrange segmented data. The object oriented function of pivot tables allowed us to dynamically arrange segment data which aided in tracking phonemic and featural correspondences. This was tested against a manual analysis of the data and it was shown to confirm, revise and produce new results.

Rodrigues		BDEC-T		
P-T	Mundurukú	P-T	Mundurukú	Total
		∅	a	1
*a	a	*a	∅	1
			a	11
			ə̃	1
			õ	1
			a̰	2
*e	e	*e	e	5
*i	i	*i	i	2
			∅	2
*ɨ	i	*ɨ	ə	1
			i	19
			ḭ	3
			j	1
*o	ɨ	*o	∅	1
			ə́/ə	1
			o	2
*u	o	*u	o	7
			õ	1
			i	1

Table 7: Rodrigues' (1995) oral vowel correspondence sets compared with those generated by the BDEC-T.

4 Conclusion

The use of spreadsheets and databases is well-established in linguistic research. However, as far as we know, the BDEC-T represents the first attempt at harnessing the functionality of pivot tables and cross-tabulation in historical linguistics. On this note, the application computational procedures in the study of sound change and comparison have made notable advances in the past decade. Relevant to this study, systems such ALINE, a feature-based algorithm for measuring phonetic similarity, are capable of automating segmentation and quantitatively calculating cognate probabilities without resorting to a table of systematic sound correspondences (Kondrak 2002). These are valuable models which test many long-standing hypotheses on the nature of sound change and methods for investigating this. While not offering an automated algorithm of this type, we chose to keep segmentation manual in order to maintain accuracy and to make adjustments where needed in the S1-S10 segmentations made in the languages. This also offers a measure of accuracy, as the pivot tables will only yield invalid results if the segments aren't aligned properly.[6]

Although not discussed in this paper, we have promising results from using the optional feature fields (F1 and F2) to generate syllable template to accompany the phonemic correspondences generated by the pivot tables. Also, the application of pivot tables in the BDEC-T has also had success in tabulating mappings between cognate and semantic sets in the Tupían languages (Peterson 2007a). Ultimately, we would like to explore innovative visualizing techniques to display the interdependent relationships between phonemes at various stages of reconstruction (through the proto-languages in the database), and the languages whose inventories they belong to. Conceptually, this would give us a (scalable) two- or three-dimensional plots or 'webs' of correspondences across the languages, perhaps implemented by recent visualization techniques such as treemaps or ConeTrees (Fekete & Plaisant 2002).

The purpose of the BDEC-T is ultimately to complement other current computational approaches to the domain of historical and comparative research by offering a practical level of interactivity and productivity in a research tool. Where automation is not necessary, the BDEC-T offers a database model that effectively enhances the functionality of the kinds of databases that are already widely used.

References

Andrew Bredenkamp, Louisa Sadler and Andrew Spencer. 1998. Investigating Argument Structure: The Russian Nominalization Database. *Linguistic Databases*, John Nerbonne, (ed.) CSLI Publications

Jean-Daniel Fekete and Catherine Plaisant. 2002. Interactive Information Visualization of a Million Items. *Proceedings of the IEEE Symposium on Information Visualization*, IEEE Computer Society, Wash., DC

Cheryl Jensen. 1989. O desenvolvimento histórico da língua Wayampí. Master's Thesis. Campinas: Universidade Estadual de Campinas.

Grzegorz Kondrak. 2002. Algorithms for Language Reconstruction. Ph.D Thesis, University of Toronto

[6]We have developed a set of 'diagnostic' pivot tables to help control against improperly aligned segmentations.

Mirian Lemle. 1971. Internal classification of the Tup-Guaran linguistic family. *Tupi Studies I.*, David Bendor-Samuel (ed.), pp. 107-129. Norman: SIL

Augusto S. Mello. 2000. Estudo Histórico da Família lingüística Tup-Guaraní: Aspectos Fonológicos e Lexicais. PhD Dissertation. Santa Catarina: UFSC

Denny Moore and Vilacy Galúcio. 2005. Reconstruction of Proto-Tupari consonants and vowels. in *Survey of California and Other Indian Languages, Report 8*, M. Langdon and L. Hinton (eds.), pp. 119-137.

John Nerbonne. 1998. *Linguistic Databases: Introduction.* John Nerbonne, (ed.) CSLI Publications

Tyler Peterson. 2007a. Analytical Database Design: Approaches in the Mapping between Cognate and Semantic Sets. *Proceedings of the 7th Intl. Workshop on Computational Semantics*, J. Goertzen *et al* (eds). Tilburg: Tilburg University, pp. 359–361.

Gessiane L. Picanço. 2005. Mundurukú: Phonetics, Phonology, Synchrony, Diachrony. PhD Dissertation. Vancouver: University of British Columbia.

Aryon D. Rodrigues. 1958. Die Klassifikation des Tupi-Sprachstammes. *Proceedings of the 32nd International Congress of Americanists*, Copenhagen, 1956; pp. 679-684.

Aryon D. Rodrigues. 1985. Relações internas na família lingüística Tup-Guaraní. *Revista de Antropologia 27/28*, São Paulo, 1956 pp. 33-53.

Aryon D. Rodrigues. 1995. Glottalized stops in Proto-Tupí. Paper presented at the SSILA Summer Meeting, University of New Mexico, Albuquerque, NM.

Charles O. Schleicher. 1998. Comparative and Internal Reconstruction of Proto-Tupí-Guaraní. PhD Dissertation. Madison: University of Wisconsin.

Creating a Comparative Dictionary of Totonac-Tepehua

Grzegorz Kondrak
Department of Computing Science
University of Alberta
kondrak@cs.ualberta.ca

David Beck
Department of Linguistics
University of Alberta
dbeck@ualberta.ca

Philip Dilts
Department of Linguistics
University of Alberta
pdilts@ualberta.ca

Abstract

We apply algorithms for the identification of cognates and recurrent sound correspondences proposed by Kondrak (2002) to the Totonac-Tepehua family of indigenous languages in Mexico. We show that by combining expert linguistic knowledge with computational analysis, it is possible to quickly identify a large number of cognate sets within the family. Our objective is to provide tools for rapid construction of comparative dictionaries for relatively unfamiliar language families.

1 Introduction

Identification of cognates and recurrent sound correspondences is a component of two principal tasks of historical linguistics: demonstrating the relatedness of languages, and reconstructing the histories of language families. Manually compiling the list of cognates is an error-prone and time-consuming task. Several methods for constructing comparative dictionaries have been proposed and applied to specific language families: Algonquian (Hewson, 1974), Yuman (Johnson, 1985), Tamang (Lowe and Mazaudon, 1994), and Malayo-Javanic (Oakes, 2000). Most of those methods crucially depend on previously determined regular sound correspondences; each of them was both developed and tested on a single language family.

Kondrak (2002) proposes a number of algorithms for automatically detecting and quantifying three characteristics of cognates: recurrent sound correspondences, phonetic similarity, and semantic affinity. The algorithms were tested on two well-studied language families: Indo-European and Algonquian. In this paper, we apply them instead to a set of languages whose mutual relationship is still being investigated. This is consistent with the original research goal of providing tools for the analysis of relatively unfamiliar languages represented by word lists. We show that by combining expert linguistic knowledge with computational analysis, it is possible to quickly identify a large number of cognate sets within a relatively little-studied language family.

The experiments reported in this paper were performed in the context of the Upper Necaxa Totonac Project (Beck, 2005), of which one of the authors is the principal investigator. Upper Necaxa is a seriously endangered language spoken by around 3,400 indigenous people in Puebla State, Mexico. The primary goal of the project is to document the language through the compilation of an extensive dictionary and other resources, which may aid revitalization efforts. One aim of the project is the investigation of the relationship between Upper Necaxa Totonac and the other languages of the Totonac-Tepehua language family, whose family tree is not yet well-understood.

The paper is organized as follows. In Section 2, we provide background on the Totonac-Tepehua family. Section 3 describes our data sets. In Section 4, we outline our algorithms. In Section 5, we report on a pilot study involving only two languages. In Section 6, we present the details of our system that generates a comparative dictionary involving five languages. Section 7 discusses the practical significance of our project.

Proceedings of Ninth Meeting of the ACL Special Interest Group in Computational Morphology and Phonology, pages 134–141,
Prague, June 2007.

2 Totonac-Tepehua Language Family

The Totonac-Tepehua language family is an isolate group of languages spoken by around 200,000 people in the northern part of Puebla State and the adjacent areas of Veracruz and Hidalgo in East-Central Mexico (Figure 1). Although individual languages have begun to receive some attention from linguists, relatively little is known about the family as whole: recent estimates put the number of languages in the group between 14 and 20, but the phylo-genetic relations between languages remains a subject of some controversy. The family has traditionally been divided into two coordinate branches: Tepehua, consisting of three languages (Pisa Flores, Tlachichilco, and Huehuetla), and Totonacan. The Totonacan branch has in turn been divided into four sub-branches: Misantla, Lowlands or Papantla, Sierra, and Northern (Ichon, 1973; Reid, 1991), largely on the impressions of missionaries working in the area. Some dialectological work has cast doubt on the division between Northern and Sierra (Arana, 1953; Rojas, 1978), and groups them together into a rather heterogeneous Highland Totonac, suggesting that this split may be more recent than the others. However, the experience of linguists working in Totonacan communities, including one of the authors, indicates that – judged by the criterion of mutual intelligibility – there are likely to be more, rather than fewer, divisions needed within the Totonacan branch of the family.

Although Totonac-Tepehua shows a good deal of internal diversity, the languages that make it up are easily recognizable as a family. Speakers of Totonacan languages are aware of having a common historical and linguistic background, and there are large numbers of easily recognizable cognates and grammatical similarities. A typical Totonacan consonantal inventory, that of the Papantla variant (Levy, 1987), is given in Table 1. Most languages of the family share this inventory, though one of the languages used for this study, Upper Necaxa, has undergone a number of phonological shifts that have affected its consonantal system, most notably the collapse of the voiceless lateral affricate with the voiceless lateral fricative (both are now fricatives) and the lenition of the uvular stop to a glottal stop, a process that has also affected at least some of the

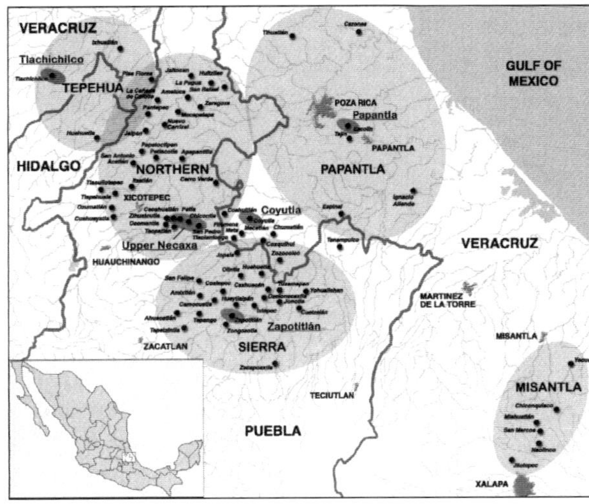

Figure 1: Totonac-Tepehua language area indicating traditional taxonomic divisions.

Tepehua languages. In Upper Necaxa, this lenition has also resulted in the creation of ejective fricatives from historical stop-uvular stop clusters (Beck, 2006). Languages also differ as to whether the back-fricative consonant is /h/ or /x/, and some languages have evolved voiceless /w/ and/or voiceless /y/ phonemes in word-final position. The phonemic status of the glottal stop is an open question in several of the languages.

Plosive	p	t			k	q	
Affricate		ts	tɬ	tʃ			
Fricative		s	ɬ	ʃ			h
Approximant	w		l	j			
Nasal	m	n				ɴ	

Table 1: Illustrative Totonac-Tepehua consonantal inventory.

In terms of vocalic inventory, it was previously thought that all Totonacan languages had three-vowel systems (/a/, /i/, /u/), and that they also made distinctions for each vowel quality in vowel length and laryngealization. It has since come to light that at least some languages in the Sierra group do not make length distinctions (in at least one of these, Olintla, it appears that short vowels have developed into a phonemic schwa), and that others do not distinguish laryngealized vowels. A number of languages, including Upper Necaxa and some of the languages adjacent to it, have developed a five-vowel system; the sounds /e/ and /o/ are recognized in the orthographies of several languages of the family even where their phonemic status is in doubt.

3 Data

There are five languages included in this study: Tlachichilco (abbreviated **T**), Upper Necaxa (**U**), Papantla (**P**), Coyutla (**C**), and Zapotitlán (**S**). Tlachichilco belongs to the Tepehua branch; the other four are from the Totonacan branch. Zapotitlán is traditionally considered to belong to the Sierra group of Totonacan, whereas the status of Coyutla is uncertain. The location of each language is indicated by grey lozenges on Figure 1.

The data comes from several diverse sources. The Tlachichilco Tepehua data are drawn from an electronic lexical database provided to the authors by James Watters of the Summer Institute of Linguistics. The data on Upper Necaxa was collected by Beck in the communities of Patla and Chicontla – located in the so-called Northern Totonac area – and data from the Papantla area was provided by Paulette Levy of the National Autonomous University of Mexico based on her field work in the vicinity of the city of Papantla. Data on the remaining two languages were provided by Herman Aschmann. The material from Coyutla was drawn from a word list compiled for Bible translation and the Zapotitlán material has been published in dictionary form (Aschmann, 1983). The glosses of Totonac forms for all the languages are in Spanish.

The dictionaries differ significantly in format and character encoding. The Tepehua and Coyutla dictionaries are in a file format and character encoding used by the *Shoebox* program. The Upper Necaxa and the Zapotitlán dictionaries are in their own formats and character encodings. The Papantla dictionary is in the RTF format. The dictionaries also differ in orthographies used. For example, while most dictionaries use k to represent a voiceless velar stop, the Coyutla dictionary uses c.

4 Methods

In this section, we briefly outline the algorithms employed for computing three similarity scores: phonetic, semantic and correspondence-based. Our cognate identification program integrates the three types of evidence using a linear combination of scores. The algorithms are described in detail in (Kondrak, 2002).

The phonetic similarity of lexemes is computed using the ALINE algorithm, which assigns a similarity score to pairs of phonetically-transcribed words on the basis of the decomposition of phonemes into elementary phonetic features. The principal component of ALINE is a function that calculates the similarity of two phonemes that are expressed in terms of about a dozen multi-valued phonetic features. For example, the phoneme n, which is usually described as a *voiced alveolar nasal stop*, has the following feature values: *Place = 0.85*, *Manner = 0.6*, *Voice = 1*, and *Nasal = 1*, with the remaining features set to 0. The numerical feature values reflect the distances between vocal organs during speech production, and are based on experimental measurements. The phonetic features are assigned *salience* weights that express their relative importance. The default salience values were tuned manually on a development set of phoneme-aligned cognate pairs from various related languages. The overall similarity score is the sum of individual similarity scores between pairs of phonemes in an optimal alignment of two words. The similarity value is normalized by the length of the longer word.[1]

For the determination of recurrent sound correspondences we employ the method of inducing a *translation model* between phonemes in two word lists. The idea is to relate recurrent sound correspondences in word lists to translational equivalences in bitexts. The translation model is induced by combining the maximum similarity alignment with the competitive linking algorithm of Melamed (2000). Melamed's approach is based on the *one-to-one* assumption, which implies that every word in the bitext is aligned with at most one word on the other side of the bitext. In the context of the bilingual word lists, the correspondences determined under the *one-to-one* assumption are restricted to link single phonemes to single phonemes. Nevertheless, the method is powerful enough to determine valid correspondences in word lists in which the fraction of cognate pairs is well below 50%.

[1] Another possibility is normalization by the length of the longest alignment (Heeringa et al., 2006).

Because of the lack of a Totonac gold standard, the approach to computing semantic similarity of glosses was much simpler than in (Kondrak, 2002). The keyword selection heuristic was simply to pick the first word of the gloss, which in Spanish glosses is often a noun followed by modifiers. A complete gloss match was given double the weight of a keyword match. More complex semantic relations were not considered. In the future, we plan to utilize a Spanish part-of-speech tagger, and the Spanish portion of the EuroWordNet in order to improve the accuracy of the semantic module.

5 Pairwise Comparison

The first experiment was designed to test the effectiveness of our approach in identifying recurrent correspondences and cognates across a single pair of related languages. The data for the experiment was limited to two noun lists representing Upper Necaxa (2110 lexemes) and Zapotitlán (763 lexemes), which were extracted from the corresponding dictionaries. Both correspondences and cognates were evaluated by one of the authors (Beck), who is an expert on the Totonac-Tepehua language family.

5.1 Identification of correspondences

In the first experiment, our correspondence identification program was applied to Upper Necaxa and Zapotitlán. Simple correspondences were targeted, as complex correspondences do not seem to be very frequent among the Totonac languages. The input for the program was created by extracting all pairs of noun lexemes with identical glosses from the two dictionaries. The resulting list of 865 word pairs was likely to contain more unrelated word pairs than actual cognates.[2]

The results of the experiment were very encouraging. Of the 24 correspondences posited by the program, 22 were judged as completely correct, while the remaining two (**ʧ:ts** and **tɬ:ts**). were judged as "plausible but surprising". Since the program explicitly list the word pairs from which it extracts correspondences, they were available for a more detailed analysis. Of the five pairs containing **ʧ:ts**, one was judged as possibly cognate:

[2]Some lexemes have multiple glosses, and therefore may participate in several word pairs.

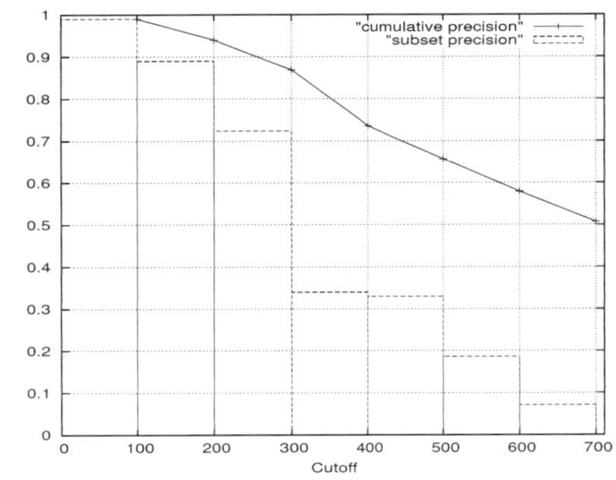

Figure 2: Cognate identification precision on the Totonac test set.

Upper Necaxa [**ʧ**astun] and Zapotitlán [aʔa**ts**astun] '*rincón, esquina*'. Both word pairs containing **tɬ:ts** were judged as possibly cognate: [li**tɬ**an]/[li**ts**eχ] '*favor*', and [**tɬ**aq**tɬ**a]/[**ts**a**ts**a] '*elote*'. Both unexpected correspondences were deemed to merit further linguistic investigation.

5.2 Identification of cognates

In the second experiment, our cognate identification program was run on the vocabulary lists containing the Upper Necaxa and Zapotitlán nouns. A large list of the candidate word pairs with their glosses was sorted by the total similarity score and evaluated by Beck. The cognation judgments were performed in order, starting from the top of the list, until the proportion of false positives became too high to justify further effort. At any point of the list, we can compute *precision*, which is the ratio of true positives (in this case, cognates) to the sum of true positives and false positives (all word pairs up to that point).

The cognate decisions were based on the following principles. The pairs could be judged as true positives only if the word roots were cognate; sharing an affix was not deemed sufficient. Compound words were counted as cognates if any of the multiple roots were related; for example, both *snowstorm/storm* and *snowstorm/snow* would be acceptable. The rationale is that a person compiling an etymological dictionary would still want to know about such pairs whether or not they are eventually included as entries in the dictionary.

In total, 711 pairs were evaluated, of which 350

were classified as cognate, 351 as unrelated, and 10 as doubtful. 18 of the positive judgments were marked as loans from Spanish. In Figure 2, the boxes correspond to the precision values for the seven sets of 100 candidate pairs each, sorted by score; the curve represents the cumulative precision. For example, the percentage of actual cognates was 86.9% among the first 300 word pairs, and 72.4% among the word pairs numbered 201–300. As can be seen, almost all the pairs in the beginning of the file were cognates, but then the number of false positives increases steadily. In terms of semantic similarity, 30% of the evaluated pairs had at least one gloss in common, and further 7% shared a keyword. Among the pairs judged as cognate, the respective percentages were 49% and 11%.

6 Multiwise comparison

When data from several related languages is available, the challenge is to identify cognate sets across all languages. Our goal was to take a set of diversely formatted dictionaries as input, and generate from them, as automatically as possible, a basic comparative dictionary.

Our system is presented graphically in Figure 3. This system is a suite of Perl scripts and C++ programs. With the exception of the input dictionary converters, the system is language-family independent. With little change, it could be used to determine cognate sets from another language family. In this section, we describe the four stages of the process: preprocessing, identification of cognate pairs, extraction of cognate sets, and postprocessing.

6.1 Preprocessing

The first step is to convert each input dictionary from its original form into a word list in a standardized format. Because of the differences between dictionaries, separate conversion scripts are required for each language. The conversion scripts call on a number of utilities that are maintained in a shared library of functions, which allows for the relatively easy development of new conversion scripts should additional dictionaries become available.

Each line in the resulting language files contains the phonetic form of the lexeme expressed in a uniform encoding, followed a gloss representing the

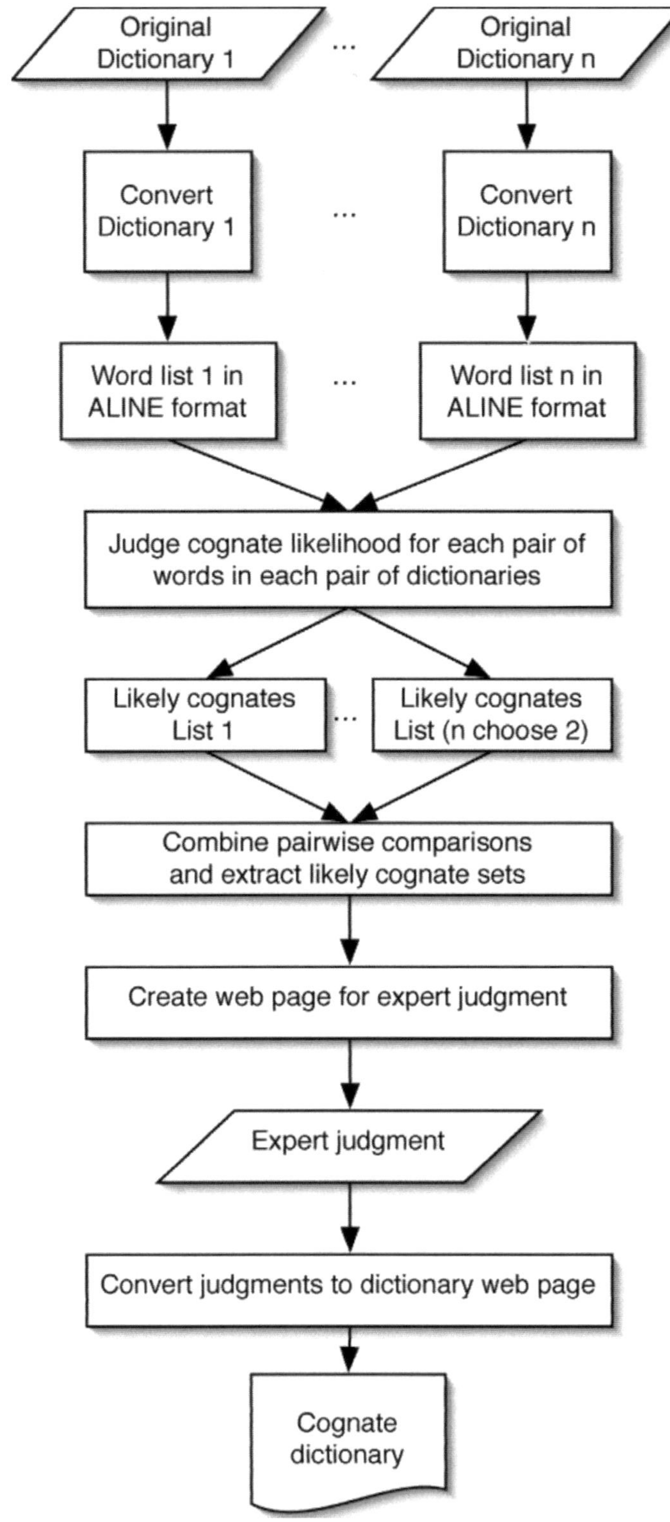

Figure 3: Flowchart illustrating conversion system

meaning of the lexeme. Long glosses are truncated to thirty characters, with sub-glosses separated by semicolons. For the present study, the conversion scripts also removed all dictionary entries that were known not to be nouns.

For the purpose of uniform encoding of phonetic symbols, we adopted the ALINE scheme (Kondrak, 2002), in which every phonetic symbol is represented by a single lowercase letter followed by zero or more uppercase letters. The initial lowercase letter is the base letter most similar to the sound represented by the phonetic symbol. The remaining uppercase letters stand for the phonetic features in which the represented sound differs from the sound defined by the base letter. For example, the phoneme [ʃ], which occurs at the beginning of the word *shy*, is represented by 'sV', where V stands for *palato-alveolar*.

6.2 Identification of cognate pairs

The main C++ program computes the similarity of each pair of words across the two languages using the methods described in Section 4. A batch script runs the comparison program on each pair of the dictionary lists. With n input dictionaries, this entails $\binom{n}{2}$ pairwise comparisons each resulting in a separate list of possible cognate pairs. These lists are then sorted and trimmed to include only those pairs that exceeded a certain similarity threshold.

The batch script has an option of selecting a subset of dictionary pairs to process, which was found useful in several cases. For example, when we discover a newer version of a dictionary, or update an individual dictionary conversion script, only 4, rather than all 10 lists need to be re-generated.

6.3 Extraction of cognate sets

The output from processing individual pairs of word lists must be combined in order to extract cognate sets across all languages. The combination script generates an undirected weighted graph in which each vertex represents a single lexeme. The source language of each lexeme is also stored in each vertex. Links between vertices correspond to possible cognate relationships identified in the previous stage, with the link weights set according to the similarity scores computed by the comparison program.

The algorithm for extracting cognate sets from the graph is the following. First, we find the connected components within the graph by applying the breadth-first search algorithm. The components are added to a queue. For each component in the queue, we exhaustively generate a list of connected subgraphs in which each vertex corresponds to a different source language. (In the present study, the minimum size of a subgraph was set to three, and the maximum size was five, the total number of languages.) If no such subgraphs exist, we discard the component, and process the next component from the queue. Otherwise, the subgraph with the maximum cumulative weight is selected as the most likely cognate set. We remove from the component the vertices corresponding to that cognate set, together with their incident edges, which may cause the component to lose its connectivity. We identify the resulting connected component(s) by breadth-first search, and place them at the end of the queue. We repeat the process until the queue is empty.

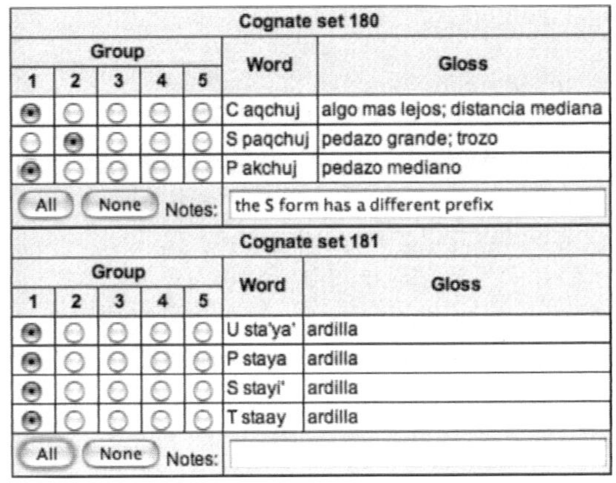

Figure 4: A sample judgment screen.

6.4 Postprocessing

The candidate cognate sets extracted in the previous stage are rendered into an HTML page designed to allow an expert linguist to verify their correctness (Figure 4). After the verification, a dictionary composed of the confirmed cognate sets is automatically generated in HTML format, with the glosses restored to their original, untruncated form. Additional cognate sets can be incorporated seamlessly into the existing list. A sample entry in the gener-

317	C	li:qama:n	el juguete; hace burla de el
	T	laaqamaan	el juguete
	S	li:qama:n	el juego; el juguete; lo maltrata; le hace burla
	U	le:ha:ma:n	juguete
	P	li:qama:n	el juguete

Table 2: A sample entry in the generated dictionary.

ated dictionary is shown in Table 2.[3]

6.5 Results

In our initial attempt to extract cognate sets from the graph, we extracted from the graph only those connected components that were complete cliques (i.e., fully connected subgraphs). Of the resulting 120 candidate cognate sets, all but one were confirmed by Beck. The only false positive involved two words that were true cognates, and one word that was morphologically related to the other two. However, although this method was characterized by a very high precision, the overly restrictive clique condition excluded a large number of interesting cognate sets.

In order to improve recall, the method described in Section 6.3 was adopted. 430 possible cognate sets of 3, 4, or 5 words were discovered in this manner. 384 (89%) of these sets were judged to be true cognate sets. Of the remaining 46 sets, 45 contained partial cognate sets. The set that contained no cognate words was composed of three words that share a cognate root, but have different prefixes.

7 Discussion

From a practical standpoint, the procedures used in these experiments provide a powerful tool for the identification of cognate sets and sound correspondences. The identification of these correspondences by traditional means is cumbersome and time-consuming, given the large amounts of data that require processing. The Upper Necaxa dictionary, for instance, contains nearly 9,000 entries, from which a list of about 2,000 nouns would have to be extracted by hand, and then compared pairwise to lists drawn from dictionaries of potentially comparable length of each of the other languages, each of which would also have to be compared to the other. Lists of potential correspondences from each pairwise comparison would then have to be compared, and so on. The algorithms described here accomplish in mere minutes what would take man-hours (perhaps years) of expert labour to accomplish manually, outputting the results in a format that is easily accessed and shared with other researchers as an HTML-format list of cognates that can be made available on the World Wide Web.

The results obtained from a study of this type have important implications for linguists, as well as anthropologists and archeologists interested in the history and migratory patterns of peoples speaking Totonacan languages. Presented with extensive and robust cognate sets and lists of sound changes, linguists gain insight into the patterns of historical phonological change and can verify or disconfirm models of phonological and typological development. These data can also give rough indications of the time-depth of the linguistic family and, potentially, suggest geographical origins of populations. At present, Totonac-Tepehua has not been demonstrably linked to any other language family in Mesoamerica. Careful reconstruction of a proto-language might reveal such links and, possibly, shed some light on the early movements and origins of Mesoamerican peoples.

These experiments have also allowed us to create the beginnings of an etymological dictionary which will, in turn, allow us to reconstruct a more accurate Totonac-Tepehua family tree. By comparing the relative numbers of shared cognates amongst languages and the number of regular sound changes shared by individual subsets of languages in each cognate set, we hope to be able to determine relative proximity of languages and the order in which the family divided itself into branches, sub-branches, and individual languages. This will shed light on the problem of Totonac-Tepehua origins and migratory patterns, and may help to answer questions about potential links of Totonacan peoples to archeological sites in East-Central Mexico, including the pyramids of Teotihuacán. Accurate determination of distance between variants of Totonacan will also help inform social policy decisions about bilingual education and government funding for language revitalization pro-

[3]The entire dictionary in its current state can be viewed at http://www.cs.ualberta.ca/~pdilts.

grams, as well as debates about orthographies and language standardization.

Acknowledgements

Thanks to Paulette Levy, James Watters, and Herman Aschmann for sharing their dictionary data. The fieldwork of David Beck was funded by the Social Sciences and Humanities Research Council of Canada and the Wenner-Gren Foundation. Philip Dilts was supported by a scholarship provided by the Government of the Province of Alberta. Grzegorz Kondrak was supported by the Natural Sciences and Engineering Research Council of Canada.

References

Evangelina Arana. 1953. Reconstrucción del prototonaco. Huastecos, totonacos y sus vecinos. *Revista mexicana de estudios antropológicos*, 23:123–130.

Herman P. Aschmann. 1983. *Vocabulario totonaco de la Sierra*. Summer Institute of Linguistics, Mexico.

David Beck. 2005. The Upper Necaxa field project II: the structure and acquisition of an endangered language. Available from http://www.arts.ualberta.ca/˜totonaco.

David Beck. 2006. The emergence of ejective fricatives in Upper Necaxa Totonac. In Robert Kirchner, editor, *University of Alberta Working Papers in Linguistics 1*.

Wilbert Heeringa, Peter Kleiwig, Charlotte Gooskens, and John Nerbonne. 2006. Evaluation of string distance algorithms for dialectology. In *Proceedings of the COLING-ACL Workshop on Linguistic Distances*, pages 51–62.

John Hewson. 1974. Comparative reconstruction on the computer. In *Proceedings of the 1st International Conference on Historical Linguistics*, pages 191–197.

Alain Ichon. 1973. *La religión de los totonacos de la Sierra*. Instituto Nacional Indigenista, Mexico City.

Mark Johnson. 1985. Computer aids for comparative dictionaries. *Linguistics*, 23(2):285–302.

Grzegorz Kondrak. 2002. *Algorithms for Language Reconstruction*. Ph.D. thesis, University of Toronto.

Paulette Levy. 1987. *Fonología del totonaco de Papantla*. Universidad Nacional Autónoma de México, Veracruz, Mexico.

John B. Lowe and Martine Mazaudon. 1994. The reconstruction engine: a computer implementation of the comparative method. *Computational Linguistics*, 20:381–417.

I. Dan Melamed. 2000. Models of translational equivalence among words. *Computational Linguistics*, 26(2):221–249.

Michael P. Oakes. 2000. Computer estimation of vocabulary in protolanguage from word lists in four daughter languages. *Journal of Quantitative Linguistics*, 7(3):233–243.

Aileen A. Reid. 1991. *Gramática totonaca de Xicotepec de Juárez, Puebla*. Summer Institute of Linguistics, Mexico City.

García Rojas. 1978. *Dialectología de la zona totonaco-tepehua*. Ph.D. thesis, National School of Anthropology and History, Mexico. Honours thesis.

Author Index

Association for Computational Linguistics
209 N. Eighth Street
Stroudsburg, Pennsylvania 18360